Praise for *Safe School Ambassadors*

"This very practical book offers an innovative and proven approach to decreasing violence in schools through student empowerment. It is the only sane solution for ensuring security in our society."

—**DEEPAK CHOPRA,** AUTHOR, *THE DEEPER WOUND: RECOVERING THE SOUL FROM FEAR AND SUFFERING, 100 DAYS OF HEALING*

"I highly recommend *Safe School Ambassadors* to all educators. In a clear, simple, and engaging style, this book makes the case and provides a practical road map for addressing the major challenge to our students' healthy development and school success: the lack of opportunities for their meaningful participation and contribution in their lives at school. The authors demonstrate how schools can 'harness' the power of students to create a safe school environment that promotes not only learning but also the social, emotional, moral, and spiritual development of young people as well."

—**BONNIE BENARD,** SENIOR PROGRAM ASSOCIATE, WESTED, OAKLAND, CALIFORNIA

"At a time when many talk about the need to stop bullying and other forms of violence, it is refreshing to encounter a book that shows us how to do so. *Safe School Ambassadors* offers a unique and powerful approach by empowering bystanders to become peacemakers, thus helping create safer schools from the inside out."

—**BARBARA COLOROSO,** EDUCATOR AND AUTHOR, *THE BULLY, THE BULLIED AND THE BYSTANDER*

"If schools are going to be safe and welcoming places for everyone, influential students must be enlisted to serve as alert and effective allies. The Safe School Ambassadors program has provided us with a well-designed student-to-student initiative that has made a positive difference in over thirty of our district's schools."

—**ALISON ADLER,** ED.D., CHIEF, SAFETY AND LEARNING ENVIRONMENT, SCHOOL DISTRICT OF PALM BEACH COUNTY, FLORIDA

"*Safe School Ambassadors* is an exciting, original vision that makes a compelling case for student-centered programming. The authors cut through the superficial solutions to where change lives and breathes: the kids themselves."

—**RACHEL SIMMONS,** AUTHOR, *ODD GIRL OUT: THE HIDDEN CULTURE OF AGGRESSION IN GIRLS*

"Bullying and youth violence are critical public health issues that have serious academic, social, and emotional costs. This book provides an antidote that can decrease acts of intolerance and create a healthy and compassionate learning community."

—DEBORAH PROTHROW-STITH, M.D., HARVARD SCHOOL OF PUBLIC HEALTH

"*Safe School Ambassadors* describes a powerful, asset-rich approach that partners school staff and students to capitalize on student knowledge and skills to change the norm at school from one of cruelty to one of inclusion, care, and concern. Any educator who is invested in young people will find this unique concept a must for their school district."

—KAREN BRESLAWSKI, STUDENT ASSISTANCE COORDINATOR, BROCKPORT CENTRAL SCHOOL DISTRICT

"This book is a 'must read' for every school leader and teacher. The Safe School Ambassadors program inspires and trains students to promote safety, respect, and compassion for others. This is the most effective program I have seen in my thirteen years as a middle school principal and assistant principal."

—KATHY COKER, PRINCIPAL, SANTA ROSA MIDDLE SCHOOL, CALIFORNIA

"I believe that *Safe School Ambassadors* represents the most innovative contemporary thinking about involving secondary students in violence prevention. I highly recommend this well-written, well-organized book and plan to add it to my collection."

—JOHN H. HOOVER, INTERIM ASSOCIATE DEAN, ST. CLOUD STATE UNIVERSITY, MINNESOTA

Safe School Ambassadors

HARNESSING STUDENT POWER TO STOP BULLYING AND VIOLENCE

Rick Phillips

John Linney

Chris Pack

JOSSEY-BASS
A Wiley Imprint
www.josseybass.com

Published by Jossey-Bass
A Wiley Imprint
989 Market Street, San Francisco, CA 94103-1741—www.josseybass.com

Readers should be aware that Internet Web sites offered as citations and/or sources for further information may have changed or disappeared between the time this was written and when it is read.

Limit of Liability/Disclaimer of Warranty: While the publisher and author have used their best efforts in preparing this book, they make no representations or warranties with respect to the accuracy or completeness of the contents of this book and specifically disclaim any implied warranties of merchantability or fitness for a particular purpose. No warranty may be created or extended by sales representatives or written sales materials. The advice and strategies contained herein may not be suitable for your situation. You should consult with a professional where appropriate. Neither the publisher nor author shall be liable for any loss of profit or any other commercial damages, including but not limited to special, incidental, consequential, or other damages.

Jossey-Bass books and products are available through most bookstores. To contact Jossey-Bass directly call our Customer Care Department within the U.S. at 800-956-7739, outside the U.S. at 317-572-3986, or fax 317-572-4002.

Jossey-Bass also publishes its books in a variety of electronic formats. Some content that appears in print may not be available in electronic books.

Library of Congress Cataloging-in-Publication Data

Phillips, Rick, date
   Safe school ambassadors: harnessing student power to stop bullying and violence / Rick Phillips, John Linney, and Chris Pack.
      p.   cm.
   Includes bibliographical references and index.
   ISBN-13: 978-0-4701-9742-4 (pbk.)
      1. School violence—United States—Prevention.   2. Bullying in schools—United States—Prevention.   3. Schools—United States—Safety measures.   I. Linney, John, 1968-   II. Pack, Chris, 1962-   III. Title.
   LB3013.32.P49   2008
   371.7'82—dc22

                                                                                            2007045000

Printed in the United States of America
FIRST EDITION

PB Printing   10 9 8 7 6 5 4 3 2 1

CONTENTS

119618

ACKNOWLEDGMENTS

THIS BOOK IS DEDICATED TO ALL THE BRAVE YOUNG PEOPLE who are stepping up, speaking up, and standing up to bullying and violence and to the adults who support them in their efforts. Our world is a more compassionate, inclusive, and peaceful place because of their courage and their actions.

We acknowledge the following individuals and organizations that have contributed, inspired, and supported us mightily in the writing of this book. They are our angels, our champions and supporters, our colleagues, our friends, and our families. We stand on their shoulders and the shoulders of all those who have stood up for justice and peace.

Community Matters, the 501(c)(3) nonprofit organization that has provided the structure for expressing the deep-seated beliefs and passion that have given rise to the work at the heart of this book.

Our "angels," those special individuals who showed up when we most needed them to gift us with their wisdom, resources, and support:

Alison Adler, who invited us to pilot the first Safe School Ambassadors program in the public schools of Palm Beach County, Florida.

Jethren Phillips, who provided his ongoing wise counsel, love, and financial support. He has been a generous donor and has tirelessly served on our board since we began Community Matters.

William Frost, who has been our board president and provided sage leadership since we began Community Matters. He has brought to our team valuable expertise in marketing, planning, facilitation, and client cultivation.

Kim Hunter, who has served on our board and provided wise counsel and generous support for our work.

Laurie MacCaskill, who was instrumental in introducing the Safe School Ambassadors program to many caring adults in southern California and helping us to expand our work into more schools.

John Liechty, whose vision and leadership helped bring Safe School Ambassadors to the Los Angeles Unified School District. Although he didn't live to see his vision enacted fully, his spirit is alive in the actions of ambassadors who are striving to reduce bullying and youth violence in Los Angeles every day.

Rick Geggie, whose generosity, spirit, and commitment to children provided us with the opportunity and funding to bring our Safe School Ambassadors program to the province of Ontario, Canada.

Our colleagues, who have provided the expertise, leadership, and support for our work:

Rick Lewis, whose generosity, spirit, and brilliance has given the Safe School Ambassadors program so much of the strength and power it possesses.

Lynn Garric, who has generously provided us the forum to share our work with so many. She has been an invaluable resource, keeping us current about county and state educational trends, legislation, and mandates.

Daryl Thiesen, a passionate advocate for youth empowerment who has made funding and information available to support Kern County, California, schools in implementing the Safe School Ambassadors program.

SuEllen Fried, who graciously invited us to bring the Safe School Ambassadors program to the Aspen, Colorado, area in tandem with her own efforts to help schools reduce bullying and violence.

Bonnie Raines and Laurie Lauer, who offered creative ideas and wise counsel on the development of the elementary version of the Safe School Ambassadors program.

Aqeela Sherells, peace warrior, who joined with us when we brought the Safe School Ambassadors program to several schools in the Los Angeles Unified School District that were experiencing high levels of violence.

Our champions and supporters, who have courageously shared our vision and paved the way for us to bring Safe School Ambassadors to their schools and communities:

Kristin Greenstreet, Jim Gilchrist, Karen Breslawski, Dave Heard, and Rory Elder, who recognized the power and potential of the Safe School Ambassadors model and tirelessly advocated for its implementation in their schools and regions.

Trisha Liskay, then counselor at Parkside Middle School in San Bruno, California, whose vision, passion, and commitment made it possible to bring ambassadors to the middle school level.

Tricia Dickinson, Spencer and Janine Sherman, Karen Solomon and Billy White, and Jethren Phillips, who have generously shared their time and their financial resources to strengthen our efforts.

Robin Sindler and the *NBC Today Show* staff, who produced the video footage that so effectively showcased the work of Safe School Ambassadors to millions of viewers nationwide April 20, 2004. Joanie and David Bruce, Ash Camp, Scott Falconer, Sun McNamee, and Allan Lundell, all of whom have contributed to the video images that tell the stories of these courageous young people.

John Beilharz and Ron Campanile, who generously devoted time and talent to developing the second generation of informational materials that helped others learn about the work of Safe School Ambassadors.

The gifted professionals who have guided and supported our research efforts: Dixie King of Transforming Local Communities; Andy Horne of the University of Georgia, Athens; Greg Robinson of California State University, Fullerton; Alexander White of Texas State University, San Marcos; John Hoover of St. Cloud State University in Minnesota; and André Birjulin and his colleagues at Omni Research and Training.

Frank Baxter, who, after learning about the powerful work of young people in making schools safer, brought our program to the attention of the Los Angeles Unified School District and advocated that district officials review it carefully.

Our training team, past and present:

We have deep gratitude for those powerful peace warriors who criss-cross the continent and show up at schools ready to connect, inspire, and teach young people why and how to be Safe School Ambassadors: Rick Lewis, Tory Capron, K'vod Wieder, Sasha Rose Schaible, Lidia Lopez, De Palazzo, Sally Clapper, Dawn Monnet, Bob Falle, Annette Schyadre, Sarah Behm, Mario Cossa, and Teddy Wright.

Our grantors:

We are especially grateful to these organizations for their support in bringing the Safe School Ambassadors program to areas of great need and helping establish the track record from which this book is drawn: the Aspen Center for Integrative Health and Children's Health Foundation; Kaiser Permanente Foundation, North and South; Wells Fargo Foundation; Y&H Soda Foundation; Codding Foundation; San Francisco Foundation; Crail-Johnson Foundation; the Eames Family Foundation; and the Polly Klaas Foundation.

Our Community Matters team, past and present:

Specific thanks to Sally Ember for her talent and writing support and to Bernadette Sproul, Jennifer O'Donnell, Helen Volhontseff, Lisa Sugarman, Brett Naftzger, Miranda Hansen, Suzanne Yeomans, and Geo Howard for their professionalism and dedication to this work and for so capably shouldering the additional responsibilities that came their way during the writing of this book.

Our editor, Kate Bradford at Jossey-Bass, who believed in our vision and invested the time, resources, and expertise to bring this book to publication.

Our families:

From Rick: My "heartner," Bobbi, for listening, supporting, and providing valuable feedback on our writing. My parents, Joe and Maxine; my children, Kris and Eric; and my grandchildren, Ethan and Sienna: they have inspired me to champion the cause of all children and young people. My gratitude and love for them knows no limits.

From John: Elsa who encouraged me and supported me in this long and worthwhile journey. Maya and Aden who remind me that young people are precious and should experience joy, freedom, and peace in every place and at every possible moment. I also acknowledge those others who have had a profound impact on me and this work including my parents, M.J. and Charles; all eight of my brothers and sisters; and my professional coach, Billy Sparkle.

From Chris: My parents, Bette and John, who instilled in me the values of working hard and giving back, and the belief that my character and actions make a difference. I also have deep gratitude for my wife, Mary, and my children, Sarah and Sam, who steadfastly supported me through countless sleepy days after late nights of writing and who remain always in my heart.

Rick Phillips
Graton, California

John Linney
El Paso, Texas

Chris Pack
Santa Rosa, California

INTRODUCTION

I moved to Los Angeles, California, from Montreal, Canada, when I was ten years old. My parents had divorced, and my mother wanted to start over and create a better life for her two sons. It was a very destabilizing period for my brother and me.

Our first home was a motel on the west side of Los Angeles. From this unfamiliar and transitory setting I entered the fifth grade. I was the new kid, from a divorced family, a foreigner with a Canadian accent. I might as well have had a "hit me" sign on my back. I was teased, punched, and made to feel that I didn't belong.

Over the next few years, my family moved around a lot. By the time I entered junior high, I was attending my third new school in three years, still trying to figure out how to fit in but not having much success. The rejection and harassment I was experiencing were taking their toll. I was a pretty troubled kid, anxious about being a target, and longing for a safe place to belong. I tried to fit in by being really friendly, hoping the other kids would accept me, and that way I could avoid being their next victim. Unfortunately, this strategy wasn't successful.

During the second week of school, I got off the bus with an "uh-oh" feeling in my gut. Walking toward my first class, I noticed some boys pointing and snickering. Following my plan of trying to get on their good side, I went up to them and sheepishly said, "Hi."

They were all wearing stickers on their shirts, with the letters "A.R.A." written on them. They began laughing, and soon other kids circled around me, chanting "A—R—A, A—R—A . . ." One of the ringleaders said, "How does it feel to know there is an Anti-Rick-Association at this school and that nobody likes you or wants you here?" His words were like bullets, piercing my sense of self and wounding me deeply. I pushed my way through the crowd, and I ran all the way home, some five miles away.

Exhausted and feeling sick to my stomach, I made it to my bedroom, collapsed, and stayed there for four days—four days of living in my own private hell—wondering, "Why me? Why did they do that? Why didn't anyone stop them?" I was so miserable and afraid that my mother couldn't get me to go back to school that whole week.

On Saturday, some neighborhood kids stopped by. They asked if I wanted to play football with them at the local park. It was just what I needed: a reason to get back in the game and back to school.

So, on Monday morning, with sweaty hands and a rapidly beating heart, I returned to school. I was relieved to discover that my tormentors had lost interest in me as a target. For them, it was all a big joke. But for me, it was a traumatic and defining moment in my early adolescence.

—RICK PHILLIPS

WHILE THIS IS THE STORY OF MY JOURNEY AS A YOUNG PERSON, it is also the reality for countless young people today. It is an archetypal tale of being mistreated by one's peers: excluded, teased, insulted, harassed, hit, punched, or worse.

Why This Book Is Needed

Despite the best efforts of educators and policymakers, mistreatment, bullying, and cruelty are far too commonplace in schools. Seventy-five percent of high school graduates report that they were bullied at school.[1] Every day, an estimated 160,000 young people stay home from school not because they have a doctor's appointment or are ill, but because they are afraid of how other students will treat them.[2] Every day millions more come to school with a knot in their gut, waiting for the next insult, intimidating look, or shove to happen to them or their friends. In schools and in pop culture as a whole, being cool has become closely linked to being cruel. Consequently a pervasive climate of unease and tension permeates schools.

There is no shortage of books addressing the problem of bullying and violence in our schools and communities. Most of these books focus on educating adults about bullying—its characteristics, its causes, and its effects. Some of these books suggest ways the school can address the problem through staff training or parent education. Others are designed to help adults teach an anti-bullying curriculum in a classroom setting. Some include a series of lessons to create awareness, empathy, and understanding among students, and others contain strategies that targets can use to defend themselves against bullying.

However, as we reviewed the literature and assessed the schools' responses to the conditions they face, we observed a troubling trend: students are too often overlooked as a resource for solving the problem. Consider the following:

- Students see, hear, and know things about their peers that adults don't.

- Students can intervene in ways adults can't.

- Students are often on the scene of an incident of student-on-student mistreatment before any adults arrive.

- Students shape and set the norms that govern how other students treat each other.

In spite of these realities, many adults don't see or tap into students' power. The remedies most books prescribe are primarily adult driven. They focus on doing things to, for, and at students rather than with them.

Safe School Ambassadors offers a student-centered departure from those tactics, an approach grounded in our experience as practitioners and our deep belief in young people as allies, contributors, and agents of positive change.

A Shared Vision

Coming from very different backgrounds, we three authors have joined together to write *Safe School Ambassadors* because we share in common:

- A concern that too many young people experience far too much bullying and cruelty at the hands of their peers and that their pain must be stopped

- A belief that young people are powerful and uniquely positioned to effectively solve this problem, breaking the cycle of mistreatment and stopping the pain

- A vision that all students, no matter who they are or where they come from, can attend a school free of cruelty, bullying, and violence; a school where they feel welcome, included, and physically and emotionally safe

Safe School Ambassadors is not about "fixing" students. On the contrary, this book is about believing in young people's ability to contribute to and be part of the solution. This book derives from our core belief that students are, as former dean of students at Indiana University Robert Schaffer put it, "not empty bottles to be filled but candles to be lit."[3] Youth development theory combined with our years of practice have shown us that when young people are provided with training, support, and opportunities, they can courageously and competently reduce violence and improve school climate.

Most schools address the problem of student-on-student mistreatment as adults see it: overt bullying and physical violence. They respond with what we characterize as an outside-in approach—one that is heavily focused on security, driven by adults, and based on rules. Although this approach appears to have reduced gun violence at school, it is not a complete solution to the problem. The outside-in approach does not effectively address the mistreatment that bubbles beneath the surface, out of sight of adults until it erupts in a form of visible violence.

Safe School Ambassadors takes a different view and looks at what students see: a vast universe of peer-on-peer mistreatment that includes rumors and relational aggression, teasing and taunting, exclusion, harassment, and more. The vast majority of this mistreatment goes unnoticed by adults. However, it has significant costs, not only for the targets but for the aggressors, the bystanders, and the school as a whole. For these reasons, this book presents a complementary inside-out approach: one that is based on current research on bullying and social norms change. This approach focuses on relationships, students, and norms.

Why go beyond security? While security can stop guns at the school entrance, it can't stop students from bringing in the prejudices, grudges, and attitudes that fuel the bullying and cruelty that students experience. Focusing on the importance of relationships builds and strengthens trust and connections among students and adults. Why can't adults address school violence effectively by themselves? Because young people know more about their peers' feelings and plans and are in a better position to address the mistreatment in their midst. Why aren't rules enough? Because young people's behavior is governed by social norms more than it is by rules. Our inside-out approach is based on the most recent research on bullying and social norms change.

The Safe School Ambassadors Program

We have used this inside-out approach as a basis to develop the Safe School Ambassadors program. Safe School Ambassadors (SSA) was developed in 1999 to help prevent and stop mistreatment and cruelty among students in fourth through twelfth grades.

As of December 2007, the program has been implemented in more than 550 schools in North America. SSA is a research-based and field-tested model that has involved more than twenty-five thousand young people and taught them how to break the cycle of mistreatment. The program engages, equips, and empowers children and adolescents with the skills, support, and opportunities they need to intervene with their peers and effectively reduce incidents of bullying and violence—in the halls, on the playground, in the lunch area, and wherever else mistreatment occurs.

Research shows that 70 to 85 percent of students have been passive bystanders to peer mistreatment. Most often, they do not intervene because they fear retaliation or don't know what to do or say. Their silence amounts to tacit consent, which reinforces an environment of cruelty and mistreatment. SSA training mobilizes the bystanders, but not just any bystanders. Socially influential opinion leaders (the students who shape the school's norms) from the diverse groups and cliques on campus are carefully identified and chosen by both the school faculty and their peers. SSA then trains these social leaders in nonviolent communication and intervention skills to prevent, deescalate, and stop mistreatment among their peers.

The SSA program is sustained through regularly scheduled small group meetings under the supportive leadership of the key adults who were trained alongside the students. These group meetings have several purposes: the ambassadors strengthen their skills to become increasingly effective; they share their experiences and exchange encouragement and support for their efforts; and they record their interventions and observations, providing important data for the school.

Schools that have implemented the SSA program report a reduction in violence, mistreatment, and tension among students. The SSA program also fosters increased tolerance and acceptance of diversity, as well as an environment that encourages higher grades and better attendance.

As Chapter Nine describes in detail, the feedback from hundreds of schools has demonstrated that students use these skills to intervene with their peers when they witness mistreatment. As a result, the behavioral norms that guide students' behavior change, and the school's social and emotional climate improves. Discipline incidents decrease, while attendance and academic achievement increase.

Making the Most of This Book

This book is written primarily for a school-based audience: school counselors, administrators, classroom teachers, teacher aides, district personnel, school board members, parents, parent-teacher associations, social workers, school resource officers, coaches, and after-school program providers. Nevertheless, the issues and strategies described in the book are equally important to all adults who offer programs and services to children and adolescents—those in parks and recreation settings, Boys & Girls Clubs, YMCAs, religious and faith-based programs, Boy Scouts, Girl Scouts, 4-H groups, summer camps, and all the other places where young people gather. In each of these settings, adults must implement effective strategies to reduce mistreatment and create environments that are physically and emotionally safe.

Safe School Ambassadors provides new research and ideas for reexamining how we see and respond to bullying and violence in schools. The book looks at how to improve school climate and provides strategies for tapping into, nurturing, and harnessing the power of young people. Although it wasn't written as a guide for implementing the complete Safe School Ambassadors program, it will help adults to connect with students as allies to help reduce bullying and violence, and it will provide key strategies for creating safer schools. We also believe the book can help you inspire your colleagues in schools and youth-serving agencies to join you in these efforts.

The book is divided into four parts. Part One focuses on the climate in schools today. It highlights the latest research and statistics about bullying, categorizes and defines the types of mistreatment, examines the costs to students and adults, and evaluates existing efforts to address the problem. Even if you are somewhat familiar with the problem of bullying and cruelty in schools, Part One will give you a solid overview and new information that will help you be an articulate and effective advocate for the strategies and approaches presented in Parts Two through Four.

Part Two provides an in-depth look at the inside-out approach, a complement to rather than a replacement for the existing outside-in approach that has been implemented in most schools. It also examines school climate, five main factors or determinants that shape it, and the role of climate in school safety, and it sets out ten keys to creating safer schools.

Part Three describes a different way of working with and being with young people, one that is based on empowerment and seeing them not as consumers but as contributors, not as problems but as solutions. The chapters in this part offer our formula for youth development and explore the role of bystanders in the dynamics of mistreatment. We also explain how to mobilize the bystanders and break the code of silence that permeates so much of today's youth culture. Finally, it presents an overview of the SSA model. It explains how SSA can be implemented in both school and after-school settings and gives examples of ambassadors who have diffused, deescalated, and prevented violence.

Part Four guides readers in how to be informed and effective advocates for the inside-out approach to creating safer school climates. Chapter Ten can help readers gain the support and buy-in of key decision makers in their school and the community. It can help those new to this way of thinking see the wisdom of empowering youth to reduce bullying and violence and to improve the social and emotional climate of all the places where young people gather. Regardless of your role or relationship to students, you can use the material to make a clear and convincing case for successfully initiating youth involvement.

Throughout the book, we present the stories and observations of students we have worked with around the country. These examples of actions by and voices from students show the problem from that student's perspective. Some of the students' names have been changed for privacy reasons. However, the statements are true, and we have tried to use the students' own words wherever possible. We also share some of our own stories, and though they are the experiences of three separate individuals, we have written them in the first person as if there were a single author.

We invite you to join us in making our vision a reality for the young people in your life, your school, and your community. Together we can engage, equip, and empower young people to transform their schools from institutions into communities characterized by acceptance, compassion, and respect.

Safe School Ambassadors

PART I

The Extent and Costs of Mistreatment and the Outside-In Response

THE CHAPTERS IN PART ONE EXPOSE THE DEPTH AND BREADTH of youth-on-youth mistreatment in schools and after-school settings, the far-reaching consequences of that mistreatment, and what schools are doing to try to stop it. In Chapter One, we describe the problem of mistreatment and how pervasive and increasingly frightening it has become in our schools. As much as possible, in this and other chapters, we bring in the voices of young people to express the reality of their experiences.

Chapter Two illuminates the vast consequences of seemingly small acts of mistreatment as we see how the problem spreads out and affects everyone: the targets, the aggressors, the bystanders, the school staff, and many others. We also take a look at the extensive financial and societal impact of this epidemic. In spite of increased security and stricter policies, many schools are experiencing declining test scores, lower attendance, poor teacher and staff morale, and a pervasive climate of tension and fear.

Chapter Three describes several of the most common strategies being used to address bullying and violence and the strengths and limitations of those efforts.

The emphasis on keeping schools safe from the outside in can reduce the use of weapons and some cases of physical violence, but they often don't deal with what causes students to want to hurt each other emotionally and physically or their desire to bring weapons to school in the first place. Many more young people are worried about having rumors spread about them, or being put down, cyberbullied, cast out, or harassed in the restroom than they are about weapons. The less visible incidents of mistreatment can keep the social climate of the school simmering with unease. Because the most common strategies used to try to create safer schools don't fully address the underlying causes, the cycle of mistreatment continues.

A Day in the Life

I don't even know how it got started, but for weeks this group of guys had been hassling me. It started with them laughing and calling me names when I walked by their lockers. They'd point at me and make faces and pretend that they were imitating me in these really weird ways. One time one of them said, "Yeah, that's it! He must be gay!" and the other guys joined in and went off on that. I felt my ears go red when they shouted, "Hey little faggot-boy. Are you going to ask Michael out on a date?" Michael is this other kid in my class that they always pick on too. There's nothing wrong with him, but they're always saying mean things about him and making up stories about him. You try to ignore it, but you can't. Other kids see it too, and you wonder what they're thinking. I hate feeling like people are judging me when they don't even know who I am or what I'm like.

I tried to avoid them by walking the long way around the halls to get to my classes, but it was almost impossible not to run into them. Every time they saw me, it would happen, and it kept getting worse. One day, I was walking home after school, and I saw them. They saw me too and turned and started walking toward me. I thought, "Maybe I should run," but then they'd make fun of me for that. And, besides, they'd have caught me anyway. So I thought I'd just try to get through whatever mean things they were gonna say. But when they got up to me, the guy who was the loudest of the group pushed me, and I fell down. I tried to get up, but there were at least three of them surrounding me. I looked around, and some other people were watching. It was just off of the school property, so there were plenty of other kids around. I waited for them to do something, but they just stood there. Then one of the guys started kicking me, and I covered my head to protect myself.

The next thing I saw was another guy put a padlock in a bandana and began to swing it around. I heard them yelling, "Hit him! Hit him!" I felt the lock smash into my elbow. The pain was unbelievable. I could hear my own bones cracking. They whooped and yelled and ran away. I tried to get up, but it hurt too much. It seemed like I was on the ground forever. I wondered, "Why did this happen to me? How come nobody tried to stop them?" Someone could have said, "Hey, you guys, chill out" or "Leave him alone," but they didn't. They just watched. Finally, a teacher and the security guy showed up, and they called an ambulance.

I still keep thinking about it. Why me? Why was I singled out? What did I ever do to them? I didn't even know those guys. And how come no one stood up for me? If this happened to me, how many other kids are scared or messed with or feel like they're lower-than-life and that no one really cares what happens to them? I don't ever want to come back to this school.

—Ninth-grade boy, New York

YOU MAY READ THIS ACCOUNT and be shocked by the brutality of the aggressors or the callousness of the bystanders. Or you might nod your head in silent acknowledgment that these kinds of incidents are a part of the lives of too many youth today. Perhaps you'll breathe a sigh of relief that this degree of visible violence is not happening to the young people in your school, community, or family. Or is it?

Visible Mistreatment: What Adults See

In the years immediately following the Columbine tragedy in April 1999, a great deal of public attention and educational policy was focused on school shootings—tragic but thankfully rare events. Over time, that focus has broadened to encompass school violence, which includes attacks like the one described at the start of this chapter. It also includes fights, robbery, hazing, use of weapons, hate-motivated incidents, and other acts that break clearly defined rules. After the terrorist attacks of September 2001, even threats of violence against people and property began to be taken more seriously. More recently, many school safety discussions have broadened to include bullying.

The statistics are sobering:

• From 1992 to 2003, the violent crime victimization rate at school for *students* ages twelve to eighteen declined from 48 incidents per 1,000 students to 28. Nevertheless, in 2003 there were still 154,200 serious violent crimes: rape, sexual assault, aggravated assault (855 average each school day), 584,500 simple assaults (3,250 average each school day), and 1.2 million thefts reported (6,620 average each school day).[1]

- During 2003, 33 percent of high school students reported being in a fight at least once in the twelve months preceding the survey, and 13 percent reported being in a fight *on school property.*[2]

- Every year between 1999 and 2003, an average of 7,400 *teachers* were victims of serious violent crime: rape, sexual assault, robbery, or aggravated assault (40 per school day), 57,200 were victims of simple assault (315 per school day), and 118,800 had property stolen (660 per day).[3]

- During the 1999–2000 school year, approximately 9 percent of all teachers (304,900) reported that they were threatened with injury *by a student* during the previous twelve months (almost 1,700 each school day).[4] In addition, during the same period, 4 percent (134,800) reported being physically attacked by a student.[5] The apparent discrepancy between this figure and the 57,200 simple assaults might be due to the protocols two different federal agencies used to gather and analyze their data; nonetheless, either number indicates a serious problem.

These are all examples of visible mistreatment: the violent or harmful student behaviors that adults actually see. However, a growing body of research suggests that these visible incidents make up a very small percentage of the broad spectrum of cruelty, bullying, and violence that is part of the daily lives of students throughout the country (Figure 1.1). As the U.S. Secret Service and Department of Education state in their guide, *Threat Assessment in Schools,* "Targeted school violence (where an attacker selects a target beforehand) is arguably only the tip of the iceberg of pain, loneliness, desperation and despair that many students in this nation's schools deal with on a daily basis."[6]

Wendy Craig is the director of the Bully Lab at Queen's University in Kingston, Ontario, and co-leads the Canadian Initiative for the Prevention of Bullying. Her research clearly shows that adults' perspectives on school violence and mistreatment are very different from students' perspectives. In their field research, Craig and her team asked school staff members, "How often do you intervene in bullying?" Most said, "All the time." However, when researchers carefully reviewed and analyzed hundreds of hours of videotape of children in school playground settings, they saw teachers intervene less than 5 percent of

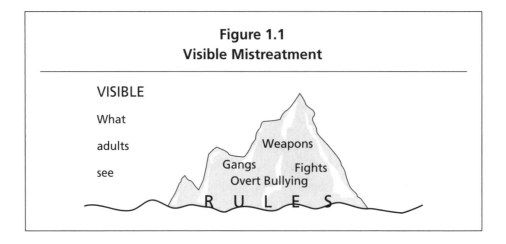

**Figure 1.1
Visible Mistreatment**

the time.[7] This huge disparity between adult perception and student experience shows that the problem of mistreatment goes far beyond the visible acts that most adults see. Referring to bullying and other forms of mistreatment, Craig notes, "We rarely see it. We don't hear it. And we don't intervene."[8]

Researchers examining the factors contributing to the Columbine High School shooting noted that students described their school as having "a lot of tension between groups . . . almost continuous conflict, anything from verbal abuse to physical attacks and violence," but the teachers and staff did not seem to notice the bullying and aggression.[9] The fact that so many adults simply do not grasp the extent or severity of the problem often leads to complacency, that is, the sense that the problem is under control, and ineffective efforts, such as stricter rules and policies about bullying, which do little to address the real problem. (These responses to the problem are explored further in Chapter Three.)

Less Visible Mistreatment: What Students See

We have met and talked with more than twenty thousand elementary, middle, and high school students in the United States and Canada. These students have described in graphic detail how students are mean to each other in classrooms, lunch areas, and common spaces; on playgrounds and athletic fields; in hallways and walkways; on buses and in parking lots. They have recounted more than fifty thousand painful and often frightening interactions that they or their peers experience daily as either targets of mistreatment or bystanders who witness it. Here are just a few of those examples:

> The other day in science class, the teacher was making up new groups, and she put this kid Mark in this one group. The other people in the group started doing and saying mean things about Mark. They'd groan and roll their eyes, and try to imitate him asking questions and saying things. The teacher told them to be quiet, but it didn't stop. A lot of what happens is not so easy to see as that was, but it happens.
>
> —Fifth-grade girl

> Oh, yeah, they say all kinds of things here. They make fun of you for being stupid, or if you seem smart, they call you a geek or a brainiac. They put you down if you wear certain clothes that are out of style. Then there's gay. People say that all the time. If they don't like you or you look just the slightest bit different, they'll say you're gay. And people will just say things like "loser" or "bitch" or "whore" to you for no reason at all, just when you're walking by. And then there's the racial stuff. They call the Mexicans "beaners" and the blacks "niggers" and the whites "crackers."
>
> —Eighth-grade boy

> These guys always hang out together. They are pretty popular. This other guy wanted to be friends with them, so they told him he had to go into the classroom and get the answers to the math test they had to take tomorrow. He didn't want to do it, but they said to him, "Look, if you want to hang out with us, you gotta do it. What are you, scared?" So he did it and got the answers for the test for them, and they laughed at him. They are always making him do stuff, and he does it. But they don't really like him.
>
> —Seventh-grade girl

> People get pushed into lockers all the time. They'll just be walking down the hall, and these bigger people will walk by and "accidentally" bump into them. Sometimes they'll fall down and drop their stuff all over the place. That's when all of them really laugh.
>
> —Ninth-grade girl

The fights, they still happen, but not at school so much. They know they'll get suspended, so they just do it on their way home. They know which way you go, and they'll wait for you if they really want to get you.

—Eleventh-grade boy

In PE, when we have to run a long course, I've seen the older and bigger guys grab the freshmen. They'll hold them by the ankles and dangle them from the bridge over the creek. I'm just glad they never got me.

—Tenth-grade boy

These anecdotal accounts provide insight into the lives of today's students, but it is the statistics that show how pervasive mistreatment is. Many studies and reports focus on bullying:

- A 2001 landmark study of more than fifteen thousand students in grades 6 through 10 found that roughly 30 percent of students were directly involved in bullying: 10 percent reported that they had been bullied, 13 percent reported that they had bullied others, and 6 percent reported that they had been bullied *and* had bullied others.[10]

- A 2003 report by the U.S. Department of Health and Human Services indicated that approximately 22 percent of students surveyed had been bullied during the current school term and over 4 percent reported that the bullying had occurred once a week or more. In the same report, 31 percent of the students responded that sometimes they had taken part in bullying, with over 5 percent reporting that they had participated in this behavior once a week or more.[11]

- A 2007 study conducted by Stanford University and the Lucille Packard Children's Hospital found that 90 percent of elementary students have been bullied by their peers, and nearly 60 percent have participated in some type of bullying in the past year.[12] Other research shows that 15 percent of all students in grades 5 through 8 report that they have been bullied on a regular basis during the current school year.[13]

Bullying is often used to describe a range of different behaviors that are better understood under the larger category of *mistreatment*. To understand the many varied kinds of mistreatment that students experience, it is helpful to examine some of the details revealed by the research—for example:

- One-third of the nearly seven thousand students in grades 6 through 12 who participated in the first national Students Speak Survey agreed with the statement, "Students say things to hurt or insult me."[14]

- A 2004 report on a five-year study of a diverse group of nearly nineteen hundred students in grades 8 through 12 offers some insights into how many students reported being:

  - Left out of activities: 67 percent (43 percent sometimes and 24 percent often)

  - Called names: 74 percent (47 percent sometimes and 27 percent often)

  - Teased: 62 percent (45 percent sometimes and 17 percent often)

  - Hit or kicked: 46 percent (35 percent sometimes and 11 percent often)

  - Threatened: 42 percent (33 percent sometimes and 9 percent often)[15]

- In a 2002 study by the Families and Work Institute, 66 percent of youth said they had "been teased or gossiped about in a mean way at least once in the last month," and 25 percent have had this experience five times or more. Over half (57 percent) said they had "teased or gossiped about someone at least once," and 12 percent had done so five times or more in the past month.[16]

- In 2002, a nationally representative survey sponsored by the National Mental Health Association revealed that 78 percent of all teens report "that kids who are gay or thought to be gay are teased or bullied in their schools and communities." More than nine out of ten teens (93 percent) hear other kids at school or in their neighborhood use words like *fag, homo, dyke, queer, or gay* at least once in a while, and 51 percent hear them every day.[17]

- The landmark 1993 study on sexual harassment commissioned by the American Association of University Women was updated in 2001 and showed remarkably little change. Based on surveys of more than two thousand students in grades 8 through 11, the report revealed that 83 percent of girls and 79 percent of boys have been sexually harassed, and 85 percent of students report that the perpetrators are other students.[18]

- A 2003 U.S. Department of Education study found that 10 percent of all sixth graders and 6 percent of all eighth graders feared attack at school or on the way to or from school, some or all of the time.[19]

- A 2007 survey conducted under the auspices of the National Crime Prevention Council found that 43 percent of teens ages thirteen to seventeen were victims of cyberbullying: the use of electronic means (cell phones or the Internet) to hurt or embarrass another person.[20]

Facts and figures like these seem to imply a sense of certainty, but in fact the numbers, especially those that come from official school reports, may not accurately represent what really happens. Several studies in England and the United States have indicated that only 25 to 50 percent of the students who are

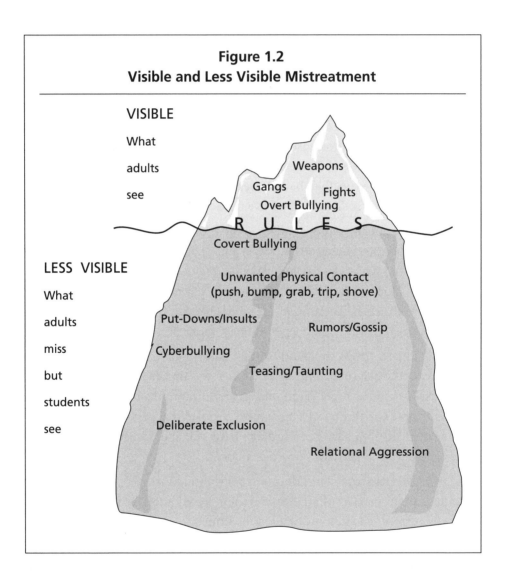

Figure 1.2
Visible and Less Visible Mistreatment

VISIBLE

What

adults

see

Weapons

Gangs

Fights

Overt Bullying

R U L E S

Covert Bullying

LESS VISIBLE

What

adults

miss

but

students

see

Unwanted Physical Contact
(push, bump, grab, trip, shove)

Put-Downs/Insults

Rumors/Gossip

Cyberbullying

Teasing/Taunting

Deliberate Exclusion

Relational Aggression

regularly bullied report the mistreatment to school staff.[21] For this reason, the problem of mistreatment could very well be two to four times what the figures in this chapter suggest.

As it is with icebergs, what is visible is at best an incomplete picture. The violence and overt bullying that most adults see are just the tip of the iceberg (Figure 1.2). As these accounts and studies show, meanness, exclusion, name-calling, teasing, gossiping, sexual harassment, and threats are all too common. Mistreatment has no zip code; it happens to students every day, in any school, in any community. It happens in public schools and private schools. It happens in inner-city, suburban, and rural schools. It happens in huge schools of 3,000 or more students where staff members struggle to learn the names of the 150 to 200 students they see daily, and it happens in schools of 300 where most students and their families have known each other for years and see each other every Sunday in church. It transcends income level, social class, and race. While school shootings are relatively rare, mistreatment happens everywhere and often.

The Players in the Drama of Mistreatment

In every example of mistreatment represented in every statistic noted in this chapter, three main roles are played out time and time again—aggressor, target, and bystander.

- *Aggressors* are the people who do the hurting, physically or emotionally, or both. This broad term includes not only bullies who use their physical power to push, hit, or injure others but also perpetrators of more subtle mistreatment, such as put-downs, rumors, and acts of exclusion. Both individuals and groups can be aggressors.

- *Targets* are the people who get hurt, physically or emotionally, by aggressors. Some researchers refer to these people as victims. However, the term *target* carries none of the emotional baggage, such as what the person might have done to deserve the mistreatment. Targets are students on the receiving end of mistreatment who may have done little or nothing to bring it on. Targets can be individuals and groups.

- *Bystanders* are the people who watch mistreatment happen. At times they actively encourage the situation, egging on the aggressor or mocking the target. At other times, they simply watch, often hoping that the aggressors won't turn on them. As Chapter Seven explores in greater depth, although the bystanders are not directly involved in the mistreatment, they play a significant role in allowing it to happen and in getting it to stop.

Mistreatment No Matter How It's Sliced

We have chosen to use *mistreatment* as an overarching term that encompasses the many ways young people hurt one another. However, it is difficult to comprehend, much less do anything about, until the types of mistreatment are differentiated. Once adults and teens develop a common language and define mistreatment in the same way, a new awareness emerges and new solutions present themselves. There are many possible ways to categorize the broad spectrum of mistreatment that students experience:

- By the issue or topic of the mistreatment (clothes or race, for example)
- By the way it is delivered (verbally, electronically, or physically, for example)
- By its effect on the target (he or she feels bad or afraid, for example)

Since we can't tame what we can't name, the choice of categories has far-reaching implications for how the problem ultimately gets addressed.

Acts of mistreatment can be grouped by topic. Teens exclude, tease, bully, and fight each other over an astonishingly wide array of subjects: hair styles, clothing styles, body size and shape, ethnic and racial background, perceived or actual sexual orientation, and still others. In addition, there are sexual harassment, hazing, and all the girl-boy interactions that generally erupt in middle school and continue through high school. The list can seem endless.

Mistreatment can also be categorized by the manner in which it is delivered. Students say and do mean and hurtful things directly to each other. They exclude, ignore, insult, taunt, threaten, blackmail, push, and fight. They talk about a person or people who are not present and start rumors that spread like a virus and can be difficult to contain and squelch. As the rise of cyberbullying demonstrates, today's teens also make full use of technology to deliver mistreatment in ways that their parents never dreamed of: e-mail, Web sites, instant messaging, cell phones, and blogs. They send text messages of hate, they post or circulate "slam books" that are repositories of a whole school's hurtful comments about one particular person, and they use their camera phones to take pictures of peers undressed in a locker room and post them on the Internet for the world to see.

Based on our extensive work with students and educators, we have found it far more fruitful to categorize mistreatment in a way that helps students respond to it effectively: by its effect on the target:

- Exclusion: The target feels left out.
- Put-downs: The target feels bad or hurt.
- Bullying: The target feels afraid.
- Unwanted physical contact: The target's personal boundaries are violated.
- Acts against everyone: The entire campus or large portions of it are affected.

Hundreds of students have told us that this framework has helped them take previously abstract and impersonal terms and make them concrete and personal. It has helped them see that they have (at times unknowingly) been aggressors themselves. And with that awareness, they have been able to begin to improve their own behavior.

Exclusion

Exclusion is a type of mistreatment in which the target is left out. He or she is ignored, shunned, rejected, or "ditched." In a young person's world, belonging and fitting in are two very important needs. Being left out, especially intentionally, is a painful emotional experience that can leave lasting emotional scars on some students and can have tragic repercussions for others. The shooters at Columbine and Red Lake, Wisconsin, high schools were the targets of exclusion.

Eric Harris, one of the Columbine shooters, wrote in his journal, "I hate you people for leaving me out of so many fun things. You had my phone number, and I asked and all, but no no no no no don't let the weird-looking Eric kid come along."[22] Obviously not every target reacts like the perpetrators of these tragedies, but it is far too easy for adults to underestimate the impact of exclusion.

Here's what students say exclusion looks and sounds like:

"Some kids made up a wall-ball game and wouldn't tell other people how to play it, so they couldn't join in."

"Once my friends and I were playing tag, and a girl came over and asked to play. One of my friends just glared at her and said, 'Noooo, I don't think so!'"

"Not letting someone sit at your lunch table. Telling him to go away and sit with his friends."

"Saying to this group of people standing around, 'Everyone's invited to the movies except for so-and-so.'"

"Go away! Why don't you swim back to the country you came from?"

"Inviting everyone to come over to someone's house and then telling one person that she can't come."

"These girls tell other girls they can't hang out with them because they are not cool at school."

"People just ignore someone. A guy will come up to this group, and they won't even turn around and say anything to him. They just keep talking and act like he's not there, even when he says something. It happens with girls too."

"Four girls were talking at lunch in the quad, and another girl came over. They stopped talking and stared at her when she sat down. They acted like they didn't want her to be part of the conversation."

"One day, these girls called me and invited me to go to the movies with them. They said to meet them there at 3:00 cause the movie started at 3:15. I got a ride down there from my brother. I was there at 3:00, but they weren't. I waited and waited. It was cold and raining. They never showed. Then I got it, and I just felt sick inside. Next day at school, they saw me and said like, 'So, have fun at the movies?' and laughed."

Put-Downs

Put-downs make the target feel bad inside: embarrassed, emotionally hurt, or inferior to others. This type of mistreatment includes rumors, malicious gossip, teasing, taunting, insulting, and pointing out someone's faults or mistakes. Put-downs are one of the most common types of cruelty teens encounter, and they are especially painful when they are done in front of others. Put-downs may take the form of a one-time, offhanded comment, or they may be repeated over and over again.

Here's what students say put-downs look and sound like:

"Did you hear that Chianna's parents are getting divorced?"

"Josh was looking at me in the locker room. I think he's gay."

"Your hair looks stupid."

"You're so gay."

"You're an idiot."

"There's way too many niggers around here."

"People laugh when someone asks a question in class."

"When the teacher made groups for a project, this girl raised her hand and asked the teacher if she could put this one kid in another group because he was too stupid."

"Kids outside the special ed class would see a kid walking into the room, and they'd say, 'Retard!' loud enough for him to hear."

"In PE, we were playing the championship game, and this other girl was saying things like 'You guys suck.'"

"People spread a rumor about this girl being a slut or that she is pregnant."

"A boy wrote a pretend love letter to this girl in the special ed class."

"One person will IM [instant message] her friend, 'Did you hear what so-and-so said?' They start this rumor, and the next day everyone is talking about it."

"There was a guy that read books a lot. Whenever these eighth graders saw him without a book, they would say, 'Hey, where's your book, school boy?' And they'd all laugh. You're not cool in our school if you get good grades."

"When someone has a different accent, other people will imitate it and laugh."

"These girls would call this other girl a bitch when she would walk by. She never did anything to them. Maybe it was because she dressed different."

"Girls will be best friends with another girl and then talk bad about her behind her back at school. They laugh about her clothes and her hair and the way she walks."

Bullying

In this type of mistreatment, the aggressor makes the target feel afraid. Bullying comes in the form of verbal threats and can also be carried out through an aggressor's body language: a look or a tilt of the head, for example. There is a power imbalance: the aggressor holds power over the target. The aggressor might be physically larger or stronger than the target, or might be part of a clique that is higher on the school's pecking order. The aggressor usually gets satisfaction or pleasure out of the encounter, and the target feels fear. The encounters between the aggressor and the target often continue over a period of time.

Here's what students say bullying looks and sounds like:

"I'm going to kick your butt after school."

"Three girls surround another girl at her locker. One girl says, 'I heard you were hitting on my guy. You better watch your back, bitch!' Then they just walk away and stare her down."

"Everyone in his group does what he says because they're afraid of him."

"These girls walk down the hall a certain way, and if they come toward you that way, you know to get out of their way. And of course, they make it so you kinda have to squeeze past them. Some guys do it too."

"These guys will just say, 'Move, punk,' and you know to move."

"My friend had her locker covered in deodorant because some people didn't like her. Everyone knew, and her books and stuff smelled for months."

"People cut in the lunch line in front of younger or weaker people who won't say anything or do anything about it."

"These guys will walk up to certain people and say how hungry they are and how they have no money, and they'll just kinda stand there around the other person until he gives them some money. They're not exactly stealing it, but he knows they'll beat him up later if he doesn't give them some money."

"This girl went around singing, 'If you're happy and you know it, kill Leanne.'"

"Groups of guys make sexual comments to girls walking by like, 'I'm gonna get me some of *that* later!' or, 'You know she wants it!'"

"These boys would like stick their feet out so I couldn't get back to my desk."

"'Bucking,' when older students make a sudden move into the face of some freshman walking by to get them to flinch or scare them."

Unwanted Physical Contact

As the term implies, in unwanted physical contact the aggressor makes some form of physical contact with a target or the target's possessions, and the target does not want the contact. In other words, it's not a game or just fooling around because at least one of the people involved doesn't like what's happening. The key element of this type of mistreatment is the violation of personal space or boundaries, although the target often feels afraid (as with intimidation and bullying) and might feel bad (as with a put-down). It can include tripping or throwing things at the target, like spitballs, bottle caps, erasers, or trash. It also could be pushing or punching the target. Unwanted physical contact includes grabbing, defacing, or stealing the target's possessions, such as the target's backpack, clothing, cell phone, lunch, or money. Physical forms of sexual harassment are unwanted physical contact. This can range from an anonymous touch on the buttocks in the hallway to date rape.

Here's what students say unwanted physical contact looks and sounds like:

"During passing period, guys grab girls' butts, and it's so crowded you don't know who did it."

"Walking home my whole sixth-grade year, this eighth grader would push me into the fence and block me from walking."

"Eighth graders kick other kids' backpacks, and flip them up."

"People put gum in other people's hair because they've done it up nice or just gotten it cut."

"They will just walk by and push you into the wall and keep on walking. Sometimes it's because of what you wear or how you look. Sometimes it's for no reason at all."

"'Coking' by pouring Coke on someone's head right after school."

"When we line up for recess or lunch, this one boy always steps on this other boy's foot. Not by accident; just slowly. If the teacher sees it, he just says, 'Sorry,' to the boy."

"Boys touch girls' hair every day in class."

"I saw a guy 'pants' this other guy. He snuck up behind him in the lunch area while he was talking to his friends and just yanked his shorts down to his knees. Lots of people saw it. It happens all the time."

"I was walking with my friend, and this eighth grader punched her and knocked her to the ground. The girl just left and walked on with her friends."

"In PE, we were playing basketball, and this girl on my team threw the ball really hard at this other girl because she thought the other girl had made a mistake."

"Some eighth graders duct-taped this kid to a tree in front of the school."

"Boys in the locker room get a younger boy and dip his head in the toilet and flush it to give him a 'swirley.'"

"I was walking with my friend when a guy screamed at me. I turned around, and two guys grabbed me and pinned me down. Another guy ran over me with his bicycle."

Acts Against Everyone

In the four types of mistreatment described, the target is usually one person or a small group who are usually known personally by the aggressor. In acts against everyone, the target is the whole school or at least a large group of students. The targets of this type of mistreatment are more anonymous than in other types, although such acts are usually spawned by specific interactions between a couple of individuals.

These examples are typical of what students experience:

"People lit a trash can on fire."

"Carving swear words into the bathroom stalls."

"People kick bathroom doors so the locks won't work."

"Writing graffiti in bathrooms. Someone wrote, 'Niggers suck,' and then other people wrote things after it."

"Breaking school windows and trashing the science classroom."

"A bunch of guys came at night and spray-painted swastikas and 'white pride' on the school."

"One kid brought a gun to school. It was loaded too."

"Calling in a bomb threat. I know some kids who really did that."

"These kids were talking a lot about making bombs and blowing up the school. They had drawings and plans and were acting weird."

"People break into other students' PE lockers and spread deodorant all over them."

"One kid said, 'This place sucks. I just wanna blow it up.' And for all I know he was gonna do it."

"Someone pulled the fire alarm, but there wasn't any fire."

Categorizing Mistreatment

Thousands of students have used these types to help them categorize what they see and experience. Through that process, they have come to see that the five types of mistreatment can be piggybacked or blended. The comment, "You can't play on our team! You suck!" contains two types of mistreatment: exclusion and put-down. More than one type of mistreatment can be present even without being spoken overtly. For example, the statement, "You'd better not sit at our table," has elements of exclusion and bullying. The target knows based on his or her relationship with that particular group that there is danger of being attacked if he or she sits at that table, and feels excluded and intimidated.

These five types are also sufficiently robust to encompass other categories of mistreatment. For example, sexual harassment is a put-down when it demeans or degrades, as when students refer to a couple of girls whose breasts are not very developed as the "itty-bitty-titty committee." It would be malicious rumors or gossip when it takes the form of slandering someone's reputation (girls are often demeaned sexually; boys are usually taunted as being too feminine or gay). It would be bullying when a boy (or group of boys) talks or badgers a girl into "going further" than she is comfortable going. And it would be unwanted physical contact if the boy touches the girl to get her to fulfill his wishes. In the same manner, racial harassment can fit into these five types of mistreatment. Saying that students of a certain racial group are dumb or lazy is a put-down. Saying to a student who appeared to be of Arab descent, "You'd better get the hell out of here you f***ing terrorist," is intimidation.

The beauty of this framework for categorizing mistreatment lies not just in its simplicity but in the way it helps students figure out how to respond to particular incidents in a helpful way. Each type of mistreatment may be best addressed by particular types of interventions, and it is important to give the students both the observation skills to recognize these types and the knowledge and intervention skills to respond most effectively.

A Culture of Cruelty

The bullying and cruelty that young people experience does not occur in isolation. What is happening in schools reflects what is happening in society in general: adults increasingly are quick to turn to anger and violence.

Consider, for example, the behavior of automobile drivers. They are generally more hurried (and harried), more impatient, and less willing to let someone merge in front of them when they are in a slow-moving line of cars. *Road rage* has become a common term, and the U.S. Congress has even held hearings on it. An automobile club study reported that incidents of aggressive driving increased by 51 percent from 1991 to 1997, and nearly 90 percent of all motorists have experienced an aggressive driving incident in the past year.[23]

Consider also mainstream media: children and youth witness a tremendous amount of violence on television. "By the time kids enter middle school, they have seen 8,000 murders and 100,000 more acts of violence on broadcast TV alone. Studies consistently show a link between media violence and violent behavior in kids."[24] This information is from Common Sense Media, an organization that reviews and rates popular media: television programs, movies, video games, music, Web sites, and books.

Beyond these explicitly violent behaviors, a casual session of channel surfing shows many other ways the mainstream media model negative behavior in a positive light. Examples of disrespectful and cruel humor abound. Many sitcoms are centered on characters who are generally snide and sarcastic with one another. Radio shock jocks enjoy record audiences and command top salaries. Their biting style has become less shocking and more accepted as the way people treat each other. Many reality shows feature individuals who score points or win for being dishonest, putting someone down, stabbing someone in the back, or demonstrating other cruel or callous behavior. Caring and compassionate acts are rarely shown on these popular programs. Consequently these negative behaviors can gain a level of acceptability by being showcased, and they become models for young people who act them out in school, at home, and in the community.

Television is not the only medium influencing the behavior of young people. Video games have become a mainstay of entertainment and social interaction for many. A recent study summed up the impact of this trend: "A meta-analytic review of the video-game research literature reveals that violent video games increase aggressive behavior in children and young adults. Experimental and non-experimental studies with both males and females in laboratory and field settings support this conclusion. Analysis also reveals that exposure to violent video games increases physiological arousal and aggression-related thoughts and feelings. Playing violent video games also decreases pro-social behavior."[25]

In an environment where it's cool to be cruel, students often gain social status and power not through compassion or strength of character but by putting down others or piling on insults. In one of our training sessions with youth, a girl at a California middle school pointed out how her school culture contributes to cruelty. In this young woman's school, being caring and kind is considered a weakness rather than a strength. She said, "If you show your emotions, if you're compassionate or kind in my school, you risk your popularity. If I'm kind to people, I can be put down for that. It's much more acceptable for me to put someone down. At my school, you'll be more popular if you're cruel."

Many young people find it difficult to stand up against this current of cruelty and are swept away by it. They are hungry for belonging, and in order to fit in and be liked, they do things they would not normally do. These otherwise normal students behave in astonishingly mean and callous ways to avoid being grouped with the "losers."

Conclusion

From 1997 to 2007, the focus of school safety expanded from school shootings, to school violence, to bullying. Many adults still have an incomplete picture of the scope and severity of bullying and violence because they do not see the extent of peer mistreatment that occurs every day in schools. Naming and defining the different types of mistreatment provide a common vocabulary that helps both youth and adults to discuss the problem and recognize hurtful behaviors. The statistics cited in this chapter illustrate national trends that shed light on the prevalence of this pervasive problem. Coupled with the stories from students, reports from staff, and perhaps even the results of any number of available school climate surveys (see the Materials and Tools in the Resources section at the end of this book), these figures can help local leaders understand the extent of mistreatment in their own schools.

However, knowledge of the problem is not enough. Only by understanding the overall effects of this bullying and violence can those involved feel some internal motivation to take action to stop it. The next chapter examines the emotional, physical, and financial costs of mistreatment for both students and adults.

The High Cost of Mistreatment

At first, you get angry and stuff and you'll get a headache, because you're so angry and stuff. And then after a while, after that you keep getting more and more angry, you feel like physical pain. When you're like violently sick and throwing up and stuff, the tightness and the pain . . . it was like that.

—JEREMY GETMAN, HIGH SCHOOL SENIOR, ELMIRA, NEW YORK

JEREMY GETMAN WAS A SENIOR AT SOUTHSIDE HIGH SCHOOL in Elmira, New York.[1] On February 14, 2001, he brought a duffel bag to school filled with pipe bombs he'd made at home. He also had a .22-caliber handgun, a sawed-off shotgun, and a book bag filled with ammunition. After ten years of mistreatment by his peers—being teased, insulted, called what he referred to as "every vulgar name you can think of," being spit on and hit, having his locker slammed shut on his hand—Jeremy Getman was going to get even. Several students became alarmed about things Jeremy had written and said that morning, and they notified school staff, who began to search the building. Southside's school resource officer, deputy Bob Hurley, found Jeremy in the school cafeteria, talking with one of the girls who barely ten minutes earlier had sought adult help. Jeremy offered no resistance as Hurley disarmed and cuffed him. The building was evacuated, the bomb squad defused the bombs, and a modern Valentine's Day massacre was narrowly averted. Ten months later, Jeremy was sentenced to eight and a half years in prison.

As this story shows, the costs of mistreatment are high. Jeremy Getman's experiences brought him to the point where he saw no alternative other than seeking revenge. His actions could have resulted in the injury or death of many students and staff at Southside. Luckily they didn't. At the very least, Jeremy lost eight and a half years of his life, and his actions have left emotional scars on many people.

Many adults subscribe to the notion that bullying and mistreatment are natural and even appropriate rites of passage that mark the transition from childhood to adulthood. Perhaps because they were once targets or aggressors (or both) or perhaps because of some inherent belief system about the process of growing up, these adults rationalize the cruelty that young people inflict on one another as a basic test of emotional strength. These adults minimize this mistreatment and its effects, using timeworn expressions like, "Everyone goes through it," "They'll work it out," or "It will make them stronger." Other adults notice the mistreatment but do nothing about it, justifying their inaction with phrases like, "Boys will be boys" or "They're just being kids." Since mistreatment has been around for generations, these responses are understandable. However, a thorough examination of the costs of mistreatment shows that they are counterproductive.

This chapter explores the emotional, educational, and financial costs of mistreatment as they ripple outward from aggressor to target, then to bystanders and the school community, and further out to families, neighborhoods, and ultimately to society as a whole. Over the past seven years, we have explored the concept of costs of mistreatment with thousands of students in schools across North America. Through a participatory process, we have guided them to scan all 360 degrees of what they can see from their individual vantage points. We have invited them to consider how mistreatment affects not only the targets but the aggressors and the bystanders, not just the students but the staff and the community as a whole. We have asked them to explore the many different dimensions of the concept of costs, including dollars and time, attitudes and beliefs, actions and lost opportunities. In school after school, urban and rural, large and small, rich and poor, regardless of ethnic composition, students have shown that they are remarkably perceptive, astute, and articulate about the costs of the mistreatment in their midst. Their words are woven into the fabric of this chapter.

Costs for Students

So many people hate on each other here. You've gotta watch your back and worry about what you say and who you look at. After a while, you just get sick of school, and you start thinking, "This place sucks."

—TWELFTH-GRADE BOY

Mistreatment has a negative impact on the social, emotional, and intellectual development of all young people—targets, aggressors, and bystanders alike. It is easy to comprehend the impact on targets: the students who are left out, teased, bullied, or assaulted. However, emerging research suggests that aggressors suffer consequences as well: loss of friends, poorly developed friendship skills, decreased empathy, an unrealistic and inflated sense of self-worth, and more. Bystanders who watch mistreatment pay a price too: they are distracted from their studies and can become desensitized and fearful.

Costs to the Targets

> Sometimes they [the targets] get depressed. Maybe they start cutting them-
> selves. Sometimes they kill themselves to make the pain stop.
> —ELEVENTH-GRADE GIRL

Several studies paint a picture of how mistreatment affects targeted students. In the spring 2002 issue of *Childhood Education,* Janis R. Bullock wrote, "Targeted students respond by skipping school, avoiding certain areas of the school (the bathroom or the playground), or, in extreme yet increasingly common cases, bringing weapons to school."[2] In two studies published in the *British Medical Journal,* researchers found that abdominal pain, headaches, bedwetting, sleep problems, anxiety, insecurity, and depression were much more common in targeted children and aggressors. Interestingly, the rates of these symptoms were highest in those who were bullied *and* in turn bullied others.[3] More recently, UCLA conducted a study of two thousand sixth graders and their teachers. The study reinforced earlier findings that the targets of mistreatment suffer a wide range of health problems, including headaches, stomachaches, and sleeplessness.[4]

Abraham Maslow's hierarchy of human needs (Figure 2.1) can help explain the results of the UCLA study. According to Maslow's work, when young people have an unmet need, their development is arrested at that stage. Instead of moving to higher developmental levels, they focus their efforts on the unmet need, not by conscious choice but by nature. Students whose need for physical and emotional safety is unmet will be unable to focus on higher-order needs such as belonging, self-esteem, or achievement.

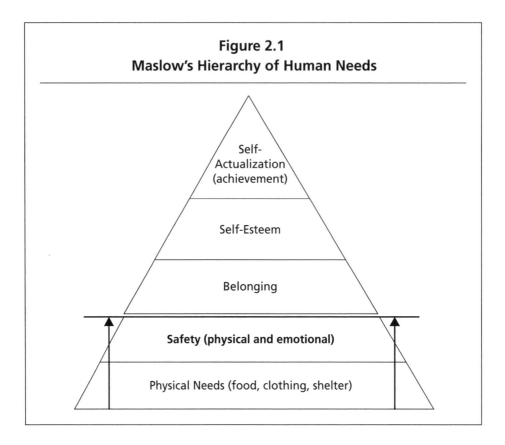

Figure 2.1
Maslow's Hierarchy of Human Needs

Self-Actualization (achievement)

Self-Esteem

Belonging

Safety (physical and emotional)

Physical Needs (food, clothing, shelter)

Other studies have shown links between students' feeling unsafe or being victimized and truancy, lower academic achievement, weapons at school, more violence, the perception of an unsafe school, fewer friends, and less happiness at school.[5] When school policies and practices fail to stop, and thus unwittingly condone, such mistreatment, they create an unsafe environment that is toxic for both staff and students.

Belonging and Connectedness   Maslow's work suggests that students who do not feel emotionally or physically safe won't be able to meet their needs for belonging. It is likely that they will feel isolated and disconnected. Recent research has begun to identify a social factor known as *connectedness*. Connectedness is the degree to which a person feels that she or he is a part of a societal unit and the people associated with it. School connectedness therefore is the degree to which a student feels that she or he belongs at, identifies with, or feels an affinity for her or his school.

In 2002, researchers released the results of the National Longitudinal Study of Adolescent Health (Add Health), the largest study of school connectedness ever undertaken. This congressionally mandated, federally funded study involved more than ninety thousand students from grades 7 through 12 in 132 schools in eighty different communities around the United States. School administrators also completed questionnaires, and the parents of 85 percent of the students were interviewed. The results confirmed that students who feel more connected to their school are less likely to experience risk factors such as emotional distress, suicidal thoughts and attempts, substance abuse, early sexual activity, pregnancy, and violent behavior.[6]

Researchers identified nine factors as root causes of connectedness:

- Classroom management
- School demographic composition
- School size
- Class size
- School type: public, private, or parochial
- Discipline policies
- Rates of participation in extracurricular activities
- Teacher qualifications
- Friendship groups among students at the school

In this exploration of the costs of mistreatment, the last factor stands out: at schools where students feel highly connected, boys and girls mix easily as friends, the tables in the lunch area are naturally populated with students of different races and social groups, and a student who usually sits at one table can sit at another table without anybody feeling angry or hurt. Conversely, at schools where students do not feel connected, the social structure is rigidly divided by race and interest. Not only would a "jock" not hang out with a "goth," but also that jock would likely harass or bully the goth, much to the amusement of bystanders.

In a school where mistreatment is the norm, there is less student connectedness, along with a lack of the positive behaviors that can directly result from connectedness. Additional research shows that the negative effects of bullying and being bullied reach into adulthood, and bullies, as well as their victims, are more likely to drop out of school.[7]

Social and Emotional Development   Maslow's work also indicates that students who are targets of mistreatment will have less confidence. They are more vulnerable to negative influences and self-destructive behavior because their self-esteem needs are not being met. Consequently these teens are less likely to take healthy and appropriate risks such as these:

- Offering ideas or asking questions in class discussions
- Reaching out to meet new friends
- Joining or trying out for new activities like sports or drama
- Asking someone for a date
- Simply being themselves

Words Can Be Weapons

Research by Stephen Joseph, a psychologist at the University of Warwick in the United Kingdom, dispels the well-known saying, "Sticks and stones will break my bones, but words will never hurt me." Although it is generally accepted that bullying lowers the target's self-esteem, his work shows that verbal abuse like name-calling can reduce targets' self-worth even more than physical attacks, like pushing or punching, and attacks on property, like stealing or destroying belongings. Joseph also found that social manipulation, such as excluding the target from taking part in games, is more likely to lead to posttraumatic stress, a recognized anxiety disorder that has serious immediate and long-term consequences. "The study reveals that bullying and particularly name-calling can be degrading for adolescents," causing post-traumatic stress. It also indicates "symptoms such as insomnia, anxiety, and depression are common among victims and have a negative impact on psychological health."

Source: H. Mynard, S. Joseph, and J. Alexander, "Peer-Victimisation and Posttraumatic Stress in Adolescents," *Personality and Individual Differences,* 2000, *29*(5), 820.

The patterns established in primary grades tend to be repeated in middle and high school, and even in adulthood. Teens who were targets of bullying in their early grades are likely to continue being bullied.[8] Those who were bullied in secondary school are likely to show signs of low self-esteem and depression as young adults, even though they are not being isolated or harassed.[9] And research also shows that students who were chronically targeted are at increased risk of schizophrenia,[10] suicide,[11] or other mental health problems.[12]

Academic Achievement

> The kids who are bullied or picked on sometimes stop trying in school, and they don't ask questions or talk much in class. If they don't ask questions, then they can't learn as much because how are they going to get an answer if they don't ask? After a while, their grades start to go down.
>
> —SEVENTH-GRADE BOY

Maslow's work also shows that targeted students are less likely to meet their self-actualization needs or achieve their potential. Students who are worried about or fearful of what might happen to them when they leave class cannot focus on what's being taught during class. Their ability to concentrate, learn, and achieve is drastically reduced. In *Emotional Intelligence,* author Daniel Goleman puts it this way: "Continual emotional distress can create deficits in a child's intellectual abilities, crippling the capacity to learn."[13]

Bullying Increases Stress

A group of golden hamsters in a lab at the University of Texas at Austin are helping to shed some light on what goes on inside people when they are worried, fearful, or stressed. In psychology professor Yvon Delville's experiments, the control group of hamster "teens" are placed in an empty cage for an hour each day. At first they are stressed by the unfamiliar environment, and their cortisol levels rise, but after a couple of weeks, they are not bothered by their hour in the empty cage and show no change in cortisol levels. In the experimental group, each young hamster spends that same hour per week in the cage of an adult male hamster, whose territorial and antisocial tendencies compel him to chase and nip at the "teen"—behavior characterized as hamster bullying. As expected, cortisol levels in the experimental hamsters rise, but they don't come down. It appears that they don't adjust to the bullying and remain continually stressed by it.

Source: Y. Delville, J. T. David, K. Taravosh-Lahn, and J. C. Wommack, "Stress and the Development of Agonistic Behavior in Golden Hamsters," *Hormones and Behavior*, 2003, 44, 263–270.

Stress is a normal and healthy response to a perceived threat to one's safety. The stress hormones like adrenaline and cortisol increase heart rate, breathing, and blood pressure so the brain can think clearly to plan a response to the threat. It is the classic fight-or-flight response that served our ancestors well but takes a toll on the brain. Blood cortisol attacks the cells of the hippocampus, the brain's center for memory and learning. As a result, it is common for targets of mistreatment to experience problems with their studies and a drop in grades. Recent research confirms that targeted students are indeed distracted from their schoolwork, which results in lower academic performance.[14] In their study of bullying, Hoover and Oliver found that 14 percent of students in grades 8 to 12 and 22 percent of students in grades 4 to 7 reported that bullying diminished their ability to learn in school.[15]

Many targets skip classes or miss entire days of school for fear of mistreatment. One study showed that 7 percent of eighth graders stay home at least once a month because of bullies.[16] Other research found that 10 percent of the students who drop out of school cite repeated bullying as the reason.[17] There is a direct relationship between attendance and academic achievement.

Costs to the Aggressors

Aggressors are individuals who initiate or inflict mistreatment on others. They appear in many guises—big and small, boys and girls, popular and unpopular, academic stars and underachievers. They are not just the "big bullies" who threaten or hit smaller, weaker students. Aggressors are also the students who inflict pain on others by intentionally excluding them, teasing them, or gossiping or starting hurtful rumors about them.

Students become aggressors for a number of reasons. They generally lack empathy and impulse control, and some have aggressive behavior modeled for them in their homes. Many don't have the skills to negotiate and resolve conflicts peacefully. Because they haven't acquired these skills, their social and emotional development suffers. Consequently they have difficulty developing and maintaining healthy relationships in school and other social settings.

Maintaining Social Position

> Sometimes they feel a lot of pressure to keep being mean, because that's what got them into that group or whatever. If they want to stay friends with them, then they have to keep doing it.
>
> —EIGHTH-GRADE GIRL

Aggressors often paint themselves into a corner. There is tremendous pressure when one is seen as top dog. Once students have established themselves as aggressors, they often feel a need and an expectation to maintain that role. Therefore, behavioral change can be difficult. Aggressors risk losing their social position if they suddenly change their behavior. In order to maintain their position, they are expected to be mean and exclude others who are perceived to be lower in the pecking order.

Because of this expectation, aggressors are less likely to interact with a diverse range of peers. Although they may have the power or ability to interact with all of their peers, they are unlikely to do so in healthy ways, especially with members of certain groups.

Aggressors believe they have to look and act a certain way to maintain their social position. They have to hang out with the right crowd, say the right things, and wear the right clothes. An aggressor who maintains a friendship with someone in a social group that is often targeted risks criticism and the loss of status. Aggressors will fight and even end long-standing friendships in order to maintain their high status.

Inflated Sense of Self-Worth   When aggressors' actions go unchecked, they come to think that mistreating others is acceptable. They often believe they are entitled to hurt others in order to meet their own personal needs. The more incidents of aggression they engage in, the more they believe that their behavior is appropriate.

This unchecked behavior gives them an inflated sense of self-worth, making them think they are more powerful and more formidable than they really are.

This inflated sense of self-worth leads aggressors to mistake fear for respect. Others tend to do what the aggressor demands of them, so the aggressor begins to believe that others behave that way out of respect. In fact, aggressors don't have authentic respect from their peers. They often see their peers as looking up to them when, in fact, their peers are simply afraid of them.

Social Consequences   Many aggressors face an uncertain future. Their developmental deficiencies, types of beliefs, and accompanying behaviors are likely to have negative consequences later in life. Aggressive behavior that becomes habitual in the early elementary years can easily become a lifelong character trait if it continues past age eight.[18] In a twenty-two-year study involving more than six hundred subjects, their parents, and their children, aggression in childhood was shown to interfere with the development of intellectual functioning and to be predictive of poorer intellectual achievement as an adult.[19] In other words, people who start bullying in childhood are less likely to finish college and get good jobs. Being a bully in childhood and adolescence has been associated with delinquency in adulthood.[20] By age thirty, approximately 25 percent of bullies who started young had criminal records.[21] Aggressors are more likely to drop out of school, use drugs and abuse alcohol, and engage in delinquent and criminal behavior.[22] A large-scale study in Sweden found that 60 percent of the boys ages thirteen to sixteen who were identified as bullies had at least one criminal conviction by the age of twenty-four. Furthermore, 35 to 40 percent of these bullies had been convicted of at least three officially registered crimes by age twenty-four. In contrast, this was true of only 10 percent of boys who were not classified as bullies. In other words, former school bullies were four times more likely than other students to engage in relatively serious crime.[23]

Recognizing that aggressors are often targets in other settings (so-called bully/victims), several researchers have looked into the costs of having any direct involvement in the dynamic of mistreatment. A nationwide National Institute of Child Health and Human Development study involving 15,686 students in sixth through tenth grades found that both aggressors and targets were more likely to engage in violent behaviors like fighting and carrying weapons than those who were only bystanders. The study also found positive correlations between those who are involved in bullying and alcohol use, smoking, and poor academic achievement.[24] In addition, targets and aggressors are more likely to be depressed than students who are not involved in bullying, which can lead to academic and interpersonal problems, and self-defeating behaviors.[25]

Costs to the Bystanders

> People are always watching what they say, so they don't make a mistake and then people will make fun of them. Same for clothes—really for everything. You don't want to make a mistake because they can make you miserable.
>
> —TENTH-GRADE GIRL

Bystanders are the students who stand by and watch others being mistreated. At any given time, bystanders make up about 70 to 85 percent of the students in a school.[26] In a study where hundreds of hours of videotaped playground interactions were analyzed, peers (bystanders) were present in 85 percent of bullying incidents.[27] When students observe this mistreatment and don't speak up, they not only give passive consent to the aggressors but also pay a significant personal price.

Sense of Helplessness

> Everyone who's watching starts to think that's just the way it is; it's normal. Then maybe they become a little more like that; they start being mean or talking bad about people. Then everyone is. It just spreads.
>
> —TENTH-GRADE BOY

Bystanders often report feeling helpless and anxious. In addition, they suffer from guilt for not taking action. As a result, they experience lower self-respect and self-confidence.

Those who repeatedly witness mistreatment can become desensitized and begin to feel less empathy toward the pain of others. As a result of this desensitization, bystanders not only stop caring but also stop noticing what is going on. For example, when they witness a student making a racial slur or getting tripped, they don't see these acts as unconscionable; they see it as business as usual. The inaction of bystanders makes mistreatment of peers become more acceptable to other bystanders, as well as to aggressors and targets.

Lowered Academic Achievement   Research shows that chronic exposure to violence adversely affects a child's ability to learn.[28] Even if children are not abused physically themselves, when they see abuse, emotional or physical, they can suffer psychological trauma, including the inability to establish vital psychological bonds with key people in their lives. W. Thomas Boyce of the University of California, Berkeley, studies the impact of stress on children. His work shows that when children witness violence in any form or fear for their own safety, that state of arousal or stress triggers a variety of physical reactions in the body that may interfere with thinking and learning because they alter brain chemistry.[29] David Sousa, author of *How the Brain Learns: A Classroom Teacher's Guide and Learning Manual,* reinforces this connection. He notes that in a peaceful school environment, students (and teachers) feel that their survival and emotional needs are met, so they are free to focus on higher-order thinking.[30] Conversely, when bystanders witness physical or emotional violence, their brain functions shift away from higher-order thinking (learning) and toward more basic survival functions.[31] When they are concerned about what just happened or what is going to happen and how they could be affected, even if they are not the direct targets, students cannot focus on learning and academic performance suffers.

Staff Costs

> My day starts at 7:45, and by 7:47 I usually have my first discipline problem.
>
> —JERRY NAVE, DEAN, SHERIDAN HIGH SCHOOL, SHERIDAN, COLORADO

In researching this book, a common theme clearly emerged from the more than one thousand hours of interviews and discussions with teachers, counselors, and administrators throughout the country: student mistreatment has a huge impact on school staff members. The most common impacts are the time required to deal with students who are mistreating other students; morale, productivity, and effectiveness; and absenteeism and turnover.

Time

> Counselors and the vice principal, they spend a lot of time dealing with this stuff, trying to help kids settle an argument so it doesn't start up again. If there's a fight, then they have to take all that time to talk with everybody and do the suspension hearings and everything.
>
> —TEACHER, GREECE, NEW YORK

Teachers, administrators, and other staff members must take time from their other duties to deal with acts of mistreatment by students. The time required may be just moments for a simple comment from a teacher during class or several hours of an administrator's time to address a major incident. Either way, dealing with discipline issues takes time away from staff members' main job: education.

Interrupted Instruction   An act of mistreatment in class requires that the teacher interrupt instruction. In many secondary classrooms, this takes the form of a quick comment that such behavior is unacceptable, and if the student continues, there will be certain consequences. The focus is on following the rules, and the aim is to maintain order in the class. The total elapsed time is probably less than a minute, but the time adds up with each incident. More significant, the attention of the class is shifted away from learning, and the flow of the lesson is disrupted. At the elementary level, it is more common for the teacher to use an incident as a teachable moment to educate the class on appropriate behavior. Although this is often valuable to social-emotional development, it takes time away from the lesson being taught.

Loss of Focus on Learning   When some episode of mistreatment has occurred, it often becomes the center of attention for students. It is difficult to get students focused on learning when they are thinking about the fight that just happened in the hallway or the argument they just heard. This affects aggressors and bystanders as well as targets. Teaching is much more difficult when students are distracted by an incident that just occurred or is likely to occur after class. This distraction factor slows the pace of learning and decreases the amount students absorb and integrate.

Need to Make Up Work   Students who have been absent from class must make up the work they missed. This may be a single assignment missed while the student was at the counselor's office to work out a conflict that erupted at lunch. It might be a full day of school that was missed because a student who'd been humiliated in the locker room feigned illness and stayed home to avoid similar mistreatment the next day she had physical education. Or it might be several days of work missed while the student was suspended for mistreating someone. Regardless of the reason for the absence, teachers must take the time to assemble the materials and explain missed assignments. Obviously this is part of the teacher's job, but it is a separate, time-consuming task added to an already full workday.

Responding to Mistreatment   When a student informs a staff member about an act of mistreatment, an often-lengthy response cycle is triggered. The kind of response depends on a number of factors, such as the severity of the incident, the type of school, and state, district, and building policies.

First-time teasing about a new haircut or a clothing choice may require only a few minutes of a teacher's time to remind the aggressor how he would feel if he were the target and to exact an apology. A sixth grader reporting that two eighth-grade boys cornered him that morning just off campus and demanded his money would likely require more of a counselor's or vice principal's time to investigate and meet with the people involved, and double that time if the investigation leads to a suspension. Alleged sexual harassment could require several hours of an administrator's time to investigate, meet with parents, and complete the required documentation.

To begin to understand the amount of time spent on discipline issues, it is helpful to examine how much time a single suspension at a high school can require from various members of the school staff and community. These estimates have been compiled from a sample of school administrators who have collectively handled thousands of suspensions:

- 5 to 15 minutes for the staff member who observed or learned about the incident to gather information and report it
- 30 to 60 minutes for the counselor, dean, or assistant principal to meet with the students involved in the incident and gather information
- 30 to 60 minutes for a meeting between school officials and parents
- 60 to 120 minutes of secretarial time to file the paperwork
- Total time: 125 to 255 minutes, or 2 to 4 hours, for each suspension

While it is virtually impossible to quantify time at a national level, it is safe to say that thousands of hours of administrative and staff time are spent each year dealing with behavior and discipline problems. Imagine if that time were instead devoted to enrichment activities or staff development.

Morale, Productivity, and Effectiveness

> Sometimes two people will bring it [trouble] into class, and they'll be arguing or whatever, and the teacher has to deal with it instead of teaching. Or sometimes it's just one person who has an attitude, maybe because of something somebody said or whatever; then they give the teacher a hard time.
>
> —NINTH-GRADE BOY

Most educators who enter the field are motivated by a strong desire to make a positive difference in the lives of young people. But new teachers quickly discover many realities that erode their altruism. Educators live with the pressure of teaching the required curriculum, grading and assessing student performance, preparing students for standardized tests, supporting young people with problems, and managing the tensions and conflicts that arise among the students in their classrooms.

Especially since the passage of the No Child Left Behind legislation in 2002, administrators and teachers are under tremendous pressure to improve students' academic achievement and performance on standardized tests. When that pressure is coupled with a seemingly overwhelming number of discipline issues, teachers can easily lose their connection to the passion and energy that led them into education in the first place. Stress goes up, and morale goes down. As a result, the school culture becomes more negative: staff members complain about their work; they make negative comments to colleagues about the school, the administrators, and other staff members; and they begin to generalize their view of parents as adversaries and of students as inconsiderate and difficult, or perhaps even ungrateful and burdensome.

As this shift happens, many teachers also become less open and more guarded. Their concern for students diminishes, their passion for teaching suffers, and they don't put as much of themselves into their work. When this happens, students end up doing the same: they don't open up and don't try as hard. Students sense when a teacher is just going through the motions. As a result, learning and performance suffer.[32]

Absenteeism and Turnover

Many teachers become frustrated working in an environment where it's cool to be cruel. As a result, schools experience increased teacher absenteeism and incur costs for substitutes. Teacher absenteeism causes decreased continuity and connectedness for students. Some teachers get so frustrated with spending their energy on discipline that they quit teaching altogether. Nationally almost 50 percent of all teachers leave the profession within the first five years of entering it. While poor salaries and inadequate support from school administration are cited as the primary reasons for leaving, the third leading cause for teachers leaving the profession is student misbehavior.[33] It takes a great deal of time to identify, interview, and hire new teachers to replace ones who have left.

Schoolwide Costs

> It [the school] gets a bad reputation, and then everybody starts thinking that your school is a bad place. And when they find out that you go to that school, they treat you like you're some jerk or gang-banger or criminal. And it doesn't feel very good.
>
> —TWELFTH-GRADE BOY

When we ask the teens we work with to reflect on how the culture of cruelty and bullying affects them, they invariably create a long list of consequences. These consequences have an impact on them, their friends, the adults, and the entire school community. Students describe two different types of tension. One tension exists between certain groups, cliques, or individuals, and the other is what they feel internally. While adults usually become aware of the conflicts between groups or individuals only after they erupt into visible aggression or violence, students experience these conflicts at their roots. Teens' stress levels go up as they watch conflicts develop out of a look or a gesture or a bump or a comment between students. The internal tension arises from the culture of cruelty—a culture that metes out steep consequences for those who commit a social misstep: wearing the wrong thing or hanging out with someone from an "out" group. The extent and intensity of the tension can vary with the demographics of the school, yet the net result of this tension is always a loss of feelings of connectedness, community, and safety. In such an environment, many students live in a constant state of fight or flight. This elevated adrenal activity interferes with normal functioning and healthy development, which is at the root of many of the schoolwide costs.

Reduced Participation and Healthy Risk Taking

> You watch and you see what happens to other people, and you think, "I don't want that to happen to me." So you play it safe, like with what you say, what you wear, what you like, what you do and even who you're friends with.
>
> —EIGHTH-GRADE GIRL

Teens we have worked with say that they or their friends feel as if they are always on guard or hypervigilant. They are fearful of saying or doing something that will make them the object of isolation, ridicule, intimidation, or attack. In this social minefield, one wrong step can result in an explosion of mistreatment or violence. Young people find it difficult to express themselves in healthy and authentic ways; for example, they may be afraid of:

- Making a joke, because someone might take it the wrong way and start a fight
- Talking with a girl or boy who might belong to a different group, whose members might get mad about the conversation
- Asking a question in class because they might appear to be dumb, or because they might appear to be too smart, and be ridiculed
- Speaking their minds in a discussion or a debate because they fear being scorned and humiliated

When students do not fully participate in class, intellectual exploration and growth are reduced, the richness of the teacher-student exchange is diminished, and the entire academic environment suffers. With today's emphasis on group projects and teamwork in the workplace, an atmosphere of fear inhibits students from developing skills they will need later in life. Fear of mistreatment prevents all students from taking healthy risks that are vital to their social and intellectual development.

Intergroup Tension

> Because people don't get to know each other, there are more rumors and prejudices about other people and whoever they hang out with. Then there are more problems and fights between different groups.
>
> —ELEVENTH-GRADE GIRL

Commonly held stereotypes reinforce and promote separation. Rumors and put-downs can develop quickly into physical violence and fights, affecting the entire school community. Mean-spiritedness spreads from one racial or social group to another, creating a school climate in which stoners don't like the jocks, whites don't like the blacks, blacks don't like the Latinos, cheerleaders don't like the nerds, Asians from one country don't like the Asians from another, goths don't like the cowboys, and so on. This culture of intolerance between groups makes many students feel unwelcome and often unsafe. In this environment, teens are less likely to venture out of their comfort zones and mix with other groups of students. They don't engage in as much cross-cultural and cross-clique dialogue, which solidifies the stereotypes and judgments students have of one another. They can go to high school for four years and never mix with people in other groups. This type of experience does not foster school connectedness and the associated positive behaviors,[34] and it does not prepare teens for today's multicultural, multiethnic workplaces. Finally, it does not help them develop cultural competence, one of the forty developmental assets identified by the Search Institute and linked to a host of thriving behaviors and success in life.

Loss of Privileges

> Because of all the stuff that's happened, the administrators now lock the bathrooms, and we don't have as many assemblies and dances as we used to. It's starting to feel more like a prison than a school.
>
> —TWELFTH-GRADE BOY

Faced with a threatening environment, adults often try to protect students and school property by adding new policies and rules that restrict student interactions. For example, schools that are worried about teen violence are less likely to sponsor dances or other social events. Ironically, such events can promote student connectedness and, in many cases, act to improve the school climate.

More rules and restrictions inhibit the increasing need that adolescents have for greater independence and self-determination. Teens resent these restrictions on their ability to connect with their peers and exercise new freedoms. When this resentment builds, morale suffers. Young people become less connected to each other and to the school in a phase of their life when those connections are critical for academic, social, and emotional development.

Disruptions in Attendance

Students, even those who have never been targets, avoid certain hallways, restrooms, the cafeteria, or other places in and around the school because they are afraid. Many students report that they or their friends avoid school altogether for fear of violence or mistreatment. In the United States, 6 percent of students miss at least one day of school a month because they feel unsafe at school or on their way to or from school. This figure has held fairly steady since 1999, when it jumped up from 4 percent.[35]

Researchers investigating the relationship between bullying and absenteeism have reported a consistent link. One study showed that among students bullied frequently (once a week or more), approximately 20 percent of boys and 25 percent of girls missed at least one day of school. In addition, roughly half of those bullied frequently reported that they had considered skipping school.[36] As stated earlier in this chapter, 7 percent of eighth graders stay home from school at least once a month because of bullies.[37] These percentages back up research by the National Association of School Psychologists that found that approximately 160,000 students stay home from school every day in the United States because they fear how they will be treated at school.[38] Many experts believe that these figures are conservative.

The students who avoid school are typically the targets. Yet bystanders also avoid school because they are afraid. We have received reports from several schools that have experienced an epidemic of absences—20 percent, 30 percent, or more—when word spread among the student population that something bad might happen on a particular day. For example, at one high school in Sonoma County, California, more than 25 percent of the students stayed home because a note scrawled on a bathroom wall corroborated a rumor that several students were planning to shoot up the school. Although the attack never happened, the fear, anxiety, and stress generated by the rumor, and the absences themselves, were all too real.

Absences affect more than just the students who are absent. They have a negative impact on the entire continuity of instruction.

Barrier to Academic Achievement

A growing body of research shows that the targets of mistreatment are not the only students whose academic performance suffers. All students are affected. Data from the California Healthy Kids Survey (Figure 2.2) shows a "very strong, positive, step-wise relationship" between perceived safety at school and academic performance.

School safety is measured by the percentage of students who report feeling safe or very safe at school. The graph is scaled to show how strongly perceived safety is related to school Academic Performance Index (API) scores. At the 20 percent of schools with the highest API scores, more than 90 percent of students also reported feeling safe or very safe. By contrast, at the 20 percent of schools with the *lowest* API scores, only 81 percent of students reported that same level of safety. The vertical area between each gridline (the horizontal dotted line in the figure) represents one standard deviation. A difference in bar heights of a standard deviation represents a large difference in terms of effect size.

Although it can be tempting to explain those findings in other ways—for example, by theorizing that students who do better on state tests are better prepared or more academically inclined because they come from families that are more educated and value education highly and that such families tend to be wealthier ones that tend to live in more well-to-do communities that are therefore safer—researchers ruled out the effects of those other variables, such as ethnicity or family income or level of parental education. They found that a decrease in students' feelings of safety is correlated to a significant decrease in their academic performance, independent of the other variables. In other words, their scores were directly attributable to feelings of safety.[39]

Students cannot and do not learn in an environment of fear. Over eight hundred studies on child and adolescent development found student academic success tied to "promoting supportive and caring relationships," "increasing student motivation and engagement," and "strengthening social norms and expectations that promote achievement."[40] If young people are valued, feel safe, and

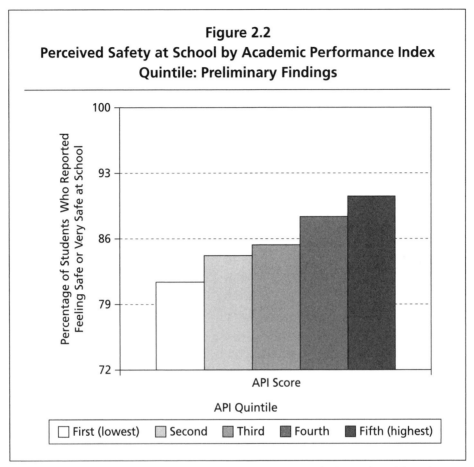

Figure 2.2
Perceived Safety at School by Academic Performance Index
Quintile: Preliminary Findings

Source: Preliminary calculations based on the California Department of Education's Healthy Kids Survey (1998/1999) and API database (2000).

are making contributions to their social environment, including helping others, several researchers argue that it is reasonable to assume that they are "more likely to be productive, caring citizens."[41]

Escalation of Pain and Violence

One other noteworthy cost of mistreatment is escalation: the social phenomenon whereby a student who has been mistreated (feels pain) gets mad (feels rage) and wants to get even (seeks revenge).[42] The existence of this dynamic has been confirmed by the more than twenty thousand students who have participated in our training sessions over the past seven years. In these settings, we describe escalation and ask, "Who has seen their friends or people they know well at school (or perhaps even yourself) get hurt, get mad, and then try to get even?" Inevitably nearly every student raises a hand. In reflecting on the rash of school shootings following the Columbine High School tragedy, Ronald Stevens, executive director of the National School Safety Center, said, "As we look at the profile of the perpetrators, the majority were first victims. When spurned, rejected, or bullied, some adolescents resort to violence."[43] As Figure 2.3 shows in detail, that violence can be directed and expressed internally or externally, or both.

In some situations, young people feel such pain that they internalize it and express it through drug use, depression, self-mutilation, or suicide. Between 1980 and 1997, there was a 109 percent increase in suicide among young people ten to fourteen years old,[44] and the third leading cause of suicide among teens is now bullying.[45] This type of suicide has become so prevalent it has come to be called *bullycide*. These young people are bullied to such an extent that that they can no longer cope and see suicide as their only escape.

When students' pain leads to anger that is expressed externally, it might show up as acting out against a peer, a parent, a sibling, or a member of the school staff, at times without apparent provocation. Targeted students may feel such intense pain and anger, or such a strong need to reestablish a sense of power, that they start fights, break things, vandalize the school or someone's home, start fires, or break into a community business.

Sometimes that pain is exacted on others in dramatic and tragic ways, as we have seen in the school shootings of the past ten years. When researchers from the U.S. Secret Service and the U.S. Department of Education examined thirty-seven school shootings from 1975 to 2002, they found that the shooters could not be profiled; they had surprisingly little in common. Some were star students, and others were struggling academically; some were popular, and others were shunned; they listened to all different types of music and came from different social groups. However, they also found that 61 percent of the attackers identified revenge as a motive for their attack, and more than half had multiple motives. Most of the attackers held some type of grievance against either their target or someone else.[46] And 71 percent of the attackers "felt persecuted, bullied, threatened, attacked or injured by others prior to the incident. In several cases, individual attackers had experienced bullying and harassment that was

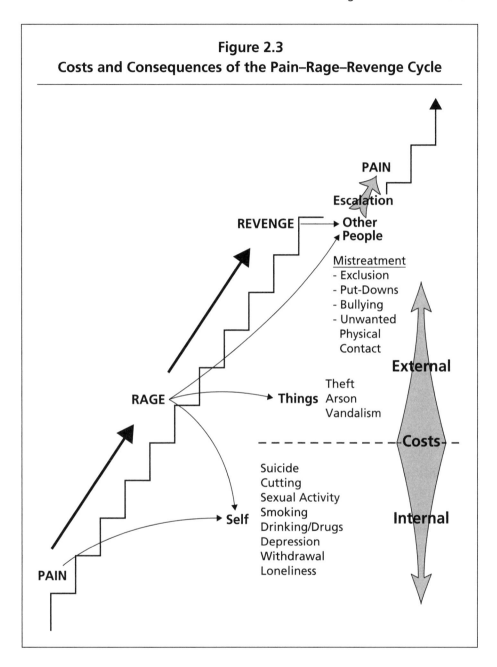

Figure 2.3
Costs and Consequences of the Pain–Rage–Revenge Cycle

long-standing and severe. In some of these cases the experience of being bullied seemed to have a significant impact on the attacker and appeared to have been a factor in his decision to mount an attack at the school," though they cautioned that they could not conclusively determine that bullying had actually caused the shooter to attack. In one case, most of the attacker's schoolmates described him as "the kid everyone teased" and reported that nearly every student had at some point "thrown the attacker against a locker, tripped him in the hall, held his head under water in the pool, or thrown things at him."[47] The fact that the bullying was well known indicates it had not, in the eyes of the target, been adequately addressed by the school, which could only have exacerbated his desire for dramatic revenge.

In this fashion, escalation perpetuates a cycle of mistreatment that casts a pall over an entire school. Students become nervous, tense, and on guard, wondering what incident might erupt. Might they get caught in the crossfire and become some of the collateral damage, physically or emotionally? In a harsh atmosphere, compassion and forgiveness are signs of weakness, hostility is accepted, and frontier justice is applauded. It's not an atmosphere that supports learning and healthy social or emotional development.

Financial Costs

Up to this point, this chapter has detailed the social, developmental, and academic costs of students mistreating others. Negative student behavior also has financial costs.

Replacing Staff

Many teachers change schools or leave teaching too soon, and the financial costs for replacing those teachers are significant. The Alliance for Excellent Education estimated that in September 2005, the cost for replacing the 394,000 teachers who did not return to the schools in which they taught the previous year could be almost $5 billion. It could cost more than $2 billion to replace the 173,000 teachers who left the profession entirely.[48]

Average Daily Attendance Funds Lost

Average daily attendance (ADA) funds are paid by states to schools based on the number of students in school. When students are absent, a school loses the ADA money it would have received had the students been in attendance. Previously we cited research by the National Association of School Psychologists showing that roughly 160,000 students stay home from school daily because they are afraid of how they will be treated at school. These absences mean that schools receive less ADA money, but just how much money?

According to the U.S. Department of Education, the average school year in the United States is 180 days long. If 160,000 students stay home out of fear each day, in a school year of 180 days there will be 28.8 million student absences due to fear:

160,000 students absent each day $\times$ 180 school days in a school year
= 28,800,000 student days lost

Although the formula individual states use for calculating actual ADA rates is complex and rates vary from state to state, an approximate national average figure is $40 per student per day.[49] By multiplying that amount by the total number of students who do not attend in a year, schools in the United States lose more than $1.1 billion in ADA funding per year:

$$28,800,000 \times \$40 = \$1,152,000,000$$

Suspensions and Expulsions

Previously we looked at the amount of staff time spent on a single suspension. Now let's look at the average cost for a single three-day suspension:

- 5 to 15 minutes for the staff member who observed or learned about the incident to gather information and report it: $40 per hour, for a total cost of $3.30 to $10.00

- 30 to 60 minutes for the counselor or assistant principal to meet with the students involved in the incident and gather information: $50 per hour, for a total cost of $25.00 to $50.00

- 30 to 60 minutes for a meeting between school officials and parents: $50 per hour, for a total cost of $25.00 to $50.00

- 60 to 120 minutes of secretarial time to file the paperwork: $30 per hour, for a total cost of $30.00 to $60.00

- Total time: 125 to 255 minutes (2 to 4 hours) for each suspension: $83.30 to $170.00

In addition to staff costs is a three-day loss of ADA funds while the student was suspended, adding $120 to the cost of the suspension. So a typical three-day suspension costs a school somewhere between $200 and $290. And the entire suspension could cost even more if school property were damaged during the incident.

If you are curious about what the costs of a suspension would be in your school, use the suspension costs worksheet here to calculate costs based on your district's pay scale.

Suspension Costs Worksheet

	Time Required	Hourly Rate	Total Cost
Staff member observing or reporting			
Meeting(s) with student(s) by counselor, dean, or administrator			
Meeting(s) with parents			
Clerical Time			
Total		NA	

According to the National Center for Education Statistics, there were approximately 3 million suspensions in the year 2000 (the last year for which these figures are available).[50] Using these data, you can estimate the yearly cost of suspensions in the United States. For this example, assume (conservatively) that 50 percent of suspensions were due to some form of student-to-student mistreatment. Also assume that each suspension was for three days. Using the amounts from the previous example, the annual cost of mistreatment for suspensions alone would be somewhere between $300 million and $435 million:

$$(3{,}000{,}000 \text{ suspensions} \times 50\%) \times \$200 = \$300{,}000{,}000$$

$$(3{,}000{,}000 \text{ suspensions} \times 50\%) \times \$290 = \$435{,}000{,}000$$

Vandalism

> All the vandalism, the graffiti and tagging and stuff, that costs money to fix and clean up. Then there's not as much money for the science labs and all the stuff that makes school not so boring, or even for books. We have some pretty old books.
>
> —TENTH-GRADE BOY

For 1996–1997, more than one-third of the nation's eighty-four thousand public schools reported at least one incident of vandalism, totaling ninety-nine thousand separate incidents.[51] But these statistics don't reveal the magnitude of the problem. While the U.S. Department of Education, major education associations, and national organizations regularly compile data on school-related violence, weapons, and gang activity, they lack complete data regarding school vandalism and break-ins. One reason for this may be that different schools define vandalism differently: some include both intentional and accidental damage, and others report only incidents that result in an insurance claim. Some vandalism is not reported at all, either because minor cases are viewed as trivial or because administrators may fear it will reflect poorly on their management skills.

Various estimates reveal that the costs of school vandalism are high and increasing. In 1970, costs of school vandalism in the United States were estimated at $200 million, climbing to an estimated $600 million in 1990.[52] And these figures don't include the significant cost of staff time to deal with the vandalism: filing insurance forms, cleanup, repair, and others.

School Security

School security has significant financial costs. Some of the costs are for purchasing, installing, and maintaining security equipment, such as fencing, locks, lighting, surveillance cameras and monitors, and metal detectors. Staff costs include hiring campus supervisors, security guards, yard duty staff, and school resource officers. They also include developing and implementing emergency response plans. In addition, staff must be trained in the proper use of security equipment and in security procedures. As part of the national reaction to the shootings at Columbine High School, the California legislature passed Assembly Bill 1113, which funneled $100 million into schools for security measures. These expenditures nationwide now approach $1 billion annually.[53]

In *School Violence: Deadly Lessons,* Francha Roffe Menhard catalogues the ramifications of this security trend in Texas.

> The state of Texas spends more than $90 million each year on school security, with most of that money used for police officers and security guards. Some eighty school districts in Texas have their own police force. Other money went for technology, including metal detectors and cameras. The statewide total spent on security averaged over twenty-two dollars per student; for example, the city of Houston spent more money on security (thirty-six dollars per student) than on sports and all non-classroom activities put together (thirty-five dollars per student). For every metal detector that schools buy, there are computers, baseball uniforms, or trumpets it cannot buy. For every police officer that a school hires, there is generally a teacher or coach it cannot hire.[54]

Incident Response Costs

Every time a fire department responds to an alarm, false or real, at a school, the community pays. Every time a police officer is summoned to a school to investigate an incident, provide support to staff, or arrest a student who is suspected of violating the law, the community pays. Every time a student uses a gun at a school, the community pays.

An overview of the costs of the Columbine shooting gives an indication of how quickly these expenditures can add up. The following expenses were reported by the *Rocky Mountain News:*[55]

- Bureau of Alcohol, Tobacco, and Firearms: estimated $185,000 for personnel and travel

- Arapahoe County: estimated $140,000 for responding units, bomb squad, crime lab, and aid in investigation

- Aurora Police: $18,859 for increased school security, emergency response team at the memorial service, increased security at the governor's home in Aurora

- Arvada Police: $98,439 for officers at the scene and detectives working subsequent investigation

- Colorado State Patrol: $263,000 for officers at the scene on April 2 and security at the memorial service

- Denver Police: $418,183 for on-scene response, replacement duty for officers dispatched to scene, increased school security, and security for Vice President Dick Cheney's trip

- Federal Bureau of Investigation: estimated $750,000 for emergency response team, SWAT, headquarters staff, lab time, special projects unit, and transferring evidence

- Jefferson County Public Schools: $2,099,154 for building and personal property losses, increased security measures, substitutes, and miscellaneous

Not counting the agencies that responded to the scene but did not provide any information to the *Rocky Mountain News,* the total comes to $8,972,995.

Legal Costs

In our litigious society, it is increasingly common for complaints about student-to-student mistreatment to end up in courts, with the parents of targeted students asking for monetary compensation for the physical and emotional pain their children suffered while theoretically in the care of the school district. When schools lose those cases, the costs of settlement create a growing financial burden, as these three examples of recent settlements show:

- $10,000 was awarded to an Oregon boy who was attacked by a group of students on the school bus in a culmination of years of bullying.[56]

- $250,000 was awarded to a Kansas teenager who suffered five years of harassment by peers who perceived him to be gay.[57]

- $300,000 was awarded to two gay students in California who were repeatedly threatened. One boy was also spat on, kicked, and punched and had his car vandalized. They were both home-schooled during their senior years because the constant harassment was too great.[58]

Beyond the monetary settlements that schools had to pay, there were substantial expenses for the time of legal professionals (district staff and lawyers hired for particular cases) to research and defend the school districts.

As more of these lawsuits are brought against schools, more settlement monies will be paid by schools and their insurers. The result will be increases in liability insurance premiums for schools that are already strapped for funds. It is not hard to see how increased insurance expenditures will draw funds away from sports, the arts, science equipment, counselors and other support staff, and other school budget items.

Societal Costs

Society ultimately pays the price for youth-on-youth mistreatment. Although the cruelty may begin in the schools, it is not contained there. It ripples out into the community and sets patterns that are played out for years to come. Aggressors and targets are likely to continue the cycle of mistreatment and violence in their jobs and their relationships.

Workplace Violence

Bullies at school are likely to be bullies in their workplaces. Bullying behavior ripples out into homes and workplaces. Many people have experienced a coworker or boss who has used abusive language or physical intimidation to manipulate others. These adult bullies are often continuing their behaviors that weren't appropriately dealt with when they were young. The results are a hostile workplace environment and lower productivity, which affects the company's bottom line.

A recent study of more than nine thousand federal employees found that 42 percent of female and 15 percent of male employees were harassed within a two-year period. This resulted in more than $180 million in lost time and productivity. What is not factored in is the cost of turnover: 82 percent of targeted people leave their workplaces. Workplace bullying also creates health care costs, borne by either employees or their companies, as targeted workers seek mental health care: 41 percent of workplace bully targets become depressed, and 31 percent of targeted women and 21 percent of targeted men are diagnosed with posttraumatic stress disorder.[59]

Family and Community

> Kids who are bullied will sometimes go home and take it out on their little brothers and sisters and hurt or bully them. Then it becomes like a cycle that never stops.
>
> —ELEVENTH-GRADE GIRL

Young people who are victims of violence are more likely to grow to be perpetrators of violence as adults.[60] Bullies are three to four times as likely as their nonbullying peers to have multiple convictions by their early twenties.[61] Bullying and aggression has a ripple effect on families and communities. A criminal record can put significant stress on a family, and some of these convictions are related to family violence. Unchecked bullying and aggression can continue in the form of relationship abuse, spousal abuse, and child abuse.[62]

It is critical to intervene in the actions of bullies early on. Intervening to reduce bullying and intimidation in schools may not only prevent bullies from developing a criminal record, it may save countless children and spouses from abuse. Not confronting bullying and cruelty during childhood and early adolescence only creates greater consequences and societal costs as these bullies become adults. Bullying is a community problem, not just a school problem. The consequences of bullying show up in relationships and over a lifetime in homes, neighborhoods, and communities.

Conclusion

Mistreatment is not "normal," it is not "part of growing up," and it does not "build character." If adults had to experience the cruelty and violence in their workplaces that many young people see and experience in their schools, workplace attendance and productivity would plummet as employees focused on surviving rather than thriving.

Mistreatment has huge costs: for the targets and aggressors directly involved, for the bystanders who watch it, and for the schools and communities that inadvertently play host to it. No one can thrive in such an environment.

As awareness of the problem and its costs has grown over the past decade, policymakers, administrators, teachers, and parents have taken some important steps to address this ongoing public health issue. The next chapter explores many of these efforts, along with their strengths and limitations.

3

The Outside-In Approach

After Columbine, our work in safety and security changed dramatically. There was tremendous pressure to make sure nothing like that happened again—anywhere. One of the first things was putting together emergency response plans for every school site; this is a state requirement. Even though we already had many measures in place, there were still a lot of changes that we made. We invested thousands of dollars in technology. We secured the perimeter of each campus and made sure that anyone coming on the campus was really supposed to be there. We hired additional security. We put video cameras on each campus. We reviewed our policies and procedures and tightened them up. We did training for all the staff. Several of our schools have even got conflict mediation programs in place, so the students are involved in working out their differences. All this has taken a lot of money, hundreds of thousands of dollars, and a lot of time.

—DAVE HEARD, DIRECTOR OF SAFETY AND SECURITY, PERRIS UNION HIGH SCHOOL DISTRICT,

CALIFORNIA

How We Got Where We Are

Before reviewing current strategies and approaches to school safety, where they succeed, and how they fall short, it's important to understand some trends that are affecting all schools. There are two factors that have come together and changed the educational environment: the Columbine shootings and the No Child Left Behind legislation. One forever altered how the public views school safety issues; the other radically reorganized educational priorities and practices by placing testing and accountability at the top of the list, far above other important issues.

Response to Columbine

The Columbine tragedy was actually the twenty-fifth incident of targeted school violence to occur in the United States since 1990.[1] However, many people view Columbine as the 9/11 of school shootings. On cable and broadcast news, Americans watched never-before-seen images of a school under siege: students jumping out of windows, students and teachers running across the school grounds with their hands in the air, SWAT teams aiming weapons at the school, bodies being carried from the building. These powerful images sent shock waves through the American psyche. Everyone was asking, "How could this happen in the safe haven of an American school?" And not unexpectedly, the incident evoked a very strong response.

Federal and state legislators immediately drafted bills about school violence and allocated additional funds to address safety and security issues. Federal, state, and local educational and law enforcement agencies issued mandates, wrote additional rules, revised policies, and instituted new programs. School districts nationwide began a far-reaching process of changing how they operated their schools. All of this effort was undertaken in reaction to a tragic and emotional incident, and it had a single goal: making sure that no student will ever again be able to enter a school building and kill others. This initial reaction and its fall-out have contributed to some of the gaps that exist in school safety efforts today. Russell Skiba, of the Safe and Responsive Schools Project at Indiana University, explains, "In the period after Columbine, we responded out of fear and often moved too quickly to put reactive measures in place."[2] Additional school shootings, including the ten deaths at Minnesota's Red Lake High School in March 2005, and the shooting of four students and the death of one at Success Tech Academy in Cleveland, Ohio, in October 2007 show that problems continue.

No Child Left Behind

Three days after taking office in 2001, President George W. Bush proposed what are arguably the most significant changes in American education since the landmark Elementary and Secondary Education Act of 1965. The motivation for this legislation stemmed from his belief that despite the nearly $200 billion expended on education since 1965, America's neediest children were still being left behind.

The No Child Left Behind Act sent powerful ripples of change through every district, school, and classroom in America.

No Child Left Behind rests on four pillars:

1. More accountability for states, districts, and schools to meet rigorous academic standards

2. Greater school choice, particularly for parents of children attending schools that do not meet required standards

3. Increased flexibility for schools and local education agencies in their use of federal education funds

4. A stronger emphasis on reading, especially for younger children, and math

An understanding of schools today requires at least a general knowledge of how several key features of the law have worked together to narrow the focus of many schools. The legislation required that states develop challenging academic standards and conduct annual testing for all students in grades 3 to 8. As states began to develop these standards, they focused first on the core academic subjects of reading and mathematics. The act also increased pressure on schools to meet reading and math requirements by allowing parents to pull their children out of schools that don't meet the standards. With this increased emphasis on reading and math, subjects like social studies and health—areas under which social-emotional development curricula are generally taught—came to be seen as less important academically. Consequently much of the teaching related to social-emotional development has been eliminated. Many teachers, especially at the elementary level, report that they no longer have time to teach communication, problem-solving, and conflict resolution skills or to conduct the class meetings that are the backbone of creating a positive and productive learning environment in the classroom. At the secondary level, many of the required and elective courses related to communication, decision making, and other social development areas have been dropped.

The act's "flexibility for accountability" rules allow some states and local education agencies to shift funds away from certain grant programs. This has had the net effect of reducing total funding for Safe and Drug-Free Schools programs administered by the U.S. Department of Education, funding that had supported many of the social-emotional and school climate improvement programs being used by schools.

Common Strategies for Creating Safer Schools

With Columbine and No Child Left Behind as a backdrop, school districts have endeavored to meet the challenge of creating and maintaining safe schools in a variety of ways. There is nothing inherently wrong with any of the strategies discussed in this chapter. Many are helpful and necessary components of effective and comprehensive school safety programs, and as noted in Chapter Two, they have reduced the more visible and extreme forms of violence at schools. Nevertheless, the continued existence (and increase) of the less visible forms of youth-on-youth mistreatment makes it clear that the current strategies do not go far enough. In addition, the presence of these strategies and the decrease in visible violence can foster the mistaken belief that the problem of mistreatment has been solved.

The balance of this chapter provides an overview of the most common ways that schools address safety and security issues:

- Disaster response plans
- Security equipment
- Security personnel
- Policies and rules
- Tip lines and boxes
- Staff development
- Classroom curricula
- Assemblies and special events
- Youth involvement programs

Disaster Response Plans

After what was seen by many as a lack of preparedness on the part of schools and law enforcement agencies, it became mandatory that schools develop plans for responding to violent incidents like Columbine, whether threatened or occurring. Often called crisis response plans or emergency response plans, they are designed to address a wide array of threats, both natural and human. The plans typically include these components:

- A thorough assessment of the vulnerability of a school's targets (people and facilities)
- Assignment of command-and-control responsibilities (who does what)
- Procedures, including code words, to lock down or otherwise secure buildings to protect students and staff
- Specialized training for key staff members
- Improving communication with emergency services agencies such as police and sheriff's departments

Districts and schools throughout the nation generally follow a similar process in creating their plans:

- State departments of education typically establish general requirements and provide templates for these plans.
- Regional or county offices of education often provide support or sponsor training for the educators who have to develop emergency response plans specific to their sites. School-based teams (typically a principal or vice principal, several classified and certificated staff members, and possibly even some parents and students) attend the training and then return to their sites to develop the plans, a process that can take weeks or months.
- After the emergency response plans have been developed, many schools test them out with mock scenarios to identify strengths and weaknesses in the plan, which are then addressed.
- Many states require annual reviews and updates of a school's plan.

Strengths Before the 1990s brought a marked increase in school shootings and other violent acts, the pool of potential threats was relatively small, well known, and limited to specific geographical areas. Schools generally focused on preparing for native natural events: hurricanes along the Gulf and southeast coasts, earthquakes in California, and tornadoes in the Midwest, for example. Disaster response and crisis management plans definitely help school personnel increase their readiness for major incidents of school violence, however statistically unlikely they are.

These plans help school administrators prepare for crises that include bomb threats, hostile visitors, hostage situations, stabbings, shootings, and weapons on campus. In creating their plans, administrators consider issues like establishing a crisis management team, an incident command system, lockdown and evacuation procedures, staging areas, dealing with the media, and more. If armed students or intruders were to enter a campus, the injury and loss of life would likely be far worse than without such plans.

These plans have helped improve schools' level of communication and cooperation with law enforcement and other agencies. Furthermore, they increase the awareness of school violence, at least on the part of those who develop and implement the plans.

Limitations   Disaster response plans require a significant investment of time, and it is difficult to calculate the precise dollar cost of creating and maintaining them. A conservative estimate of direct time costs to develop and approve a plan would be twenty-five hundred dollars for an average school; yearly updates can easily cost five hundred to a thousand dollars. This estimate does not take into account the time for site-based training and rehearsal, or the significant resources state and county education departments allocate to help districts and schools create the plans and monitor compliance with regulations.[3] For example, in Virginia, the Fairfax County Public Schools have developed the 188-page *Crisis Management Workbook,* only one part of its nationally recognized school emergency response effort.[4] The relatively small number of incidents of targeted school violence gives disaster response plans a fairly high cost-to-benefit ratio.

Time and money are also required to train newly hired school personnel, either on-site by school leaders or off-site in special workshops and training. This investment too has an opportunity cost: time and money spent on training and testing disaster response plans is time and money not spent helping teachers and other staff members in a number of ways—for example,

- Learning to use new teaching resources and curricula
- Developing strategies for meeting the academic and social-emotional needs of an ever increasing number of students with special challenges, for example,

students who are still acquiring English language skills and students with identified emotional or behavioral problems

- Refining and sharpening their skills and strategies for classroom management and discipline

Because they focus on more catastrophic events like shootings and bomb threats, these plans can distract school leaders from addressing the more pervasive but less visible forms of peer mistreatment and can contribute to a false sense of having solved the problem. An effective crisis management plan is a good tool, but it is not a complete solution.

Security Equipment

Another dimension of schools' responses to violence is their investment in equipment, typically:

- Video surveillance systems
- Lighting
- Antigraffiti coatings for frequently tagged areas
- Fencing and gates that help define and secure the perimeter of a school
- Locks and other access control systems
- Metal detectors, both handheld and walk-through types

Locks are the most common security devices across all school levels and video surveillance cameras the second most common type of equipment in use in high schools. In a 1999 survey of California school districts conducted by the California Research Bureau, 29 percent of the districts used surveillance cameras on school buses, 22 percent used them on campuses, and 13 percent used them to monitor other school property. These figures represent a huge increase since a previous survey in 1996 and set the direction of the trend. Research has also indicated that the most common security goal listed by schools nationwide is installing video surveillance cameras.[5]

Strengths   If they work and are used properly, fences, gates, locks, and access control systems can keep out dangerous or unwelcome persons and can decrease potential violence from outside intrusions. Antigraffiti coatings can make maintenance of a frequently tagged area much easier. Metal detectors serve two purposes: helping security personnel screen for weapons and serving as a deterrent to individuals who might want to bring a weapon to school. Cameras can and have helped identify and apprehend individuals who have committed acts of violence against people or property. And highly visible security equipment installations send a message to staff, parents, and community members that the school is being proactive about security.

Limitations   The most obvious drawback to the installation and use of security equipment is cost. A study of the school security market showed that the national expenditure on school security equipment, including video surveillance, access control, and weapons detection systems, reached $570 million in 2000 and was estimated at $985 million for 2005.[6] In addition to the initial costs for installation, schools face ongoing costs for operating the system, including monitoring of video cameras, maintenance (repair and replacement), and training.

Districts that have invested in security equipment face another challenge: the policies and procedures of implementation. The sheer number of people who use a school building make this a significant and daunting challenge, because they create a virtually unlimited number of ways that policies and procedures can be circumvented. For example, a school that was concerned about the entrance of unauthorized persons (for example, a deranged passerby, angry parent, or former student) might choose to implement a policy requiring that all doors be locked during the school day except for the front door near the office. This door would then have to be monitored, and procedures would have to be adopted for checking the identity of visitors and reason for their visit. Once inside, would they be escorted or allowed to wander freely through the building? To allow hundreds or possibly thousands of students to enter the building during a short period at the start of the day, it is likely that other entrances would need to be opened and then monitored. But monitored for what? What criteria can be given to the monitors that are reasonable and enforceable? Certainly a police officer at the entrance can spot a raving lunatic, but most school attacks are mounted by people familiar to the staff of the school who have legitimate reasons for entering and do not raise any eyebrows unless their belongings are searched. The vast number of backpacks, duffel bags, and instrument cases brought into a school on a daily basis make searching them all a logistical nightmare. And even if a school were to have random searches as a deterrent, any enterprising student would likely be able to get a fellow student inside the building to open an unsupervised back entrance at a specified time to permit him or her to bring weapons or bombs into the school. As our nation's recent experience with airport security shows, establishing security through equipment not only requires rigorous and disciplined implementation; it requires that the people on the inside be one step ahead of the people on the outside who are developing a multitude of creative ways to get in.

Moreover, a growing body of evidence suggests that these approaches might not have their intended effect. Researchers examining data from interviews with nearly seven thousand students found that increased security tended to *cause* an increase in school disorder, a conclusion widely supported by other research. In other words, metal detectors, locked doors, locker checks, security guards, and staff members' watching halls seemed to foster the violence, gang activity, personal attacks, and thefts that administrators hoped to avoid.[7] While adults see the installation of security equipment as evidence that the school is being proactive about safety, many students believe that security equipment sends the message that students are neither trusted nor responsible. They report that these measures make them feel less safe and often create a self-fulfilling prophecy.[8]

Security Personnel

The community-oriented policing movement of the 1980s and 1990s aimed to increase the flow of information and build better relationships between police officers and the community members they serve and protect. This was accomplished largely by getting many police officers out of their cars and back on foot or bicycle patrols, which made them more accessible to community members. In the same manner, almost all schools have responded to the escalating threat of violence by increasing the number of adults who watch or supervise students when they are not directly under the charge of their classroom teachers.

While elementary schools may still refer to them as yard duty staff, it is now common for middle and high schools to hire campus supervisors who walk around campus before and after school, as well as during lunch and other breaks. In addition, schools often ask or require that administrators, teachers, and support staff members maintain a presence in the hallways or common areas during breaks between classes. Their job is to look for signs of trouble and intervene before things escalate into visible mistreatment. These adults also try to build relationships with students to foster open lines of communication, which can help them gain information about a planned incident or obtain compliance during one.

To supplement what their staff can do, schools often partner with local law enforcement agencies to place more officers or deputies on campus. The federal government has funded some six thousand police officers assigned to schools.[9] Sometimes these officers are assigned to one or several schools on a full-time basis. Other officers on campus might be associated with community-sponsored programs, such as DARE (Drug Abuse Resistance Education).

Strengths   By making it possible for adults to intervene when flare-ups begin, security personnel can help lower the number of major discipline problems. In March 2004, the Associated Press reported that the New York City Department of Education released data showing that over the previous three months, violent incidents at twelve of the city's most dangerous schools had declined by 9 percent. Administrators attributed the drop to the increased presence of police officers in those schools, officers who could quickly get to the scene of a fight and intervene before it escalated.[10] Their presence may also act as a deterrent, although research has yet to confirm a direct causal relationship.

Having more adults around the school can make it physically easier for students to report a weapon or a planned fight. However, they are not more likely to do so until they have developed a positive, caring, and trusting relationship with one or more of those adults. Research has shown that developing these relationships is more effective in reducing violence than is security equipment and stricter rules.[11] It remains a significant challenge to train adults to build those relationships rather than simply focus on catching rule breakers.

Limitations   One of the biggest limitations to increasing security personnel is cost. Since its inception, the Office of Community Oriented Policing Services (COPS) within the U.S. Department of Justice has provided nearly $700 million to state and local law enforcement agencies to hire and train over sixty-one hundred school resource officers.[12] District costs are above and beyond these federal funds. For a comprehensive high school of two thousand students with three campus supervisors, the annual cost could reach close to $100,000.

Another limitation to this approach is that adults cannot be everywhere. They cannot see or hear what every student is saying or doing. Even when adults are present, they cannot effectively address all the mistreatment that occurs because they don't recognize many behaviors as mistreatment. Many of the most powerful put-downs and threats are communicated with subtle gestures or words that adults don't recognize. Students repeatedly report that the presence of adults simply drives the mistreatment to a different place and time, away from adults. And as with video surveillance, having security guards everywhere also sends a message that adults do not trust young people.

Policies and Rules

At all levels—federal, state, local, and individual schools—there has been a distinct change in the policies and rules aimed at maintaining a safe school and controlling student behavior. Between 1999 and 2001, at least eight states considered or adopted legislation directing schools to develop antibullying policies or programs.[13] By 2004, at least seventeen states had enacted twenty-seven bullying-related statutes.[14] As a result, tough new policies and rules have been issued, and existing ones have been clarified so there can be no misinterpretation of their meaning or the consequences for breaking them. School staff have been charged with enforcing and interpreting the rules strictly. In addition, the consequences for breaking rules are generally severe and are enforced with no exceptions.

This zero tolerance discipline is intended to send a message by severely punishing both major and minor infractions. Zero tolerance has been incorporated into federal education policy, and 94 percent of public schools report having a zero tolerance policy for firearms, 91 percent for other weapons, and 79 percent for violence.[15]

Some examples of these tougher policies and rules in school settings include:

- Subjecting students to random searches of their backpacks, clothing, or lockers on entry to the school or at any point during the day

- Broadening the definition of illegal substances to include prescription medication and over-the-counter products

- Extending the list of weapons to include penknives, plastic cafeteria knives, and other objects

- Suspension or expulsion for violations that were once considered minor

Strengths Well-written rules and policies help schools make a clear statement about what is acceptable behavior and what is not. Studies have shown that awareness and perceived enforcement of school rules are associated with a decrease in school violence.[16] A key tenet of the internationally recognized Olweus's bullying prevention program is that the rules forbidding bullying must be clearly communicated to all members of the school community and must be applied in a fair and consistent manner. Furthermore, a school's legal liability is reduced when all the rules and policies are clear and applied consistently.

If the process of revising and clarifying school rules includes all the key stakeholders—staff, parents, and students—and is facilitated well, there can be several positive outcomes:

- The school develops a common code of behavior that all stakeholders understand. This is especially important because students often come to school with disparate standards of acceptable behavior, which they derive from their family systems and ethnic or cultural heritage. In our training sessions, after the discussions and activities that focus on defining bullying, it is not uncommon for a student to say something like, "This was helpful, because before we had this discussion, I didn't really get that pushing people around like that [or other mistreatment] was bullying. I mean, that's how my dad [or mom or older brother or sister] treats all of us."

- Students who are involved in the process of setting the rules understand where those rules are coming from and why they are necessary, and thus they are more likely to obey them.

- Teachers throughout a school are more likely to have consistent behavioral standards.

- Parents are more likely to reinforce at home the standards that are being used at school.

Limitations By their nature, rules are best suited to governing observable behaviors and specific language, which make enforcement practical. But rules have limited applicability and effect in arenas where observation, monitoring, and enforcement are difficult. The prevalence of bullying on school buses illustrates this point, as does the rise in cyberbullying, which happens outside students' school time and in the anonymous world of cyberspace.

Cyberbullying also shows how challenging it is to use rules to mitigate the negative effects of fast-moving pop culture. School districts have suddenly found themselves needing to issue policies that extend the definition of bullying into a realm of behavior (expression) that is traditionally and justifiably protected by the Bill of Rights in the U.S. Constitution. Certainly precedent and community standards provide a basis for writing rules that prohibit the more offensive behaviors such as racial slurs, but in the vast majority of incidents of student-on-student mistreatment, what makes the behavior offensive is either its context (for example, who heard the insult and laughed) or its effect on the target (for example, the target was bothered or hurt by it). Rules that attempt to govern this kind of behavior often become unenforceable platitudes like, "Be nice" or "No mean comments." Rules simply cannot govern the attitudes that are at the root of much mistreatment.

Rules and policies have other unintended consequences. In a survey conducted by the National Association of Attorneys General, students reported that they generally appreciated the tougher rules and security measures. However they did not feel safer and, in fact, often felt less safe.[17] Rules that are not enforced become meaningless, so educators must spend a significant proportion of their time being police, which takes time away from educating and puts them at odds with the very students they are supposed to be helping. Furthermore, although students are allowed to plan dances and school spirit events, they are almost completely left out of the process of making school rules. Consequently when rules and policies are toughened, students generally feel that these things are being done to or for them, not with them. This disempowerment decreases students' willingness to comply with such rules, which ultimately makes them harder to enforce.

Zero tolerance policies appear to have little value. Researchers examining data from the Add Health study noted in Chapter Two found that "students in schools with harsh discipline policies report feeling less safe at school than do students in schools with more moderate policies."[18] Other research conducted through Indiana University Bloomington's Center for Evaluation and

Education Policy also found no evidence that zero tolerance policies improved school safety. Nor have these policies made any impact on the behavior of antisocial and violent youth who are the intended targets of their message. Unfortunately, many truly innocent students have been caught in the cross-hairs of zero tolerance enforcement, which forces administrators to ignore the understandable and legitimate legal distinction between wrongful intent and innocent intent.[19]

For example, in June 2001, Lindsay Brown, a senior at Estero High School in Estero, Florida, was prohibited from attending her graduation, even though she was a National Merit Scholar and honor student who had never before been in trouble. Brown was suspended a few days earlier when an observant adminis-trator noticed a kitchen knife on the floor of her car in the school parking lot. Brown claimed the knife fell out of a box when she was moving.[20]

In an incident in March 2001, Kara Williams, a freshman at Rio Rancho High School in Rio Rancho, New Mexico, was summoned to the office because she and a friend were not in class at the time another student reported smelling pot smoke in a bathroom. Without her consent, her backpack was searched by a school security guard, and a penknife with a one-inch blade was found. Due to the district's zero tolerance policy, Williams was suspended for ten days or more, pending a hearing. When hearing an appeal from Williams's mother, the principal stated that his hands were tied by the district's zero tolerance policy, which meant that he could not consider that the knife was never removed from a key ring that was zipped inside her purse, which was inside her backpack. The key ring belonged to her stepfather, who lent it to her the day before when she discovered that she'd lost her house key; she had no target in mind or motive to use the knife.[21]

Hundreds of similar stories have been reported, and research suggests that these controversial applications of the policy are not aberrations but the direct result of the zero tolerance philosophy.[22]

Tip Lines and Boxes

Tip lines and boxes are designed to get students who know something about a potentially dangerous incident to share that knowledge with adults who presumably can do something about it. By maintaining anonymity, these strategies recognize the social risk that students take by coming forward.

Schools and districts use a wide variety strategies, ranging from simple tip boxes in a library or office to participation in a national tip line program that includes MTV-style public service announcements broadcast on the school's closed-circuit TV. Posters publicize the service, and rewards are offered to increase students' willingness to use it.

Most states have established a telephone tip line service, along with many school districts or regional entities such as county offices of education. For example, in Sonoma County, California, school districts have collaborated with their insurance provider to set up a twenty-four-hour toll-free number for students, staff, or community members to call if they are aware of any actual or potential threats to students, staff, or school property. Reports can be anonymous, and information is passed on to the relevant district for handling. Rewards are offered to those who report people who are proven to be responsible for threats or crimes. The tip line number is publicized through notices sent home, posters at schools, and a variety of school-related products like pencils and cups, which are distributed during assemblies or other presentations about the tip line.

Strengths   Law enforcement agencies have long held the premise that it makes sense to get those who know something about an incident to share their information with those who can do something about it. Involving the school community and the larger society to help monitor or report crimes or other misbehavior is certainly an important strategy for preventing or stopping these incidents. Most seasoned teachers, counselors, and administrators will acknowledge that students typically know more about their peers' thoughts, feelings, and plans than adults do. And tip lines are one way of encouraging involvement and empowering students to take action that can have a positive effect on their schools.

In their analysis of the thirty-seven school shootings that occurred from 1974 to 2000, a joint team from the U.S. Secret Service and the U.S. Department of Education found that "prior to most incidents, other people knew about the attacker's idea and/or plan. In most cases, those who knew were teens—friends, schoolmates, siblings, and others. However, this information rarely made its way to an adult."[23]

Limitations   That same report recognized some of the limitations inherent in getting students to tell adults about their peers' plans and activities. It went on to recommend that schools break down barriers in the school environment that might inadvertently discourage students from coming forward (for example, the us-versus-them mentality of many students) and develop a variety of avenues by which students could notify adults of potentially dangerous incidents in a way that maintained anonymity.

In practice, tip lines and boxes present several challenges:

- The time, effort, and cost to inform students of the location of the boxes and helping them to remember the tip line number
- Gaining enough useful information from a report to act on it in an effective and timely way
- Sustaining interest over time without spreading paranoia
- Finding a response system that balances the need for immediate action with the high costs of having a dedicated person available around the clock

Beneath those factors lies an even more fundamental challenge of getting students to use the system. There are several reasons they do not come forward with information:

- Students don't trust that their anonymity will be preserved, which could result in some form of retaliation.
- Students don't think the adult will believe them.
- Students believe adult involvement will make the situation worse.
- Students feel a stronger sense of allegiance to their peers than to adults and thus choose to honor the code of silence.
- Students don't feel a sense of ownership or responsibility toward their school.
- Students feel apathetic and don't think the incident or issue is their problem.

Staff Development

Another way schools have responded to the epidemic of mistreatment is to raise the awareness and skills of staff members through training. This type of training tends to be more issue focused and typically occurs in staff development sessions ranging in length from one hour to a full day. In addition, some states require training in addressing bullying as part of the certification process for teachers. Some courses are provided online.

Some states are mandating in-service training specifically directed at addressing mistreatment, bullying, and violence in schools. For example, the California Department of Education has contracted with professional trainers to offer workshops on bullying in each county. School principals and counselors typically attend the training sessions, which have these goals:

- Increase their knowledge of the problem of bullying
- Help them develop school policies and strategies to combat the problem
- Encourage them to take further steps to combat the problem, for example, conducting training for their staff members to help them recognize bullying and develop strategies for intervening effectively

In addition, there are workshops that focus on security technology, creating disaster response plans, developing school policies directed at student mistreatment and violence, and other security-related topics.

Strengths   These efforts raise staff awareness of some of the problems and help them gain a deeper understanding of the consequences of mistreatment. Because of the training programs and models, more adults have become knowledgeable and aware of the overall problem inside and outside the classroom.

Well-done training and high staff commitment can result in stronger and clearer rules prohibiting mistreatment, positive changes to classroom management practices, better intervention skills, and increased communication between adults and teens.

Limitations   Because of standardized testing and a more intense concentration on academic success, staff development monies are being directed toward improving instruction, especially in reading and math. In addition, there has been a reduction of the number of in-service days and hours, and training budgets have been cut.

As a result, there is a general lack of staff development going on in this important area. A three-hour workshop once every few years is not sufficient to address an issue of this magnitude and significance. Although it might raise awareness, this kind of training can't go far enough or deep enough. It typically does not provide adults with the skills they need to recognize and understand the subtler forms of mistreatment and to intervene in an effective way.

Classroom Curricula

Dozens of curricula teach impulse control, anger management, assertiveness, empathy, conflict mediation, and other positive social skills and values; some focus specifically on bullying. Many of these curricula are excellent. They typically consist of lessons and activities that are delivered by classroom teachers over several weeks or months. These curricula are often used as part of a social studies, life skills, or health unit.

One widely used model for seventh graders consists of four lessons. The first one reviews basic concepts and definitions of bullying and presents students with several strategies for responding when they observe bullying. It includes class discussions and involves students in generating examples of how they could use the strategies. It also includes homework that challenges students to observe positive behaviors in their peers. The second lesson addresses concepts of empathy and inclusion, using a similarly multifaceted approach that includes role-plays. The third lesson is designed to motivate students to take a stand and speak up when they witness bullying. The fourth lesson focuses on sexual harassment.[24]

Strengths   If high-quality, age-appropriate curricula are selected and the limitations discussed in the next section are addressed, the results can be very positive, and students can learn important social skills. Especially at the elementary and middle levels, good curricula can help students learn how to communicate with one another (for example, to use "I-statements" to articulate their feelings and needs, speak without blame, and listen without judgment) and how to resolve disagreements and solve problems without fighting. Lessons can also help students become more aware of the problem of mistreatment, how their behaviors can contribute to it, and how to respond when they are targets or witnesses of it. Research on certain well-designed curricula has shown positive changes in students, including increased social competence, reduced aggression, and decreased tolerance of social exclusion and meanness.[25]

Limitations   By nature, the bulk of curricular instruction is done by teachers, but in these subject areas especially, students are more effective teachers of their peers. Perhaps the most significant and disturbing limitation is the finding by some researchers that it may be counterproductive for teachers to instruct students, especially boys, how to behave.[26]

Proper and effective use of curricula designed to prevent bullying and improve student behavior and interactions has a number of challenges:

- Selection is limited, especially for middle and high schools, since most curricula are designed for elementary students.

- Cost can be a deterrent: equipping a single school with a reasonably priced curriculum and providing teacher training can cost several thousand dollars. A ten-school district can easily expend twenty to forty thousand dollars.

- Training in the proper use of these curricula can be time-consuming, and these trainings are often negotiated to be shorter than is ideal. Training is usually conducted when the curriculum is purchased, so staff members hired after that time frequently do not receive adequate training. Materials are often lost or misplaced during personnel changes, and it is not uncommon for the newly arrived teacher to lack a complete set of materials. In addition, there is often a considerable amount of time required for teachers to prepare to instruct students in these programs.

- These curricula take up instructional time during the school day. Many are complex and require more time than most teachers have. With the accountability focus of No Child Left Behind, many districts are unwilling to sacrifice instructional time in reading and mathematics to topics that aren't on standardized tests.

- Since these courses do not fit clearly into one department's jurisdiction, it can be difficult to find teachers for them at the secondary level. Scheduling can also be challenging since many are not full-semester courses.

- Because these units are rarely a regular feature of the school day or week, students can perceive them as unimportant or insignificant add-ons, which further reduces the transfer and integration of knowledge, and thus the overall impact of the curriculum on student behavior.

Assemblies and Special Events

These activities are typically high-energy, high-drama events that last from one hour to an entire school day. Many have an interactive element that encourages participants to relate to one another in new and powerful ways. Some include instruction, but most are guided or structured experiences. Some of these events are run by school staff who have participated in a special training, but most are conducted by professionals who are contracted to come to the school site.

Many of these events can be classified as "scared straight" productions. Usually a person who has done or experienced something wrong or dangerous tells the audience about his or her experiences and encourages them to choose another path. For example, the father of a boy who was killed in a gang-related drive-by shooting appears on stage with the grandfather of the shooter; they talk about their pain and loss and the futility of violence, and encourage students to see past differences to find common ground and resolve disagreements without violence.

Other events are designed to challenge some of the stereotypes and prejudices students may have about peers in another clique or social group. One widely used event typically takes place at lunch and involves students' eating with other students outside their customary social circle. Sample questions at the tables stimulate and guide discussion, and in some cases specially trained students facilitate.

Another day-long event involves about a hundred students and twenty adults (staff members and parents) who participate in highly emotional activities that are designed to heighten participants' sense of what they have in common despite outward appearances. Through the design of the event, the skill of the leader, and the intensity of the subject, the process frequently raises strong emotions as students realize the pain they have caused and helps them make amends with those in the room whom they have hurt in the past.

Strengths Well-designed events and assemblies can stimulate, awaken, and energize participants. They can increase awareness of the problem and the costs of mistreatment. By touching the emotions of participants, these programs can inspire them to be more compassionate and respectful and can open the door to new possibilities for how students interrelate.

These events can also stimulate schools to deepen their commitment to the issues that have been identified and experienced. They can serve as a stepping-stone or gateway to more ongoing and systemic efforts to address the problem of mistreatment.

Limitations   Cost can be a significant factor, with schools spending twenty-five hundred dollars or more for a day-long program.

Most of these one-time events have little or no follow-up or ongoing activities to support participants after the professional leader is gone. Consequently the positive impact typically diminishes quickly. Consider the person who makes a New Year's resolution to lose weight: regardless of how inspired and committed the person was in the moment of making the promise, he or she will likely encounter challenges in carrying it out and will need encouragement and practical support down the road. Many commercial weight-loss programs are so effective because they are able to provide that support, which is the key to the legendary success of Alcoholics Anonymous and other twelve-step programs that help people change addictive behaviors.

Some students who have had intense experiences in such events are left emotionally raw and vulnerable; it then becomes the responsibility of school staff members to notice this and arrange adequate support for these students. Otherwise they can feel betrayed and angry, and can take that anger out by sabotaging the intent of the program.

One-time programs make it easy to believe that the event has addressed the problem. But no single event can solve a complex problem such as mistreatment. Events need to be embedded within the context of a comprehensive effort to address behavioral norms and improve the school climate as a whole.[27]

Youth Involvement Programs

Some schools and districts are making the shift to see their students not just as consumers but as contributors. They are recognizing the importance of engaging students in significant ways and are increasing their roles in the overall school safety effort. The primary avenues being used are typically described as peer programs.

Peer helping and counseling programs usually begin with students' self-selecting into the program, although some students are invited to join the program by a faculty member. New peer counselors receive training in interpersonal skills that will help them on the job, such as observation, empathy, and active listening. Once trained, peer counselors help other teens through informal conversations with friends and during regularly scheduled "office-hour" sessions. The aim of these interactions is to help students handle the stresses and challenges of their lives—parents divorcing, boyfriend or girlfriend problems, pressure from peers to smoke or drink or behave in certain ways, academic pressure—in healthy and positive ways.

Peer mediation and conflict resolution programs have a similar selection process, though in some programs, an effort is made to recruit students from a cross-section of the school's population. These students receive basic training in communication skills, as well as in a specifically structured mediation and negotiation process.[28] Mediators guide the disputants through a predetermined format to identify and understand the issues in their dispute. At the end of the mediation, the disputants usually sign an agreement that specifies what each of them will do in the future.

Some states have embraced this approach. Ohio, for example, has created the state-level Commission on Dispute Resolution and Conflict Management that supports schools in developing conflict resolution programs. A recent survey showed that approximately 44 percent of the state's thirty-eight hundred public schools had some form of peer conflict resolution program.[29] Other estimates put the national average closer to 15 to 20 percent, so although these programs are growing, they are still not the norm in American schools.[30]

Strengths   Good peer programs can have a positive impact on school and classroom climate. However, any program is only as good as the worst of its components: the training, the materials, and the abilities of the people running it. If the adviser is knowledgeable, skilled, and committed and the school administrators are supportive, peer programs can effectively teach important life skills to participants and those with whom they work.

Conflict resolution programs have been shown to increase students' academic achievement, positive attitudes toward school, assertiveness, cooperation, communication skills, and other beneficial life skills and values.[31] Students in conflict mediation programs used better negotiation and conflict resolution strategies.[32] Scholars and practitioners alike generally agree that more research into the effectiveness of peer programs needs to be conducted.

Limitations   Peer counseling and conflict resolution programs are known to have limited impact on many types of mistreatment. The 2001 U.S. Surgeon General's Report on Youth Violence found that conflict resolution programs were not effective in preventing violence, specifically murder, stabbing, and shootings.[33] Even in more benign forms of mistreatment like bullying and teasing, peer helping has a limited effect, largely because mistreatment is marked by an imbalance of power: only one of the parties wants things to change. In such cases, a typical conflict resolution or mediation process can be deceptive and even harmful to the target.[34] For example, the aggressor can gain information about the target's inner feelings, which can increase the vulnerability of the target and become the subject of future aggression. Or, the aggressor can "fake it" during the meeting in order to satisfy the mediator figure but afterward return to the old pattern of behavior. As a result, the target has a false sense of resolution and gets hurt again.

Furthermore, having a peer program on campus does not mean that it is being used by students or that those student encounters are effective. Success often depends on the personal commitment of the program advisor and the degree of training and support this person provides to the students involved. Sometimes there is a lack of resources to provide proper training. In such cases, well-intentioned advisors might buy a book or video and conduct training themselves, which can compromise the quality and effectiveness of the program.

Conclusion

With all of these strategies available, it would be reasonable to conclude that schools have the tools they need to reduce the problem of mistreatment and create a social-emotional climate where all students can feel safe and can perform at their best. Nevertheless, the problem continues to be pervasive, and its costs are staggering.

What is wrong? Why are schools not achieving the results they should expect? A close examination reveals how two trends have produced a responsibility gap that well-intentioned educators have struggled to close with an outside-in approach that by its very nature cannot succeed alone. As one eighth-grade boy said, "Yeah, we have security cameras in the hall but everyone knows they can fight behind the lockers where the cameras can't see. We're not dumb."

The first trend is that over the past few decades, schools have taken on a greater responsibility for the social-emotional development of youth. This was not by design but due to significant changes in society, including these:

- For many teens, the influence of religious faith has faded. Most of today's young people spend much less time in religious practice than their parents did.

- American society has become more mobile, and the influence of the extended family has decreased. As families move to a different town or state, fewer live near their extended families, which means less support from—and less influence by—grandparents, aunts, and uncles.

- As families move with increasing frequency, the influence of the neighborhood is not as strong. They say it takes a village to raise a child, but when there's no village, what happens?

- Women have become a major part of the workforce. A stay-at-home mom is no longer the norm. The influence of the nuclear family is reduced as both parents work, often at multiple jobs, to make ends meet.

Most young people today spend their largest single block of time at school. The burden of teaching social skills that used to fall on the church, the community, and the family is now being placed on schools.

The second trend is the push toward accountability, standardized tests, and increased focus on core academic subjects like language and mathematics. The No Child Left Behind Act is the leading edge of this movement. In its wake, little room is left for teaching subjects like communication and conflict resolution skills or for helping students to build bridges of understanding between the different social and/or racial groups on a school campus.

When these two trends combine, they create a troubling responsibility gap between the social institutions that once taught essential social skills and the schools that no longer have the mandate, and thus the resources, to do it. The results are evident: the problem and costs of mistreatment are growing.

Educators have been left in this gap with the daily responsibility for managing the behavior of millions of students and creating safe learning environments. Understandably, as they have worked to close the gap with limited resources, they have focused on the most obvious problem: visible mistreatment. Their efforts, detailed in this chapter, can be characterized as primarily focused on security, driven by adults, and based on rules and policies (Figure 3.1).

While this outside-in approach to safety does appear to have reduced physical violence at schools, it has had a limited effect on the less visible forms of mistreatment: the exclusion, put-downs, and bullying that students see but adults typically don't. Metal detectors allow security officers to check the guns at the door, but the students pass right through and bring with them their attitudes, prejudices, and grudges. Despite rules to the contrary, students create social norms that say it's cool to be cruel.

Consequently these less visible incidents of mistreatment that occur below the waterline keep the social climate of the school simmering with unease until it boils over in a more visible incident that breaks a school's rules. This eruption triggers the school's react-and-discipline strategy: catch those who break the rules, and discipline them with detentions, suspensions, or expulsions. Since these responses don't address the underlying causes of the eruptions, it is only

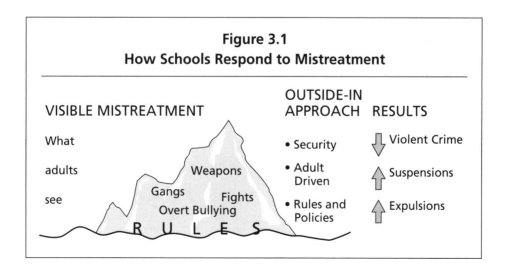

Figure 3.1
How Schools Respond to Mistreatment

VISIBLE MISTREATMENT

What

adults

see

Weapons
Gangs   Fights
Overt Bullying
R U L E S

OUTSIDE-IN
APPROACH   RESULTS

• Security   Violent Crime

• Adult
  Driven   Suspensions

• Rules and
  Policies   Expulsions

a matter of time before more eruptions occur and the cycle continues. Breaking this cycle requires a new approach to solving the problem of mistreatment, one that reconciles the often competing goals of academic achievement and youth development. This new approach recognizes and harnesses the power of the very people who fall through that responsibility gap: the students themselves. The chapters in Part Two explore this complementary inside-out approach, and show how it reduces incidents of mistreatment, increases students' sense of safety, and promotes both academic achievement and social-emotional learning.

Building Safer Schools from the Inside Out

PART TWO OF THIS BOOK DETAILS A DIFFERENT YET complementary approach to creating safer schools, but then goes further. It offers readers the chance to understand the importance of school climate: how climate not only enhances school safety but sets the stage for effective learning and success, not just in school but throughout life.

Chapter Four introduces our inside-out approach to safer schools, which places students at the center of all efforts to improve school safety because they are in the best position to do so. Not only are they the primary targets and aggressors, they are the bystanders who by default are the "first-responders," and whose action or inaction has a profound impact on each act of mistreatment. The chapter includes a discussion about how to harness students' power by identifying the social groupings and cliques of their world and taking proactive steps to build a network of positive relationships between them. It also compares and contrasts the impact of rules and norms on human behavior, identifies three norms that impede efforts to reduce the mistreatment discussed in Part One, and sets the stage for enlisting students to change those norms.

Chapter Five expands on our complementary inside-out approach by looking more deeply at the context in which those norms exist. It explores the very nature of "school climate" and why it is important to school safety, citing recommendations from the U.S. Secret Service and Department of Education. To help schools use this powerful strategy, Chapter Five discusses five determinants of school climate, and shows how one state has adopted climate benchmarks to support and guide educators to bring climate out of the realm of theory and into practice. The chapter includes ten keys to a safer school climate, a more comprehensive framework that schools can use to assess and guide their school safety efforts. The final section of the chapter shows how climate is a cornerstone of efforts to create schools that are both high achieving and safe. It articulates the double-win of climate: how it improves both physical and emotional safety *and* supports the social-emotional learning needed to balance the current emphasis on academic achievement, which equips students for success not just in school but throughout life.

chapter

4

The Inside-Out Approach

As we looked at what we were doing, we realized that we were doing a lot of the right things, but it wasn't quite enough. There was something missing from our approach. And as we looked more closely, we saw that we had not found an effective way to harness the power of the students. The history of school violence has taught us, in most crisis events, our students heard what was going to happen before it happened. Where schools have failed was not having a climate and environment where students feel safe in sharing information on what is going to happen before it happens. Even with our modern technology, the most effective intervention to school safety is communication and human relationships.

—DAVE HEARD, DIRECTOR OF SAFETY AND SECURITY, PERRIS UNION HIGH SCHOOL DISTRICT, CALIFORNIA

THE HEART OF THE INSIDE-OUT APPROACH TO SCHOOL SAFETY is the students: their relationships with one another and with adults, their involvement in all aspects of creating a positive school climate, and their role in creating and maintaining the social norms at their schools. The inside-out approach consists of three main elements:

- Relationships—creating, improving, and maintaining positive connections or bonds between and among all students and staff

- Student-centered solutions—drawing on young people's strengths by involving them in real decision making and putting them at the center of preventing and solving problems

- Norms—recognizing that while adults make the rules, it is the students who create, maintain, and can change the social norms that govern their peers' behavior

83

Table 4.1: Approaches to School Safety

Outside-In Approach	Inside-Out Approach
• Security	• Relationships
• Adult driven	• Student centered
• Rules and policies	• Norms

It contrasts with the outside-in approach discussed in Chapter Three, which focuses on security, is adult driven and is based on rules and policies (see Table 4.1).

Relationships

The security focus of the outside-in approach helps a school respond to the acts of mistreatment and violence that are above the waterline of the iceberg in Figure 1.2 and thus are visible to adults. By contrast, the relationship focus of the inside-out approach helps a school deal with the vast universe of mistreatment that seethes below the waterline, out of sight and earshot of most adults until it erupts into a visible incident that triggers a disciplinary response. Bill Bond, the former principal of Heath High School in Paducah, Kentucky, where a student shot and killed three peers and wounded five, noted that "it's not a hardware issue any more. It's about the relationships between the people in the school."[1]

Relationships grow out of the interactions between people. They begin with familiarity and contact, which can deepen knowledge and lead to understanding, which increases respect and fosters trust. Building relationships in a school setting involves creating ongoing opportunities for young people from varying social and ethnic groups to get to know one another, learn about each other's cultures and traditions, share common experiences, and build healthy and long-lasting positive connections based on understanding, respect, and trust.

In today's schools, especially at the secondary level, it's common to focus on relationships only when they become problematic—tension grows between groups, words are exchanged, tempers flare, and the battle lines are drawn. This lack of proactivity occurs because educators are held accountable for other priorities that they feel are more pressing, such as improving test scores, and some believe that building relationships and improving test scores occur separately.

But many educators realize that the nature and strength of the relationships on a school campus affect many other aspects of the educational experience: the quality of the learning, the number of discipline incidents, and the overall feeling of safety and security, usually referred to as school climate. Researchers have found that improving and strengthening the relationships among young people and among various social groups is fundamental to creating safer schools.[2] When student-to-student interactions are generally positive, tensions are reduced, trust is increased, and the amount of mistreatment declines. These all contribute to a more positive atmosphere, which in turn supports learning and academic achievement. Other research has found that the ability to form social networks among students may be more crucial as a determinant of academic and personal success than any other single factor.[3]

Improving relationships between young people is complicated by the ways youth gather and arrange themselves at schools. They create their own version of something like the United Nations. Each school is made up of different "countries" or groups of students, each with its own language, customs, beliefs, and biases. There are similar cliques or groups at almost every school, with labels such as the preps, the jocks, the skaters, the goths, the geeks, the populars, the druggies, the band nerds, and others that are based on race or ethnicity. These groupings generally begin to emerge in upper elementary school and solidify in middle and high school. They can be pictured as a very complex Venn diagram, with some circles intersecting others and some standing alone. The clustering of these cliques and groups often fosters a competitive social environment in which jockeying for position and power can lead to increased tension and, in many cases, can trigger violence. Just as building positive diplomatic relationships between and among some countries is challenging, trying to build positive connections among some students or groups is often difficult.

To reduce tension and encourage more positive interactions among the diverse and sometimes antagonistic student groups on a campus, it is first necessary to identify each of those different groups and determine who their leaders are. The Groups and Cliques worksheet can serve as a starting point in this identification process. It may be helpful for several staff members to complete their own worksheets and then compare results. Those who complete the worksheet should try to observe and interact with students in free-form, large-group settings before or after school or during recess, nutrition break, or lunch.

Groups and Cliques Worksheet

Name of Group or Clique	Description of Group (Include Activities and Interests, Mode of Dress, Other Distinguishing Characteristics)	Names of Leaders or Key Members of the Group	Groups This Clique Might Interact with Positively	Groups This Clique Might Interact with Negatively

Students are likely to have a different perspective on the school's social groupings and hierarchy, so it is valuable to involve them in this identification process. Student views can be incorporated into this process through focus groups or less formal conversations with adults they already know and trust, like counselors, yard duty staff, or campus supervisors. Naturally curious and sometimes suspicious of adult motives, students typically want to know why they are part of this process. Let them know that the goal is to help build and strengthen the relationships between students, help everyone get along, and reduce tension and potential, or actual, violence on campus and in the community.

With the groups and their members identified, it is easier to promote interpersonal relationships in a deliberate and thoughtful manner. Knowing who's who in the campus social structure and who's aligned with whom makes it possible for staff members to deliberately reweave the fabric of relationships on campus by including key students from these different groups in relationship-building activities.

The late John H. Gardner, founder of Common Cause, often talked about "familiarity through participation" as a way to "increase one's connection to their community." How is familiarity achieved? How can young people become more affiliated with their schools and their peers? Many researchers have found that intercultural goodwill is best achieved through frequent and sustained contacts—academic, extracurricular, or social—between and among students.[4]

We often tell students that *it's hard to hate someone when you know their story,* an idea we first heard in a conference keynote given by Margaret Wheatley, a noted author, innovative social scientist, and international leadership development expert. This resonates deeply with virtually all youth, especially when they've been through a facilitated relationship-building experience with other young people who are in different cliques within the school. Placing students in a situation where they get to know the stories of the other students and get to tell their own stories helps to lower barriers and break down stereotypes, an important first step in reducing peer-on-peer mistreatment. Isabel, a tenth grader in Arizona, had this to say: "I used to think about some of the people in the room—that they were just stuck up and mean. After getting to know everyone in this room, I now know who you really are. I have more in common with people in here than I thought. I feel like I have a bunch of new friends that I now respect, and I will keep remembering that as I see you every day."

The relationship-building process can be stimulated and supported by one-time events like these:

- Mix-it-up days, where students are encouraged or assigned to sit at different tables at lunch in order to converse with students outside their customary social circles.

- Multicultural or diversity days, designed to increase students' awareness of, and eventually their understanding and appreciation of, different cultures. Although these days can be organized in many ways, they often resemble fairs that use demonstrations, films, and activities to introduce students to the food, dance, clothing, customs, traditions, and history of the cultural groups represented in a school or community.

- A Challenge Day or similar process that uses powerful exercises to break down barriers and stereotypes and stimulate relationship building across cliques and groups.

When these opportunities for interaction are available, students develop more positive relationships. As they gain familiarity with one another, their knowledge and understanding grow, and their previously held biases and stereotypes are reduced, all of which are necessary for building a compassionate and welcoming school community.

Though events such as these are valuable, by themselves they don't go far enough. Many schools report that their impact diminishes too quickly, sometimes within a few weeks. A more effective way to foster familiarity and affiliation for all students is to combine these events with ongoing thematic experiences that are interwoven through the curriculum and extracurricular activities. For example, themes like tolerance and diversity, prejudice and discrimination, respect, and nonviolent conflict resolution often arise in the previously described experiences. These can be further explored through themed units that might be taught in a social studies or language arts setting for one or more weeks, a process that often further deepens relationships between students. (For an example, go to www .tolerance.org/teach/index.jsp and click on "Kits & Handbooks" or "Classroom Activities.") It is also possible—and richly rewarding—for students to explore those themes via integrated thematic instruction (ITI). This comprehensive school improvement model was developed by Susan Kovalik in the 1980s to increase student performance and teacher satisfaction. The full model, or at least its central premise, can be used by staff members to identify ways to link instruction in several subjects through themes like those described previously. Using the theme of intolerance as an example, the following could occur:

- Language arts teachers might be able to suggest books in which characters experience intolerance; these could be read and discussed, possibly using specific questions that link the characters' experiences to situations students encounter in their lives.

- Social studies teachers might identify incidents of intolerance or historical figures who experienced intolerance; these could be researched and studied, perhaps using primary source material, and then presented or situations could be reenacted.

- Teachers in other disciplines like art and music, or even math and science, might identify projects or activities that tie into the theme and could be conducted during the same time frame.

Although it is tempting to look for an external resource that prescribes such integrated instructional opportunities, experience suggests that a more successful and sustainable theme unit is developed when staff members develop it themselves from what they know.

Developing more opportunities for adolescents to know one another in positive ways can help improve school safety and school performance. When students are no longer rigidly bound by their affiliations to their cliques, groups, and gangs, they can cross social borders and interact with one another more easily, and the entire school climate improves dramatically.[5]

Student-Centered Solutions

Although adults play a major role in efforts to create safe school environments, adults cannot achieve that goal by themselves. They simply miss too much of the below-the-waterline mistreatment that adversely affects climate and often escalates into visible violence, both because they cannot be everywhere students are and because even when they are present, the subtle looks or signs one student flashes to another are hard for adults to detect. Furthermore, adults have limited influence over students in matters of behavior, especially after elementary school.

Young people must have a pivotal role in efforts to reduce mistreatment and improve school climate for many reasons. They have the power of numbers: students outnumber adults ten to one at most schools. They also have an understanding of the mistreatment that is going on in their schools on a more personal level: students are the vast majority of targets and aggressors in incidents of mistreatment on school campuses, and if they were not involved themselves in a particular incident, they probably know someone who was. They also have the power of knowledge: they see, hear, and know things about their peers' feelings and plans long before adults ever do. And they are typically the first responders: they are on the scene of mistreatment long before adults arrive. Moreover, they have the power of relationship: they can intervene in ways adults can't because they have influence over their peers that adults simply don't have. And perhaps most significant, students largely determine the social norms that govern their peers' behavior; this means that they can permit mistreatment to occur despite the existence of rules that prohibit it, or they can oppose mistreatment and thereby help to stop it.

The power students generally lack is the positional power held by the adults who are in charge of the schools and other institutions that students attend. Devising and successfully implementing student-centered solutions to mistreatment or any other problem requires that adults share—which means relinquish some of—their power to make the meaningful decisions about how those institutions are run. Noted educator, philosopher, scholar, and media theorist Marshall McLuhan is credited with observing, "There are no passengers on Spaceship Earth—we are all crew." In an adult-driven model, the adults are the crew, and the students are the passengers. In a student-centered model, the students and adults together are the crew. And as crew members, students can play responsible roles as collaborators and decision makers in making schools safer. These roles might include sitting on a climate committee or helping to shape school discipline policies and practices.

However, it is not enough to have one or two students sit on a school safety committee or advisory board. Adults have to create multiple opportunities for more students to do more and feel ownership of the process of building a positive school climate. Students can be involved in creating safer schools in a number of other ways—for example:

- Link Crew for high school and Where Everyone Belongs (WEB) for middle school. In these transition programs, older students welcome and orient incoming students to the school through activities and small-group meetings conducted at the beginning and end of the school year and other key points in between.

- Conflict mediators. These programs create a structure that students can use to work out their interpersonal disagreements and resolve arguments with support from specially trained students.

- Safe School Ambassadors. This program engages the socially influential opinion leaders of a school's diverse cliques and equips them with skills they can use with their friends to prevent and stop mistreatment and violence, shifting the social norms of the campus in a positive direction.

- Many of the other activities described in the ten keys to a safer school climate presented in Chapter Five.

It is important to undertake these student-centered efforts for the right reasons: not for adults but for students, not in response to a problem but out of recognizing that young people are a tremendous resource. This paradigm shift for most adults is discussed in greater detail in Chapter Six. When this shift is made and a school becomes more student centered, everyone wins. Research based on the California Healthy Kids Survey has identified three primary components that promote healthy development and successful learning in young people:

- Caring relationships

- Messages of high expectations

- *Opportunities for participation and contribution* [emphasis added][6]

These components support the healthiest, most successful outcomes for youth in all settings. Fostering positive relationships and creating opportunities for students to become actively involved are two of the elements of the inside-out approach. The third element is the social norms that govern student behavior, which are created and maintained largely by students.

Norms

In contrast to the rules focus of the outside-in approach, the inside-out approach is built on the power of norms to shape, guide, and influence behavior. A norm is a standard or pattern seen as typical for a particular group: "When in Rome, do as the Romans do." Norms are understood and passed along in the absence of any written rules. Rules are written and discussed; norms are enacted and rarely discussed.

The dynamic interplay among rules, norms, and authority figures can be clearly seen in the behavior of drivers on freeways. The posted speed limit is the rule, and everyone knows it. When traffic conditions permit, most drivers exceed the speed limit by ten to twenty miles per hour; that is the norm and it is quite different from the rule. When a highway patrol or police officer enters the highway, the rule overrides the norm and traffic slows to the posted limit, but when the officer exits, the norms become the governing force once again.

I had an experience while conducting a training at a school in Colorado. The training day fell on the same day as the school's picture day. Most of the students weren't dressed up. In fact, they were dressed somewhat grungy, and it seemed odd that none of the students bothered to dress up for their annual picture. When it was time for these students to get their picture taken, many of them took their backpacks with them. This seemed unusual, but it turned out that these students had their dress clothes in their backpacks. They would go to the restroom and change into their dress clothes just before having their picture taken. After the picture was taken, they would return to the restroom, change back into their grungy clothes, and stuff their dress clothes back into their backpacks. At this school, the norm for this particular group was to dress a certain way. Students learned this behavior by watching what others wear or by listening to what students say about what others are wearing, or by being put down themselves for what they wear. Young people don't determine the norms for just what they wear or how they look. They also determine the norms for how students treat one another.

Every school has rules and policies that define and prohibit specific types of mistreatment. Despite these rules and severe consequences for rule breakers, mistreatment has not gone away; in many cases, it has even escalated. However, as we have seen and research has shown, rules and consequences for rule breakers are not the sole determinants of student behavior, regardless of the intentions of the adults who made the rules. For example, in our work with thousands of youth, we often ask if their schools have rules about foul language. Invariably, the answer is yes, and students can explain in detail the consequences of breaking those rules: getting benched, serving detention, attending Saturday school, and so on. However, when we ask, "Who's heard someone get cussed out at school by another student?" a forest of hands goes up. This apparent contradiction illustrates the difference between rules and norms and reveals what really governs students' behavior: the norms.

Adults make and enforce a school's rules, and when adults are present, student behavior conforms to those rules. However, as with drivers on the highway, once the authority figure departs, the norms take over as the primary influence of behavior. This dynamic presents school safety planners with an interesting dilemma: either ensure that adults are present everywhere on campus all the time to enforce the rules or shift the school's social norms.

A school's social norms are shaped largely by the students. If it is considered acceptable to push a weaker student into a locker or harass and abuse a special education student, then these behaviors will happen a lot regardless of the rules prohibiting them or the consequences for violating those rules. But if the social norms dictate that it is not acceptable to mistreat others, those negative behaviors will decrease, even in the absence of rules that prohibit such behavior and even without severe consequences for violating those rules.

Unfortunately, many of the norms governing student behavior are for the most part not very positive—for example:

• *Cool to be cruel.* Cruelty has become the norm in many schools, especially at the secondary level. Meanness—displayed physically through fighting, pushing, or tripping or displayed verbally through insults, sarcasm, or other destructive humor—is often rewarded with a "high five" and increased social status within the immediate peer group or popularity within the school as a whole.

• *Code of silence.* Many students feel strong pressure from peers to refrain from reporting actual or potentially hurtful or dangerous situations to adults. This norm is expressed through directive statements made by one student to another—statements like, "Don't be a snitch, man" or "We don't rat out our own." The code of silence is a code of honor, broken at the risk of expulsion from the social group. Although individuation and separation from adults is a natural part of adolescent development, the code of silence is fueled by a lack of meaningful contact between students and adults. It is also fueled by a fundamental disempowerment of youth in virtually all aspects of society, which grows out of a lack of meaningful and important roles for youth. In essence, many youth feel unneeded in adult society, and so they withdraw further into their own youth culture.

• *Bystander mentality.* Many students feel more comfortable watching something rather than becoming involved in it. This norm stems in part from the disempowerment, which results in students' feeling that the school is not really theirs, which leads them to ask, "So why should I get involved?" It also stems from students' general sense of disconnection from the particular people involved, which comes from the lack of strong relationships between the students who identify with different groups in the school. This norm also stems from the messages most children begin to hear very early in their lives, messages conveyed by parents and the larger culture: "Mind your own business," "That's not your problem," and even, "Don't talk to strangers."

Students have a significant role in shaping and perpetuating these norms, and social norms theory and practice strongly suggests that students can take the lead in reshaping them more positively.[7] In fact, they must. They must speak up and send different messages: that hurting someone else is not okay, that speaking up for each other is a valued act, and that courage in the face of injustice is important. When certain students do this, the behavioral norms can change, and school mistreatment and violence can decrease. Chapters Seven and Eight provide a more detailed explanation of who these students are and how they can be enlisted in a successful norms-change process.

Conclusion

Once a school has recognized the value and benefits of the inside-out approach and taken concrete steps to reallocate its resources toward that end, the next phase has begun. The school faculty and staff, in collaboration with the students, have laid the groundwork necessary to foster and maintain a positive school climate. The inside-out approach—building positive social relationships, involving its students integrally, and recognizing students' impact on creating social norms—offers both the foundation for and a proven way to build a safer school climate.

chapter

5

Building a Safe School Climate

WORKING IN AND WITH SCHOOLS FOR SEVERAL DECADES, we have learned how important climate is to creating safe schools. In an era when educators are held accountable for two main goals—academic achievement and a safe campus—climate is often seen as an afterthought to be attended to once the campus is secure and students are making adequate yearly progress on state tests. This chapter makes the case for reframing climate as a core strategy for achieving those two goals.

School Climate

Although it can be defined in a number of ways, the *climate* of a school is a very broad measure of the sense people have or what they feel when they are at the school:

> School culture and climate refers to the sum of the values, cultures, safety practices, and organizational structures within a school that cause it to function and react in particular ways. Some schools are said to have a nurturing environment that recognizes children and treats them as individuals; others may have the feel of authoritarian structures where rules are strictly enforced and hierarchical control is strong. Teaching practices, diversity, and the relationships among administrators, teachers, parents, and students contribute to school climate. Although the two terms are somewhat interchangeable, *school climate* refers mostly to the school's effects on students, while *school culture* refers more to the way teachers and other staff members work together.[1]

When assessing the climate of a school, it can be helpful to look at particular aspects of the daily interactions among students (see Figure 5.1), for example:

• Groups and cliques: When they are rigidly defined and impermeable, and members of one group view members of others with suspicion and hostility, the climate is unsafe. When there is a fabric of relationships that connects students on a deeper level, and members of one group can comfortably approach and interact with members of others, the climate is safer.

• Disagreements: When disagreements easily escalate into full-scale conflicts, and the friends of one disputant are drawn in to be mean to or even fight with the other disputant and his or her friends, the climate is unsafe. When disagreements are resolved peacefully, when there is a modicum of tolerance and forgiveness in the air, and when students give each other the benefit of the doubt and cut each other some slack, the climate is safer.

• Watching one's back: When students are on edge and have to watch their backs to dodge physical or verbal blows that might come from almost anyone at any time, the climate is unsafe. When students are more at ease and don't need to watch their backs, knowing that it's not the norm to be mean or attack one another at this school, the climate is safer. Better still are students watching *each other's* backs: they stand up, step up, and speak up to support and take care of one another.

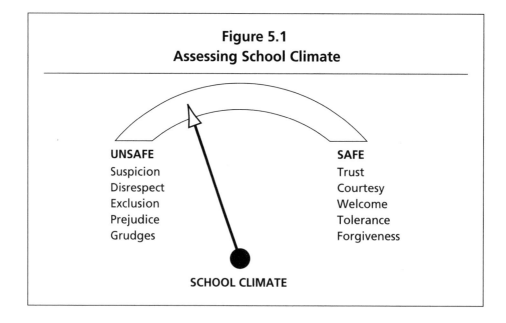

**Figure 5.1
Assessing School Climate**

UNSAFE
Suspicion
Disrespect
Exclusion
Prejudice
Grudges

SAFE
Trust
Courtesy
Welcome
Tolerance
Forgiveness

SCHOOL CLIMATE

- Speaking up in class: When students are (or fear being) judged, ridiculed, or even attacked for the questions they (want to) ask or the opinions they (want to) express in class, the climate is unsafe. When students can tolerate, understand, and even embrace the "dumb questions" and opinions that challenge their own beliefs, the climate is safer.

Although these examples provide some concrete reference points, they are not the only indicators of school climate. Accurately assessing a school's social-emotional atmosphere should include interviews or focus group discussions with students and staff, and possibly even a climate survey instrument administered schoolwide or to a representative sample of the school population.

Why Is School Climate Important?

As it affects school safety, this question is answered by the *Threat Assessment Guide,* developed by the U.S. Secret Service and Department of Education in the aftermath of the Columbine shooting to help schools prevent violence:

> Cultures and climates of safety, respect, and emotional support can help diminish the possibility of targeted violence in schools. Environments in which students, teachers and administrators pay attention to students' social and emotional needs—as well as their academic needs—will have fewer situations that require formal threat assessments.[2]

In other words, they'll have less violence because there are fewer incidents of mistreatment to spark them.

The *Guide* goes on to state, "The principal objective of school violence-reduction strategies should be to create cultures and climates of safety, respect, and emotional support within educational institutions."[3] Without a deep institutional commitment to building and maintaining a positive school climate, any program to resolve conflicts, increase tolerance, or reduce bullying is just an add-on, subject to the vagaries of funding or changes in school or district administration. With a focus on climate, these efforts become integral parts of a comprehensive approach to keeping school safe.

But climate is important for other reasons, too. Focusing on school climate allows educators to leap over the horns of the classic dilemma that catches so many: with limited dollars and instructional minutes, do we focus on academic achievement or youth development? Too often these are seen as opposing or competing goals. However, if youth are to develop into responsible adults, educators and community members must address students' social and emotional development as well as their cognitive development. Concentrating on improving school climate allows educators to address both aspects simultaneously.

Nel Noddings spent twenty-three years as a teacher and administrator before serving on the faculty of Stanford, Columbia, Colgate, and Eastern Michigan universities. An expert on caring and its impact on education, Noddings describes the impact of a caring climate in this way: "At a time when the traditional structures of caring have deteriorated, schools must become places where teachers and students live together, talk with each other, take delight in each other's company. My guess is that when schools focus on what really matters in life, the cognitive ends we now pursue so painfully and artificially will be achieved somewhat more naturally. . . . It is obvious that children will work harder and do things—even odd things like adding fractions—for people they love and trust."[4]

The No Child Left Behind (NCLB) law and concomitant policies and regulations, with their increased emphasis on academic accountability and testing, have resulted in schools' spending a disproportionate amount of time and resources on students' academic development at the expense of social and emotional development. The Center for Education Policy reports that 71 percent of the fifteen thousand school districts in the United States have reduced the number of instructional minutes devoted to history, music, and other subjects not included in NCLB accountability measures to open up more time for reading and math.[5] The report goes on to recommend that "the Secretary of Education should use her bully pulpit to signal that social studies, science, the arts, and other subjects beside reading and math are still a vital part of a balanced curriculum."[6] The virtually complete absence of social-emotional development from this report and the mainstream discussion of NCLB reform indicates how low a priority it is in most of the educational arena. This lopsided emphasis on cognitive development is like lifting weights to get in shape but working the muscles on only one side of the body. Though the one side gets stronger, the whole body ends up out of balance, and the overall results aren't successful. The authors of one recent study of NCLB noted that "reallocation of resources away from health-related programs and activities that support learning may actually undermine children's academic performance in the long term."[7] To give this discussion a more personal perspective: if your car broke down in a relatively deserted place late at night and a group of teens were walking toward you, which would matter to you more: what their eighth-grade math scores were or whether they learned at an early age the importance of respect, compassion, and helpfulness?

Research consistently shows a strong correlation between positive school climates (ones that foster resilience) and academic achievement (higher grades and performance on standardized tests), attendance (low absenteeism), school connectedness and belonging (and associated thriving behaviors), and positive student behavior (fewer incidents requiring disciplinary action like suspension).[8] For example, researchers examining the effects of school reform in Chicago found that schools with high trust levels were three times more likely to report gains in reading and math scores, and schools in the top quartile on standardized tests had higher levels of trust. Schools with low levels of trust showed only a 14 percent chance of improving in their academic measures.[9] Researchers analyzing data from California's standardized tests and the Healthy Kids Survey found that schools with high test scores had positive climates; their students experienced lower levels of violence, victimization, and alcohol, tobacco, and other drug use and higher levels of physical health, caring relationships, high-expectation messages, and opportunities for participation and contribution.[10]

Intuitively this makes sense: students who feel welcome and valued will want to come to school. Those who feel physically and emotionally safe will more naturally ask questions, engage in discussions, and be better able to focus on learning. Students who respect others and have the skills for nonviolent conflict resolution will be less likely to fight when differences lead to arguments.

"EQ, or emotional intelligence, is as important as IQ for success in today's workplace."[11] This quote highlights another benefit of a positive school climate. As students learn, through lessons and practice, what's required to create and maintain a more positive school climate, they learn the skills (like communication and problem solving) and develop the values (like tolerance and patience) that are required for success in the workplace, in relationships, and in life. As former Lockheed Martin CEO Norman Augustine said, "We have to emphasize communication skills, the ability to work in teams and with people from different cultures."[12] The double win here is that when students acquire these building blocks for a positive school climate, they not only increase their odds for success in life, they also improve in the indicators commonly used to assess educational success today: student behavior and discipline, attendance, and academic achievement.

A focus on school climate offers something for everyone. The proponents of increased social-emotional development can support it because this focus emphasizes relationships and relationship skills. Those concerned about security and discipline can support it because students with social skills get along better, which means fewer conflicts escalate into discipline incidents that require adult intervention; a focus on school climate also specifically includes addressing physical security issues. And those concerned about academic achievement can support it because when interpersonal conflict incidents decrease and students have more and better relationships with each other and with adults on campus, attendance and academic achievement increase.

These threads are reinforced by the findings of a team of researchers at the Search Institute who probed the issue of school climate. They have found that a positive school climate increases students' sense of belonging by meeting their affective needs and increases their academic efficacy, in part by supporting their confidence, which in turn boosts their achievement motivation and sets the stage for them to become lifelong learners.[13]

The effects of a positive school climate on staff are also noteworthy, especially because they address many of costs of mistreatment that affect staff, as discussed in Chapter Two. A positive school climate increases teachers' sense of efficacy, which increases teacher satisfaction. Together these effects reduce teacher turnover and help improve the learning climate for students.

Five Determinants of School Climate

What actually influences or determines the social-emotional climate of a school? To facilitate a discussion of this far-reaching topic, it is helpful to group the factors that influence the climate of a school into five categories:

1. *Community factors:* The values, beliefs, and practices that are evident outside the walls of school and home, particularly the value a community places on its children and youth and how its members invest time and resources to support youth development

2. *Family factors:* The values, beliefs, and practices that are instilled and reinforced in children by parents and other relatives, especially regarding how

to behave with adults in authority and peers and what value is placed on education, tolerance, communication, and nonviolence

3. *Organizational factors:* The values, beliefs, and practices demonstrated by a school's policies, lines of and access to communication and authority, opportunities to participate in decision making, size, physical layout, adult-student ratio, class size, and number of students, among others

4. *Staff factors:* The values, beliefs, and practices demonstrated by the ways school staff relate to each other and to students, their classroom management and discipline practices, and the priority individual staff members place on building and strengthening relationships

5. *Student factors:* The values, beliefs, and practices that are demonstrated by how students relate to one another and to adults in authority, how they prioritize education relative to other experiences in their lives, their attitudes toward acquiring and building relationship skills like communication and conflict resolution, and how their behaviors and choices are influenced by the other four factors

Community Factors   Schools reflect their communities in a multitude of ways. Sometimes they reflect attitudes and priorities of previous years or even decades; sometimes they respond to the present and change with the times. The values, beliefs, and practices that are evident outside the walls of school and home, particularly the value a community places on education, have a profound influence on the climate of schools within that community. Some of these values are evidenced in the ways a community allocates or votes to allocate tangible resources: How much funding is made available for parks and recreation? For education? For other youth-focused programs and services? Some of these values are shown in the types of labor contracts and advancement policies offered to teachers.

Other values are shown through the kinds of jobs that are available to youth, and how youth are regarded and treated by their employers, coworkers, and customers. When adults take an active interest in youth development in the workplace, those young employees experience the sense that they are valued and respected, and they carry that into their schools. When members of the public who are being served by youth in restaurants and stores treat young people with respect—as people rather than as servants—those young people learn to treat others in their school the same way: as people to be respected regardless of differences. Youth sense what the community's values are through these and other displays, and then respond to these values both in and out of school.

Family Factors   Family factors refer to the values, beliefs, and practices that parents, other relatives, and guardians instill and reinforce in children, especially regarding how to behave with adults in authority and peers and what value is placed on education. When the adults who raise a young person work collaboratively with the school faculty and staff to create the best environment for their child's education, everyone benefits. Parental or guardian involvement in schools is a vital element in positive school climate development. One of the best descriptions of the influence of family on children's beliefs can be found in "You've Got To Be Carefully Taught," a song written by Richard Rodgers & Oscar Hammerstein II from the musical "South Pacific." Written at a time in U.S. history when the bombing of Pearl Harbor made many Americans at least deeply suspicious, if not blatantly hateful, of anyone who looked remotely Asian, the song satirizes how families pass intolerance on to their children.

> "You've Got To Be Carefully Taught"
>
> You've got to be taught to hate and fear.
> You've got to be taught from year to year.
> It's got to be drummed in your dear little ear.
> You've got to be carefully taught.
>
> You've got to be taught to be afraid
> Of people whose eyes are oddly made,
> And people whose skin is a diff'rent shade,
> You've got to be carefully taught.
>
> You've got to be taught before it's too late,
> Before you are six or seven or eight,
> To hate all the people your relatives hate,
> You've got to be carefully taught!
> You've got to be carefully taught!

When adults raising children make efforts to demonstrate acceptance, have diverse friends, and relate positively to a variety of people, their children develop cultural competence that leads to an understanding of our interdependence. When youth have learned to be open-minded and compassionate, they are more likely to be willing to stand up against mistreatment based on prejudice or bias.

Organizational Factors   A school's buildings, size, organizational structures, policies, and processes for decision making all contribute to the overall climate of a school. Student behavior is influenced in subtle yet powerful ways by the physical environment of the school: color, light and lighting, the general level of cleanliness, the presence or absence of student and adult art, the overall appearance and "feel" of a school (for example, whether it more closely resembles a community or an institution). While a thorough discussion of these factors is beyond the scope of this book, it helps to note that as funds become increasingly difficult to find, less is spent on the cleaning, maintenance, repair, and renovation of facilities. And even when funds are available, too little attention is paid to creating spaces that are inspiring and full of beauty (as perceived by students). The result is that students sense that someone, somewhere, doesn't care so much for this place and think, "So why should I?" They may show their awareness of the school's deficiencies in the ways they treat peers, staff, and the facility itself. When the school environment is clean and attractive, students are more likely to take better care of their surroundings and each other. In addition, when students participate in improving the school environment, such as creating artwork and murals for the walls or planting flowers, they tend to feel more empowered and by doing so improve school climate.

Organizational structures include the hierarchies, departmental divisions, oversight, reporting, and lines of communication that staff and students are expected to conform to, know their places in, and respect. Within and permeating each organization's structures are the ways these are sensed by the people involved in them: within a school climate there could be departmental, division, or grade-level microclimates, with barriers or welcome mats.

Policies, and processes for decision making, are some of the working parts of organizations. The ways policies and decisions are made create experiences of inclusion or exclusion, respect or disrespect among those affected by them. The development of a policy could and should include many voices, including representatives of all affected by that policy, in order for an organization to be considered "receptive" and "empowering." The ways participants feel about policies and decisions greatly influence school climate.

Staff and students participate in the life of the school as an organization in varying ways, and the success of a school depends on the quality of this participation.

Staff Factors   Staff factors refers to the values, beliefs, and practices that are demonstrated by the ways school staff relate to each other and to students, their classroom management and discipline practices, and the priority individual staff place on building relationships and school climate. Although students largely create and maintain the social norms that govern peer interaction, young people do take a number of behavioral cues from the adults in the school. Specifically, students notice how adults treat students and interact with one another, and then emulate or react to those behaviors. In our Safe School Ambassadors program training, students describe how they've been put down, shamed, bullied, or even physically assaulted by staff members. Staff typically chime in with examples of their own and ask if we can do the same antibullying training with the entire staff.

Even in schools where faculty and staff treat one another and students with respect, the hustle and rush of the school day, the seemingly competing priorities for time, and many other demands on school personnel dampen their desire to create positive relationships with one another and with students beyond what is absolutely necessary for day-to-day functioning. Therefore, a school that recognizes the value of relationships and their effect on school climate builds time into every day for adults and youth to interact in positive ways: for teachers and administrators to relate to students more informally and frequently, not just when they have academic needs or have been referred for discipline problems. Many school schedules include time for class meetings and group time, or individual conferences, which foster positive relationships among students and between staff and students. The quality and quantity of these relationships directly influence the school climate.

Though somewhat difficult to define and quantify, staff morale is something everyone feels and senses, and it directly affects school climate. The energy, attitudes, and general friendliness of staff members influence how it feels to be at a school. Staff members also have the choice to foster and support student involvement and empowerment or to be negative and stand in the way of these efforts. When administrators and faculty are in agreement about the importance of positive school climate and make it a high priority, everyone benefits.

Interestingly, though, many schools do not think to include time for staff to build a sense of team with one another. Staff development time is usually devoted to improving a teacher or staff member's ability to perform job functions. When it does include time for creating and maintaining positive staff relationships, staff morale and school climate improve.

Student Factors Though students are influenced by the preceding four factors, they each are individuals with their own emerging values, beliefs, and practices— young people who make their own decisions about what they say and do on a daily basis. Their words and actions give students a key role in determining school climate.

On a purely numerical basis, students have roughly ten times the influence adults have. But perhaps more significantly, although adults make the rules, students influence and set the social norms that govern peer interactions.

Student factors that influence school climate include a student's:

- Ability and desire to relate to other students across social borders
- Level of skill in communication, impulse control, empathy, and conflict resolution
- Cultural competence and acceptance of differences
- Willingness to "let it go" rather than fight about it
- Level of involvement or willingness to intervene rather than be passive when mistreatment is occurring
- Sense of empowerment and degree of involvement in school decision-making processes
- Overall attitude toward education and desire to be in school

While these factors give students tremendous influence over the climate of a school, there is something else that makes them the best leverage point for improving school climate: the fact that they are youth. First, they are readily available, present at every act of youth mistreatment that occurs in a school. They are motivated: their inherent self-interest makes them *want* to be in a safe climate. They are willing: they generally don't say "it's not in my job description" as some staff do and they don't have "work-to-rule" issues. Whereas adults are more measured in their decision making, youth have a can-do go-for-it attitude that supports immediate action and results. And, youth have a natural affinity for risk and challenge, all of which make them ideally suited to be on the front lines of school climate improvement efforts.

Before moving on to more specific ways schools and communities can improve their school climate, the following section looks at the ways school climate definitions and benchmarks for success are being standardized.

Climate as a Standard

Although policymakers are coming to see the importance of school climate, it has not yet been codified as a standard in the same way that reading, math, and other subjects have been. Until this happens, schools that are held accountable to meet standards will always struggle to make school climate the focal point it needs to be. Nonetheless, progress is being made. For example, the Ohio Department of Education has developed an extensive set of school climate guidelines. By establishing them, these state-level leaders and policymakers are reinforcing that it's *not just a good idea* to "create environments where every student feels welcomed, respected and motivated to learn" but that schools have an *obligation* to do so. The Foreword plainly states the importance of climate, noting that "conditions for teaching and learning must be right or they [students] will not learn what they need to know to succeed and graduate."[14]

Though voluntary, these nine guidelines raise climate to a new level of importance for district and site administrators.[15] The guidelines cover many aspects of education, including overall operations, school-community partnerships, continuous improvement, real and perceived threats to safety, students' sense of belonging, skills and involvement of parents, involving students in decision making, and the quality of school food service. Through thirty-six specific benchmarks, they provide more than two hundred concrete measures schools can use to plan and assess their efforts to create a safe and positive climate. Among the benchmarks are these:

- 4C. Policies and procedures have been developed to effectively improve communication and resolve conflict among staff, staff and administration, staff and families, and staff and students.

- 5E. Policies and procedures are in place regarding positive ways to prevent violence, resolve conflict and effectively deal with bullying, harassment and violent acts.

- 6C. Students experience a warm and caring school climate.

- 6D. Students are provided opportunities to develop positive behaviors.

- 8A. Students are given meaningful roles on school and community committees to learn new skills.

Ten Keys to a Safer School Climate

The five determinants discussed earlier in this chapter outline broad groups of factors that shape and influence a school's overall social-emotional climate, but they do not make it easy for schools and districts to identify and develop strategies for creating learning environments that are safe—both physically and emotionally. The ten keys that follow provide a framework for long-term planning and development of a school safety plan that focuses on involving youth with adults in creating safer schools.

The two overarching goals of this process are to create safer schools and increase youth empowerment and involvement. Several of these keys provide excellent opportunities for increased and ongoing student involvement. Other keys are typically the exclusive domain of adults, so involving students in these areas will require commitment and perseverance, along with good youth development practice, as described in Chapter Six.

Some schools might already be strong in one or more of these key areas. Other schools might not even have realized that particular keys are factors in improving school climate and have done little with them to date. Even fewer will already be strong in all ten keys or already have involved youth in as many as possible. We hope that by presenting these descriptions and some examples, all schools will move in the direction of increasing youth involvement and strengthening all ten key areas, and thereby create safer learning environments for their students and staff.

Ten Keys to Safer Schools

Key 1: Establish school-community partnerships.

Key 2: Start a school climate team.

Key 3: Set clear behavioral standards, policies, and procedures.

Key 4: Improve the physical environment.

Key 5: Empower students as agents of social change.

Key 6: Implement diversity activities.

Key 7: Create opportunities for the least engaged youth.

Key 8: Support social skills curricula and instruction.

Key 9: Conduct teacher and staff training.

Key 10: Encourage parent involvement.

 ### Key 1: Establish School-Community Partnerships

School violence is not a problem of schools alone. As the next chapter shows in greater detail, successfully meeting the developmental needs of youth requires a comprehensive, communitywide effort best coordinated by a school-community partnership that includes law enforcement, faith groups, businesses, government, senior citizens, community-based and youth-serving organizations, along with students, teachers, administrators, and parents.

Potential Actions

1. Convene the key stakeholders, including youth representatives.

2. Articulate a common vision of a safe school in youth-friendly terminology.

3. Explore how each constituent group can work toward that vision in a coordinated way, and involve youth in many aspects of that work as described in several of the following keys.

4. Make and carry out specific action plans, some with youth as leaders or mentored by adults to be leaders.

5. Report successes and problems.

6. Meet on a regular basis to provide ongoing training and support.

👍 **The Challenge**

- Creating cohesion among people with very different perspectives, experiences, and styles of communicating and decision making.

☞ **Tip**

- Select an experienced facilitator who can work effectively with the group to establish ground rules for communication and decision making, encourage participation, and resolve differences. This helps ensure that these meetings are productive and that participants' enthusiasm and commitment grow as they see that their actions produce results.

 ## Key 2: Start a School Climate Team

A site-based school climate team, composed of students, staff, teachers, administrators, school resource officers, and parents, should be formed and meet regularly to monitor school climate and suggest strategies for improvement. The team provides a forum in which all stakeholders can voice their concerns and work with key decision makers to implement specific actions that promote safety and prevent violence in the school. Because students are the primary aggressors and targets of school violence, they have a critical role in the success of the solutions developed.

It is also important to give the team opportunities to stop along the way to reflect on their experiences—to note progress, accomplishments, or positive outcomes—so that everyone feels that their input and effort have been worthwhile. When the mission is very large and complex ("Prevent School Violence") or involves trying to have fewer of something negative (interpersonal conflicts that lead to fights), it can be hard for the team to see its effects without methods for assessing progress and naming milestones along the way.

Potential Actions

1. Convene stakeholders to form a school climate team; provide training and other support so the team can function effectively.

2. Assess the climate using climate surveys, focus groups, or interviews to identify strengths and gaps.

3. Prioritize needs, and select projects to meet them. These could include projects or activities identified in Key 6: Implement Diversity Activities.

4. Create ongoing opportunities, such as monthly open forum meetings and suggestion boxes, for staff, students, and other stakeholders to voice concerns and provide recommendations for ways to improve the climate.

👌   **The Challenge**

• Sustaining youth and adult involvement, commitment, and momentum in the absence of a crisis.

☞   **Tips**

• Take actions that lead to quick successes. Have high-visibility activities that lead to equally high-visibility results several times during the school year.

• Make sure the activities are part of a coherent plan that addresses the gaps identified in the school climate assessment and strengthens connectedness and relationships.

 Key 3: Set Clear Behavioral Standards, Policies, and Procedures

Every school community needs clear standards of behavior that all members know and accept. These standards also must have clear consequences for those who step outside the boundaries of acceptability, and these consequences must be consistently applied.

Potential Actions

1. Assemble representatives of all sectors of the school community, including students, to forge consensus on the standards, consequences, and policies affecting student and staff behavior and discipline.

2. Start a teen court for handling certain discipline issues.

👍   **The Challenge**

• Getting past the perception held by many students that adults won't listen to them, take their ideas seriously, give them significant roles, or share power with them in meaningful way.

☞   **Tip**

• Engage key students—those respected by their peers—in this process through one-to-one conversations. Then hold several dialogue sessions to solicit students' views.

 ## Key 4: Improve the Physical Environment

As was mentioned in Chapter Three, although every school needs to make sure that its students and staff are protected from the most likely potential threats—student weapons on campus, armed intruders, or other unwelcome visitors—new fencing, locks, cameras, and metal detectors are not the only ways to make the physical environment support school safety. This outside-in approach must be used, but only as one strategy among several.

In addition to specific security measures, the overall quality of the physical environment has a huge impact on how students feel at school. Is the lighting harsh or warm? What about the colors used? Are the halls and common spaces sterile, or do they contain plants, student art, projects, and awards? Are the grounds clean or littered? What happens when there is graffiti? How quickly do repairs occur? Are there safety issues and risks that remain unaddressed? Are there sufficient resources to devote to inspections, repairs, and cosmetic improvements to the building? The answers to these and other similar questions are part of a general self-assessment about a campus's physical plant that contribute to making decisions about improving school climate from this perspective.

Potential Actions

1. Use surveys, focus groups, or other age-appropriate means to gather students' thoughts about their perceptions of actual and potential threats, weak or blind spots, and ways to increase the physical security of the campus, as well as its overall feeling of warmth.

2. Remedies might include new or improved fencing, gates, locks, lighting, cameras, radios, or metal detectors, as well as new policies and procedures for visitors and lockdowns, for example. They might also include new paint, student murals, new lighting, and freshened decor.

3. Compile the ideas of students, staff, and professionals into a comprehensive report that lists threats and their probability of occurrence, along with proposed remedies and their costs. Do a cost-benefit analysis. Seek comments from all stakeholders.

✑ The Challenge

• Recognizing that physical security improvements will not do everything necessary to ensure a safe campus. Although those remedies can address potentially dramatic and costly threats, such events are only a small portion of the daily milieu of acts that erode students' sense of safety and impede learning. Creating and maintaining a warm, supportive, and friendly physical environment will greatly increase students' sense of safety at school.

☞ Tip

• Don't wait to complete this part of your plan before starting to address the issues raised in the other keys.

• Put up posters and banners with positive messages on the walls; many social-emotional learning curricula come with these already included.

• Involve students in designing, selecting, and carrying out climate improvement projects. Their participation increases their sense of ownership, which means they'll take better care of the improvements.

• Many state and county offices of education, as well as state and national educational associations, have networks of resource people who can help with both sides of the physical environment coin: security and threat assessment, and the more affective design factors.

Key 5: Empower Students as Agents of Social Change

Every school can benefit from an organized team of students—the socially influential opinion leaders of its diverse groups and cliques—who are committed to notice hot spots and trained to cool them off. Students who have the observation skills to notice exclusions, put-downs, teasing, relational aggression, bullying, harassment, and other forms of mistreatment, 95 percent of which go unnoticed by adults. Students who have been trained in powerful nonviolent communication and intervention skills can interact with their peers to prevent and stop this mistreatment when and where it happens: on the bus, in the yard, at lunch, in the locker rooms and restrooms, in the halls, and on the fields.

Potential Action

- Create a team of social change agents on campus. See Chapters Eight and Nine for one way to do this.

👍 The Challenge

- Gaining administration and faculty support for this type of program.

☞ Tip

- Demonstrate the program's benefits in terms meaningful to key decision makers: fewer discipline problems, suspensions, expulsions, and increased academic achievement.

- Provide training for students to develop skills in whatever areas they are being asked to take on (for example, meeting facilitation, tutoring, nonviolent communication, oral presentations) to develop their ability to be successful.

 ## Key 6: Implement Diversity Activities

Infuse the entire school with ongoing activities that promote dialogue, understanding, and respect for differences. These activities will have greater impact when they are not stand-alone but are consistent with themes woven into the curricula. These efforts will decrease the tensions between the cliques and interest groups on a campus.

Potential Actions

1. Convene a group of teachers, students, and administrators to identify opportunities for integrating the theme of diversity into as many curricular areas as possible—books read and essays written in language arts classes, social movements and examples from history in social studies

classes, projects using different media in music and art classes, and so on. See also Key 8: Support Social Skills Curricula and Instruction.

2. Have trained students or adults lead structured class discussions, forums, lock-ins, trainings, and other experiences that address issues of diversity, tolerance, bigotry, prejudice, and hatred.

3. Recognize youth and adults who have helped to sow the seeds of tolerance and respect, build bridges of understanding, improve the school climate.

4. Bring in community members of different backgrounds to tell their life stories to groups of students and staff, so they can develop an understanding and appreciation of people who are not exactly like them.

👍 The Challenge

- Integrating these activities across subject areas and making them ongoing school traditions.

☞ Tip

- Involve students and community members in the planning and implementation.

Key 7: Create Opportunities for the Least Engaged Youth

Athletics, academics, and traditional activities do not meet the developmental needs of all students. And in today's schools, far too many students feel disengaged, left out, and isolated. Research presented earlier shows that those who lack a sense of belonging are at greater risk for dropping out or acting out. Therefore, it is mutually beneficial to create new and diverse opportunities for these least engaged youth to reconnect with their school and community. Initiate dialogue, and ask these students what they want to become involved in and how they want to become involved.

Potential Actions

Create opportunities for these students to do any of the following:

- Be mentors
- Be tutors, and teach a skill to others
- Learn a skill

- Start a business
- Serve those in need
- Build a skate park or ropes course
- Plan events and other needed activities

👍 **The Challenge**

- Avoiding the perception that "they're doing this *to* me, *for* me, *at* me."

☞ **Tip**

- These students are often reluctant participants. Many have had little experience working with adults in a positive way, so reach out. Seek to understand them through honest dialogue, and work with them in partnership to set and achieve common goals.

Key 8: Support Social Skills Curricula and Instruction

Especially in the elementary grades, students benefit from active teaching of the skills that equip them to communicate effectively, establish solid friendships, and resolve their differences nonviolently. This can be accomplished directly through lessons that teach these skills, and it can also happen more indirectly through class meetings and other strategies, like cooperative learning, that teachers conduct on a regular basis.

Consistent messages in all social-emotional learning curricula and in all classes are vitally important. A school must encourage and support consistent teaching and use of this curriculum, and all staff and faculty should demonstrate their commitment to it.

Potential Actions

1. Have your school safety team or climate committee (see Key 2) form a work group or subcommittee to address this issue.
2. Survey staff members to find out what they are using and doing and what other resources they know about.
3. Engage staff members in dialogue about where and how these resources and strategies could be incorporated into their own teaching practice.
4. Visit other schools to learn from their approaches.

5. Involve staff members in decisions about what resources to purchase and what practices to adopt.

6. Provide training, including opportunities for practice and mentoring, and include youth in these whenever appropriate.

✍ The Challenge

- Securing the buy-in of all staff to use one approach or program in multiple grade levels and content areas or departments so the messages are simple and consistent schoolwide, and keeping interest high.

☞ Tip

- Don't isolate the teaching of social skills in one classroom or department. Meet with all staff to look for ways these skills can be incorporated into content or process schoolwide (such as class meetings or discussions). Agree as a staff to experiment with these new methods, and discuss successes and challenges on an ongoing basis.

- Contact the curriculum resource specialists at your district and county offices of education.

Key 9: Conduct Teacher and Staff Training

Whether they are classroom teachers or bus drivers, attendance secretaries or administrators, counselors or librarians, all adults have a role to play in building and maintaining a positive, healthy, and safe school climate. Unfortunately most adults aren't able to see most of the student mistreatment around them and don't have enough options to intervene effectively when they do notice it. Saying, "Hey, cut that out!" is only one tool in a potentially big tool kit.

Moreover, many adults fail to take advantage of readily available opportunities to build positive relationships with students beyond the content of schoolwork. These relationships not only improve the climate of the school and students' sense of connection to it, they become the gateways students use to report information about fights, weapons, or other potential harm to people or property.

Potential Actions

Conduct training to help staff members:

- Better understand the problem and costs of youth-on-youth mistreatment
- Strengthen their skills for developing relationships with students
- Strengthen their skills for observing and noticing mistreatment
- Strengthen their skills for intervening in mistreatment in creative, positive and effective ways

👍 **The Challenge**

- Staff will think to themselves with dismay, "Not another in-service!"

☞ **Tip**

- Acknowledge what they are already doing well. Defining what does *not* need to change helps them feel needed stability in the midst of transition, which helps them relax and embrace new ideas and practices.
- Show staff members how it will benefit them in terms of increased student performance and motivation and fewer discipline issues.
- Involve them in planning and delivering the training.
- Don't just present information and forget about it. Action speaks volumes, so get individual commitments to implement new knowledge and skills. Provide support and hold people accountable.

 ## Key 10: Encourage Parent Involvement

Since parents significantly influence students' opinions, values, and interaction skills, parent understanding and support are essential for any successful school safety plan. But booster nights and open houses usually draw only the familiar faces of the highly engaged parents, so schools must find other ways to connect with parents, especially those not actively involved in their children's education.

Potential Actions

1. Initiate opportunities for local neighborhood involvement like parent dialogue nights, an activity often conducted in homes to discuss issues

of bullying and ways students may be treating each other, cohosted by a parent, student, and the school-community partnership (Key 1) or school safety team (Key 2).

2. Help parents become informed about and get involved in safe school climate funding, policies, programs, and staffing of positions related to school safety.

👍 **The Challenge**

• The many demands on parents' time.

☞ **Tip**

• Start small. Rather than host one-time-only schoolwide events, design a series of smaller-scale, more intimate gatherings that aim to involve parents in a specific neighborhood or whose students share a particular interest or class.

• Make the invitation personal, and personally. Don't rely exclusively on posters, flyers, and mass e-mails.

• Make the activity or meeting safe, friendly, relevant, and productive. For example, consider the native language likely to be spoken by those parents, and make sure you have the resources to conduct the meeting in that language.

These ten keys can unlock the doors to a campus where youth feel empowered, are empowered, and work with adults to build a safer, more supportive, and more positive school climate. As that happens, the school becomes a place where all youth and adults feel welcomed, respected, understood, and safe and students and staff pursue learning and educational excellence with enthusiasm and commitment.

Having It All

> I believe that we can address the social, emotional, and health issues facing youths at the same time that we maintain our focus on academic success.
>
> JACK O'CONNELL, SUPERINTENDENT OF PUBLIC INSTRUCTION, STATE OF CALIFORNIA[16]

All educators want safe schools, and Chapter Three summarized the outside-in strategies aimed at physical safety that are typically the mainstay of most school safety efforts today. Chapter Four outlined a counterbalancing inside-out approach to safety that is aimed at improving school climate (see Table 5.1).

Table 5.1. Two Approaches to School Safety

Safety	Physical Safety	Climate
	Outside-In Approach	Inside-Out Approach
	• Security	• Relationships
	• Adult driven	• Student centered
	• Rules and policies	• Norms

Educators are held accountable not just for safety but for achievement, and have long debated the best strategies for helping students learn. What has become clear is that more of the same is not better. Intensifying our focus on academic achievement and physical safety without paying sufficient attention to the social-emotional and climate components will not significantly increase achievement or safety. Strategies such as longer school days, academic kindergartens, and more tests will not by themselves increase our students' learning. Investing more resources in security cameras, guards, metal detectors, and enforcement of tougher policies will not, on their own, increase the safety of our schools. Not only are the costs prohibitive, but the prevention effects have also been proved to be minimal. "No Child Left Behind" and "Zero Tolerance" have failed to reach their stated goals. It's time for something different.

It's not a question of changing the goals—learning and safety are the right goals. It's a question of methods, of strategy. Therefore, this book proposes a different strategy, one not based on security cameras, but on compassion.

Whereas the outside-in approach can *at best* lead to a reduction in weapons on campus and increased physical safety, the inside-out approach can lead to a safer school climate, *and increased academic achievement as well.* Because safety is the foundation for learning, climate becomes a cornerstone of efforts to develop schools that are both high-achieving and safe (see Figure 5.2).

Using an inside-out approach that focuses on climate:

• Requires the fostering of social-emotional skills. For students to build the interpersonal relationships that are the backbone of a positive and healthy school climate, they must acquire the *skills* of emotional and social intelligence: to read others, to listen and articulate, to be accepting, to suspend

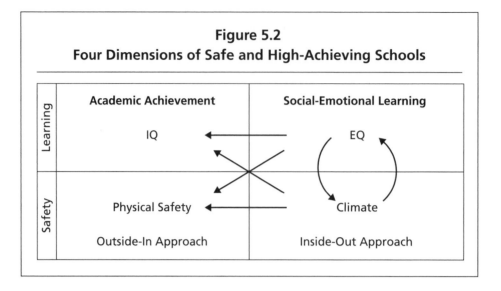

Figure 5.2
Four Dimensions of Safe and High-Achieving Schools

	Academic Achievement	Social-Emotional Learning
Learning	IQ	EQ
Safety	Physical Safety	Climate
	Outside-In Approach	Inside-Out Approach

judgment, to remain open, and so on. This process gives students something they want—the skills and opportunities to develop positive relationships with one another—and counterbalances the generally lopsided focus on academic achievement common in schools today.

• Promotes emotional safety. As students strengthen their social-emotional skills *and* develop more constructive relationships with one another, they become better able to care for one another, and this increases their motivation to do so. This active caring shifts the social norms in a positive direction, which reduces the mistreatment that occurs below the waterline in Figure 1.2. Reducing occurrences of mistreatment, in turn, decreases the number of incidents that threaten physical safety.

• Enhances physical safety. When students feel positive affiliations with each other and to the school, they are more willing to intervene to prevent or stop fights and other acts of physical aggression, and they are more likely to report to adults information about threats, fights, weapons, or other crimes.

• Creates conditions for improved academic achievement. When school is a place students want to be, they are more engaged in learning. When they are not distracted by cruel rumors, insults, fights, and fear, they are more focused on learning. And, when students feel more positively connected to their teachers, they are more motivated to learn. All of this improves achievement.

This is the double-win of focusing on school climate: it greatly enhances school safety and sets the stage for effective learning and success, not just in school, but throughout life.

With a strong commitment to and focus on building a safe school climate, schools can bring together often competing goals under one big tent. There is room for academic achievement *and* social-emotional learning. There is room for the outside-in approaches described in Chapter Three, *and* room for the complementary, climate-focused, inside-out approach described in Chapter Four. Once decision makers see how their goals are interdependent, they will be more willing to invest equally in all four goals.

Nevertheless, it is too easy for adults to fall back into the familiar but limiting view of youth as consumers and the practice of excluding youth from the decisions that affect them. The next chapter helps guard against this tendency by presenting guidelines for empowering youth to work with adults to address issues of safety.

PART III

Youth as Social Change Agents

THIS PART OF THE BOOK SHOWS HOW THE INSIDE-OUT approach introduced in Chapter Four can be applied to the problem of mistreatment outlined in Part One. Its focus is on the practical application of sound principles to produce powerful results.

Chapter Six outlines a new way of working and being with young people that's based on empowerment: students are not seen as consumers but as contributors, not problems but solutions. It provides guidelines for doing that in the classroom and through schoolwide programs and activities. The chapter highlights our own formula for youth development and explains how to put that formula and theory into practice.

Chapter Seven examines current research that emphasizes the importance of bystanders in the aggressor-target-bystander triad. It provides information that shows how to use our youth empowerment model to mobilize bystanders to break the code of silence and become proactive in intervening in the cycle of mistreatment.

Chapter Eight describes our research-based, time-tested, best-practice model, the Safe School Ambassadors program, which shows how students can take the lead in stopping mistreatment in schools. Chapter Nine showcases the concrete results of these students' efforts, including the voices, experiences, and stories of actual ambassadors in the field.

Empowering Youth

6

> One can imagine a field with the adolescents on one side of a line drawn on
> the earth and the adults on the other side, looking into each other's eyes.
> The adults reach their hands across the line and welcome the young people
> into adulthood.
>
> —ROBERT BLY, *THE SIBLING SOCIETY*

IN ANY SOCIETY, ADULTS BEAR THE RESPONSIBILITY of ushering youth across the threshold of adolescence into adulthood. To do so successfully, we, the adults, must reach out to engage our youth and build bridges of understanding. We must invite young people to join us at the table of leadership and equip them with the skills and support to be successful as leaders, mentors, role models, and agents of change. Once they are involved and able, they are empowered. It is at that point that we can share responsibility for our communities and schools with our youth.

Taking the inside-out approach from theory to practice means that students play a significant role in schools' overall efforts to reduce bullying and violence and improve school climate. For students to take on this role, they must be truly empowered, with the ability and authority to participate in decision making and take action to improve their lives and the lives of others. This means that adults must provide meaningful opportunities for significant youth involvement.

Youth empowerment, a key component of youth development, addresses the basic needs of all young people to have purpose, power, and place. Empowering youth, usually described as helping students grow into capable, connected, and contributing citizens, is often a key goal of most schools. Yet when we examine how most schools attempt to achieve this goal, we see that it is easier to say than it is to do. When schools include young people, they often draw on the same individuals or types of students: high grade point average (GPA), good social skills, college bound, good role models. They do not select youth from the nontraditional groups on campus. Even when schools do involve a variety of students in a model program, empowering young people is not accomplished through a single program or activity.

Far too many adults apply a medical model to the way they view youth: the "patient" is sick, and the "doctor" has to "cure" the "patient." Subscribers to this model believe that the main way for adults ("doctors") to educate or interact with ("cure") young people ("patients") is to focus on their problems ("illnesses"). This model is adult driven and based on deficiencies (what's wrong with students) rather than strengths (what's right with students—for example, their abilities, skills, knowledge, and perspectives).

Youth empowerment is only partially achieved by selectively sharing power with students when it serves adults or addresses a specific hot-button issue, such as needing students to help deal with graffiti or decrease racial tensions. Comprehensive youth empowerment begins by cultivating a fundamental belief in the ability of children and youth to accomplish great things, a belief in the inherent strengths of our young people. This belief must be enacted in the ways we live, relate, and behave; in these ways, the belief becomes systemic rather than situational.

Empowering youth requires seeing students through a strength-based lens, not a deficit-based one. When we build on their strengths and join these strengths with our own, we can form powerful alliances with young people. In this way, we can engage, equip, and empower them with the skills, opportunities, and support to create and maintain safer schools.

To bring youth empowerment from words to deeds, we must start with the willingness to examine our current thinking, attitudes, and practices carefully and make necessary changes. We must also be open to looking critically at our individual actions and be willing to alter our behaviors.

Our approach to empowering youth has been greatly influenced by the contributions of pioneers in this and related fields, such as Karen Pittman in youth development, Bonnie Benard in resiliency, David Hawkins and Richard Catalano in risk and protective factors, Peter Benson and the Search Institute in developmental assets, and Daniel Goleman in emotional intelligence. We are grateful to them and the many other champions of youth who have provided us with inspiration, foundations, data, and direction. Without their theories, research, and practice and without their courage, we wouldn't have seen the path we needed to walk or had the confidence to blaze these new trails.

Many adults view students as receivers of knowledge that is imparted by teachers and other educators. In the adult-driven model, students play a passive role. In order to solve many youth-related issues, teens need to be seen as active participants, not passive receivers. Having students be actively involved is the basis for a student-centered solution. Robert H. Shaffer, former dean of students at Indiana University, said, "We must view young people not as empty bottles to be filled, but as candles to be lit."[1]

As demonstrated by the work of the Search Institute, focusing on young people's assets reinforces and promotes their strengths and unleashes their power. It makes some fundamental shifts:

- From providing programs only to building relationships
- From a focus on troubled or at-risk students to all students
- From blaming others to claiming responsibility

Our experience has shown that when given responsibility, most young people act responsibly. We and others have seen that when given the opportunity, the tools, and the support, youth can become major contributors and problem solvers. They bring to bear a unique creativity, knowledge, and points of view that address problems and issues in ways that no adult can. Professionals who subscribe to a positive, strength-based youth development model believe empowering youth can be an overwhelmingly effective strategy in the fight against youth-on-youth mistreatment. This strategy is most effective for addressing not only mistreatment but many other youth-related issues when it moves from being a discrete initiative to being an integral part of the school culture: the way we do things around here.

Bonnie Benard, a leading researcher, describes youth development as the process of creating the environments, opportunities, and relationships that support a young person's social, emotional, physical, moral, and cognitive development.[2] We believe that empowering young people is an integral part of the process.

The Youth Development Formula

Our experiences putting youth development into practice provided the impetus for creating our youth development formula. This formula offers a clear and compelling vision that is understandable to educators, parents, students, and the community at large. Our formula also demonstrates that youth development is essential to educational mandates and the drive for high academic achievement. Educators are not only charged with the responsibility for ensuring that students are successful academically, but also with the duty of educating youth to be good workers, good neighbors, and good citizens. Therefore, youth development is a critically important pillar that supports the overall mission of education.

Our formula for youth development is:

$$3P + 3E = 3C$$

The three Ps are:

- Purpose

- Power

- Place

The three Es are:

- Engage

- Equip

- Empower

The three Cs are:

- Capable

- Connected

- Contributing

In the next sections, we describe each of these components in detail and how they add up to youth development.

The Three Ps: Developmental Needs of Youth

Purpose, power, and *place* are important developmental needs of all young people and are fundamental to helping youth grow into independent and contributing adults. Meeting each of these needs creates the primary building blocks for healthy youth development.

Purpose *Purpose* is having an intention, a goal, or an idea of what we want to accomplish. It inspires us to make things happen. Youth who have a sense of purpose are motivated to get up in the morning because they have a reason to do so. They want to accomplish something, or they know they have something to contribute. They feel that others rely on them, and they rise to meet those obligations and expectations; they know that their roles are vital in the big picture or that their actions are supportive in important ways to people in their lives.

When youth lack purpose, they often lack the drive to do anything, let alone strive for something important. The apathy that is often attributed to today's young people is due in some part to a lack of purpose. When youth lack inspiration, they often lack direction and are easily influenced in negative ways. Peer pressure is particularly potent with students who lack a clear sense of purpose.

Power *Power* is feeling and being capable. When youth know that they have the ability to make choices and decisions and take actions that lead to desired results, they see themselves as effective. Having power therefore means knowing that they have an internal locus of control and believing that they can manifest some of what they want. The healthy recognition of and avenues for expressions of power are core building blocks required in a young person's development.

If young people aren't provided prosocial opportunities to express and experience their developmental need for power, they are likely to seek power in health-compromising and antisocial ways: participating in violence, using alcohol and other drugs, and becoming sexually active at young ages, for example.

Place *Place* is a sense of belonging and a feeling of being part of an accepting social system. It is not a physical space. For young people to have a positive sense of place, they must experience both an adult community that actively cares about them and opportunities to belong to peer groups. Youth also need to know that the adults they encounter in school, after school, and in the community recognize, care about, respect, and value them.

Often youth seek a sense of place by trying to get approval from peers and doing things to gain acceptance into a clique, a social group, or even a gang. For youth, peer acceptance is critically important. If young people don't feel welcome, safe, or included by both peers and adults, they are more likely to act out in negative ways: do poorly academically, become truant, drop out, or vandalize the school are some of the choices they may make.

Without positive affiliations with both adults and peers, youth have no sense of place. A positive peer culture with a climate of caring and connectedness fostered by adults gives youth a sense of place.

The Three Es: Strategies for Meeting the Needs of Youth

After identifying the developmental needs of youth, adults should examine how they can support young people in meeting these needs. The three strategies in the formula for addressing these needs are *engage, equip,* and *empower.*

Engage   *Engage* has two aspects: reaching out intentionally and broadly to all youth and inviting them to participate. *Engaging* students means adults must provide opportunities for youth to be directly included in the school and community. Educators need to cast a larger net to capture the input of all students, especially those who are nontraditional and the least involved.

Although many schools provide a range of extracurricular opportunities for teens to participate in—student government, sports, music, drama, academic clubs, and others—many young people do not participate in any of them. In our experience, we have found that typically only half of the student population, from elementary through high school, participates in some form of extracurricular activity.

Disengaged or unengaged youth are usually in the forefront of feeling alienated from their lives and their communities, schools, and families. A lack of positive engagement leads to passivity, apathy, inaction, and eventually withdrawal. Isolated, alienated youth are often the ones most at risk for engaging in risky behavior and violent acts, as well as mental health problems such as depression, eating disorders, and suicide.

Educators and parents need to create alternative ways for students to become involved and connected. These new choices must speak to the needs of the students who do not currently engage in traditional extracurricular activities. Examples are opportunities for service, such as cross-age tutoring and mentoring programs; inviting usually noninvolved students to participate in leadership, planning, and safety committees; and creating recreational activities that are outside the usual sports. Reaching out and asking students for their thoughts and seeking their ideas and interests can go a long way in broadening their involvement in school.

If students are going to sustain a commitment, their motivation can't be purely altruistic or externally derived. It is a rare student who will take these actions because "it is the right thing to do" or it helps someone out. Many youth want to know, "What's in it for me?" We have found that an effective way to engage young people is to tap into this enlightened self-interest. By asking questions that elicit their goals, problems, and interests, adults can discover what actually motivates young people and then offer them activities and involvement that match what they need. Students then realize that remaining uninvolved has personal costs. When youth learn that their passivity and silence are no longer desirable or acceptable options, they become ready to step up, take action, and get involved.

Equip   *Equip* means to provide students with the tools, opportunities, and support they need to become fully empowered contributors. Equipping students means setting them up for success. If you ask youth to be leaders, you must give them opportunities to learn and practice leadership skills. If students are asked to attend meetings to share their opinions, adults must set the meetings at times that work for young people. If young people are asked to intervene when they see mistreatment, they must be taught the skills to intervene safely and effectively.

Waking up or motivating students and then depriving them of the opportunities to acquire appropriate skills to manifest this engagement can lead to disappointed, frustrated, and resistant youth who are unlikely to contribute because they do not know how to be effective. To continue the process begun by engaging youth, we must equip them to make their involvement possible.

Empower   In the formula, *empowering* students means that adults collaborate in decision-making processes and ensure that youth that youth participate fully in all aspects of decision making regarding issues that matter to them. This often means assisting youth to develop the confidence and skills necessary to share decision making meaningfully with adults. When youth are empowered, they will want to and be willing to take action. Adults must make sure that empowered young people have timely opportunities to make real differences in ways that reflect their convictions and maximize their involvement.

This does not mean that youth should be given sole responsibility for all decisions that affect them. Young people need adult guidance and support. Adults should not relinquish, because youth are not ready to assume, all the power or control of school situations or decisions. In her article, "Examining Empowerment: A How-To Guide for the Youth Development Professional," Angela J. Huebner wrote, "'Empowering teens refers to a PROCESS through which adults begin to share responsibility and power with young people. It is the same idea as teaching young people the rules of the game. Youth development professionals are helping young people develop non-academic competencies that will help them to participate in the game of life. Because it is a process, empowerment is something that is achieved over time, not overnight."[3]

Engaged, equipped, and empowered youth are poised to make a difference. Adults must offer them chances that are appropriate and provide options with increasing responsibility.

The Three Cs: Positive Outcomes for Youth

According to the equation set up by the formula, when the three Ps (purpose, power, place) are combined with the three Es (engage, equip, empower), the outcome is usually positive. Students grow to be *capable, connected,* and *contributing.*

Capable   *Capable* means being competent, and in the case of students, it includes being able to achieve academically and interact well with peers and adults. Being capable also means being able to use good judgment and make clear decisions. It includes cultural competence and is derived from having the skills to manage emotions well and get along with many kinds of people in a variety of situations.

When youth are deprived of any of the three Ps or the three Es, they do not become fully capable. Fostering capable youth is a key goal of positive youth development.

Connected   *Connected* means making and maintaining positive relationships. Connected young people have friends, belong to one or more social groups, and feel that they are important members of the school community. Being connected also includes having positive relationships with caring adults at school and in the broader community.

Disconnected, unaffiliated youth who have been deprived of key relationships in their lives may not be able to fully develop into healthy adults. It is critically important that all youth be given opportunities to create and maintain meaningful and positive relationships. When students lack meaningful relationships with at least one trusted adult and one trusted peer, research shows that these students are at greater risk for responding to their problems with violent reactions. Students who are isolated and also experiencing mistreatment at school are often unable to cope with additional losses or personal pain without becoming violent, and some have become school shooters. There is strong evidence that this is the main characteristic that many of the recent school shooters have in common.[4]

Therefore, in our work with schools, we strongly encourage school faculty and staff to be attentive to creating and maintaining positive relationships with students and to ensure that every student has at least one trusted adult he or she can speak with about subjects beyond curriculum. We help adults become more "hall-friendly" and invite schools to make it part of the hiring process to find adults who build and add to students' assets, including having strong, positive connections with students.

Contributing   *Contributing* means that teens see themselves as valued members of their schools, as resourceful people who can and do reach out and improve the lives of others. However, effective contributing also requires that adults see teens the same way, especially the adults who hold the positional power to determine how teens can participate in their schools and communities. Unfortunately, many adults often miss these valuable resources because of the way they have come to view youth.

Hundreds of times in our work, we have asked adults, "Why do we need our youth?" Most answers focus on the future: the role today's youth will have tomorrow in carrying on the traditions, leading the institutions, and caring for the current generation of adults as they age. Few adults see how much teens are needed now. Youth need to be viewed as contributors and resources to help adults end the cycle of cruelty and violence in America's schools. Calling on adolescents and employing them as central figures in the fight against this mistreatment encompasses a fundamental rethinking of how we view young people. Rather than seeing youth as part of the problem, they need to be viewed as part of the solution.

Contributing arises from holding these core values: giving back, helping others, and having an ethic of service and volunteerism. Contributing students see it as their responsibility to stand up and speak up for those who are less fortunate or are targets of mistreatment.

Having a purpose, knowing their own power, and experiencing a sense of place while being engaged, equipped, and empowered will lead to youth as capable, connected contributors. It is in all of our best interests to create these developmental opportunities for youth.

Developing Healthy, Caring, Responsible Youth

All young people need support to overcome the risks and challenges they face. Some of this support can come from external sources, such as positive relationships with a parent, relative, teacher, friend, or a neighbor. Inner resources are also important and must be developed, as seen in our formula, previously so that youth may provide some of their own internal support. Students also need to develop certain internal traits or characteristics—a positive view of their future, a commitment to learning, restraint, and responsibility—to help them navigate the risks and challenges they face.

These relationships, characteristics, and opportunities that help young people survive and thrive have been identified as developmental assets. Through nearly fifty years of research, the Search Institute in Minneapolis, Minnesota, has identified forty developmental assets that can be viewed as the building blocks for developing healthy youth. These include external factors that are supplied by the people and institutions that have contact with the youth, factors like meaningful relationships with three or more adults beyond their parents or guardians. They also include internal factors that youth acquire through their life experiences, like valuing diversity and having a positive view of their personal future. The Search Institute has surveyed over 2 million adolescents, ages twelve to eighteen, in rural and urban communities in the United States and found that youth with more of these developmental assets are more likely to thrive and be resilient in the face of risks. They are also less likely to engage in risky or violent behavior.

The power of the assets isn't only about reducing risky or negative behavior. The more assets young people have, the more likely they are to exercise and eat right, value diversity, and perform well in school. Young people with more developmental assets not only show decreased negative behaviors but also demonstrate increased positive behaviors and attitudes. And those with more assets are more likely to thrive and grow up healthier, more caring, and more responsible.[5]

Students Need Meaningful Roles

When students are seen as resources and given opportunities to be contributors, the degree of positive connectedness to the school increases significantly. Furthermore, when youth are equipped and empowered to address important issues and experience successes, they continue developing in prosocial ways.

Here are two stories of students who found and valued their increasingly important roles in other students' lives:

Eddie was a sixth-grade boy who read two grade levels below his expected reading level. He was teased repeatedly by his peers. As a result, he was often sullen and withdrawn and had spotty attendance. His teacher asked him to be a cross-age tutor to second graders. In that setting, instead of being two years behind, he was two years ahead. Through helping a younger student, his self-esteem increased, as did his behavior and attendance at school.

Simon was a troubled child who came to the attention of the counseling office. He was small for his age and teased maliciously by his peers. The dean told the boy's story to Rose, a high school junior who did cross-age mentoring. The dean worried that Simon might drop out of school and asked that Rose meet with him. Rose agreed to work with Simon over the next several weeks. One day, Rose's friends wanted her to skip school and go to the lake, because it was a beautiful, hot day. She refused to join them. Rose told them, "This is the day that my mentee, Simon, is expecting me in the library." She didn't skip school because she knew she was needed and felt she had a positive role to play.

What these two true stories have in common is that both students knew they had a purpose. They felt that they had a reason to go to school, and this knowledge led to their feeling connected and empowered. Knowing that they make a difference in someone else's life promotes an ethic of healthy citizenship for these students and potentially a lifelong commitment to service. These young people will become the volunteers of the future, contributing to their communities in significant ways.

The youth empowerment strategies adults use can include having students examine and help rewrite rules and policies, serve on a climate committee, and design and conduct activities with their peers to increase tolerance and respect for diversity, to name just a few. With sufficient structure and support, students can play key roles in presenting at workshops and training sessions for staff and parents. If the strategies are used with care and integrity and in accord with basic tenets of youth development, they can benefit not only the students directly involved but also the school as a whole. Involvement in these activities will increase students' sense of ownership and connectedness to the school and can improve the overall social and emotional climate. However, effectively and sustainably managing these strategies for increasing students' involvement requires a thorough understanding of how young people develop: What are some of the driving forces and needs of adolescents? What are the best ways to support youth development?

Youth: The Most Underused Resource

Young people are a resource waiting to be valued and used. There are four practical reasons for involving young people in the solution to mistreatment:

- *The power of numbers.* In most schools, there are approximately ten students for every staff member.

- *The power of knowledge.* Young people see, hear, and know things that adults don't. A code of silence exists between young people and adults: students know about certain things that they do not share with adults.

- *The power of relationships.* Young people can speak to each other in ways adults can't. Young people, particularly in middle and high school, also listen and respond differently to their peers than they do to adults.

- *The power of norms.* Young people determine which behaviors are considered acceptable and which are not. These same young people also have the power to change established social norms.

The chapters in Part One of this book showed that the problem of mistreatment significantly outweighs the resources that adults can marshal to address it. The problem can be solved only if youth are involved and play a more significant role than they have to date. To be successful, those involvement efforts must use the guidelines of the youth development formula: reach out and engage a broader and more diverse student population, equip them with skills and support, and empower them with meaningful roles so they can effect social change. When educators commit to using this formula, they will be able to harness the power of youth to produce safer schools, and they will be more likely to graduate capable, connected, and contributing citizens.

The balance of this chapter shows how the youth development formula can be applied in the classroom and through schoolwide programs and initiatives.

Youth Empowerment in the Classroom

The classroom in many ways is a microcosm of the school, so it is difficult, if not impossible, for a schoolwide youth empowerment effort to succeed if students feel disempowered in the classrooms in which they spend upward of 85 percent of their school time.

The process of creating and maintaining an empowering classroom begins with the teacher making a thorough and honest self-assessment. To assess their internal attitudes, beliefs, and ideas, they should ask:

- As the teacher, am I a benevolent monarch or a facilitator and guide?

- Do I see my students as resourceful: capable of good behavior, good judgment, and good problem solving?

- Do I teach curricula or subjects, or do I teach people?

- Do I welcome questions and challenges to the information I present, or do I get annoyed by them?

To assess their external behaviors, communication, and teaching style, they can ask these questions:

- To what degree do I build in opportunities for students to get to know me and their peers as people?

- To what degree is my classroom (for example, the furniture itself and the way I use the space) set up to support this relationship building?

- Do I teach communication and cooperative learning skills in addition to teaching my subjects?

- Do I think that student relationships must not disrupt the learning process so they must be kept outside the classroom? Or do I believe that student relationships are essential to the learning process in that they support effective cooperative learning, permit meaningful discussion and debate, and create a class climate that supports all members?

The results of that assessment could lead the teacher to make some personal changes. After making these personal changes or while these are becoming new habits, an honest examination of one's classroom management and governance decisions and styles should happen. While personal and classroom management adjustments are occurring, teachers have other options for empowering students, and we list some of those choices at the end of this section.

According to the youth development formula discussed earlier in this chapter, empowerment is one of the strategies used to help youth develop positively. When a teacher decides to make his or her classroom an empowering one, the needs of youth for purpose, power, and place must be addressed. Here are some ways this can be done on a day-to-day basis.

Personal Interactions

Empowering teachers take the time to be physically, mentally, and emotionally present in hallways, lunch areas, and other nonteaching settings. They get to know the names of the students they see daily, whether or not they are in their classes. This requires diligence: paying attention and learning the faces first, then making eye contact and nodding, then saying "Hi" or "Hey" in passing, and then finally taking the plunge and stopping to ask the student's name.

Next, hall-friendly teachers initiate conversations that allow them get to know something about those students—their interests and hobbies, some family facts, and what matters to them—and then disclose appropriately about themselves. These disclosures are what make it a conversation rather than an inquisition or interrogation. For example, the teacher asks a question, listens attentively and actively, asks a follow-up question, listens attentively and actively, and then shares a relevant idea, opinion, or tidbit of personal information if warranted and if the conversation seems to flow that way. Later that same day or another day, these teachers take time to follow up, asking questions or checking in about the topics or situations the student previously discussed.

Building positive relationships with students is the overarching goal of the personal changes that lead to having an empowering classroom. Some of the internal changes the teacher needs to make include acknowledging that students walk into each class not just as minds waiting to soak up the knowledge the teacher is excited to share but as young people with their own feelings, priorities, and beliefs:

- Feelings—perhaps excited that the good-looking boy looked at her and smiled, or scared because that group of guys gave him a "watch your back" look

- Priorities—perhaps being much more interested in the rumor about two students getting into a fight after school today or being preoccupied with the homecoming dance tomorrow night

- Beliefs—perhaps believing that the class or subject is irrelevant or pointless, or that the teacher is a jerk and insensitive because of a low grade just given on a recent paper

Often these and other issues get in the way of learning and sidetrack or sometimes completely derail even the best lesson plans. Recognizing the inner lives of students and taking time to acknowledge, empathize, or address their concerns is an outer change teachers can make in their behavior and ways of communicating with students. Feeling and showing respect for and interest in students' experiences are both inner and outer changes teachers can effect. For example, when a student comes into class very excited about something he or she has just heard and has a hard time settling down to class after the bell rings, the teacher could say, "I can tell that you're very excited right now, and I do want to hear about your news. Could you put it on hold until we hand out and discuss last week's test results, and then you can share with the class?" This demonstrates for the students that the excitement is acceptable and that the teacher is interested. Knowing that talking about this exciting news will occur can give students a chance to practice patience, develop trust, and grow to understand the reasons for postponing discussions without feeling disregarded.

Classroom Management

Empowered students help shape how the classroom runs. This might take the form of naming the norms or expectations of classroom behavior, or co-creating a set of working agreements or ground rules, along with the consequences for violating them, that are all within boundaries set by the teacher and school and reflect teacher and school rules and policies and community laws rules and norms. Collaborating with students to set norms and rules as well as consequences is an excellent way to involve students and generate buy-in to these policies. This involvement also addresses the students' needs for purpose and power.

In a classroom in which youth are empowered, students feel ownership of the learning process, which not only reduces the time and energy teachers must spend on classroom management and discipline but also increases students' motivation to learn what's being taught, which means they're learning more. Students who are involved in decision making and co-create the classroom atmosphere develop a stronger, more positive affiliation to their classes and therefore meet their need for place, to belong.

The process of empowering students in a classroom also includes reexamining the job of the teacher. Empowering classrooms meet students' needs for purpose, power, and place, so the teacher's job may become slightly different and more encompassing. The following summary describes the ways empowering classrooms are established.

Classroom Management

- The teacher is the facilitator and a guide, but still has the final authority.
- Students are crew members who help with the classroom management and discipline to the limits of their skill and ability, as age appropriate, and within the boundaries set by teacher, school, and community.

Learning

- The teacher is the facilitator, guide, and content expert (based on demonstrated knowledge) who does the following:
  - Praises accomplishment as well as effort, progress, and growth
  - Encourages inquiry and independent thinking; understands that student interests influence subject matter
  - Presents, tells, and listens or responds to student ideas, needs, and challenges to teacher information
- Students are crew members who help with the planning and decision making, and even the teaching and assessment.

Relationships

- The teacher and students are connecting for mutual benefit, that is, bidirectionally.
- The student-student connection is essential to the learning process in that it:
  - Supports effective cooperative learning
  - Permits meaningful discussion and debate
  - Creates a class climate that supports class members

Other Empowering Strategies

Classroom meetings, circle time, and other discussion opportunities, especially if they are held regularly, offer further ways for students to meet their needs for purpose, become more engaged, and continue to increase their empowerment. Another benefit is that students will spend more time on task when they know their time to be heard is upcoming. Offering students meaningful and regular roles in the classroom through rotating or ongoing task assignments that students can perform meets their needs for purpose and place, engages them, and equips them with new skills as well. The decisions a teacher makes about how students are seated, their access to equipment and supplies, and how they are expected to behave determine what the classroom atmosphere is expected to be. When students are allowed to see and speak with one another, become involved in group or paired work projects, get their own supplies and use equipment as needed, and are trusted to be responsible with these "privileges," the atmosphere is one of cooperation and lively learning. All of these are important components that determine the level of empowerment students will develop in that classroom, and these are excellent and easy ways for a teacher to demonstrate commitment to student empowerment in the classroom.

Implementing some of these strategies will go a long way toward the goal of meeting students' needs for purpose, power, and place in the classroom and toward helping them feel, and be, empowered members of their school community. They then take greater responsibility for the well-being and safety of everyone in that community.

Seven Elements of Effective Youth Empowerment Programs

In this part of the chapter, we move from theory into practice, outlining seven critical elements required for successfully launching and sustaining a youth empowerment program outside a classroom setting, such as the Safe School Ambassadors program described in detail in Chapter Eight.

If you already have a program that empowers young people to play a pivotal role in school climate change, you can use the seven elements to assess your program's effectiveness. In doing so, you might see that adding or enhancing one or more of these elements in your program could strengthen or enrich your current efforts.

Elements of Effective Youth Empowerment Programs

- Element 1: Identifying a point person, program coordinator, or advisor
- Element 2: Gaining school site buy-in
- Element 3: Engaging students and adults
- Element 4: Training students and adults
- Element 5: Providing ongoing support and supervision
- Element 6: Collecting data to measure program effectiveness
- Element 7: Acknowledging and celebrating the efforts of participants

Element 1: Identifying a Point Person, Program Coordinator, or Advisor

The process of creating effective youth empowerment programs begins with identifying a person or people in a school who are passionate about youth empowerment. Perhaps this person also has seen a need for youth involvement in solving schoolwide problems, such as youth-on-youth mistreatment. This person is often a teacher, counselor, or administrator, but could also be a parent. Sometimes the point person is more than one person—a committee that includes students and is focused on youth-empowerment opportunities.

Without a point person or people, few initiatives can begin, much less succeed. A committed person or group needs to be in place to advocate for the program and champion it to the faculty and administration. The point person not only needs to be committed but must be an effective spokesperson for the actions to be taken. Speaking one-on-one, in small groups, or at a faculty meeting is a major part of the job description of this initiator. Often this main contact becomes the program coordinator or advisor who manages the implementation and arranges for ongoing youth participation. If not, the point person would then hand off the leadership to that advisor when the youth empowerment activities begin.

A local youth-serving agency had a grant to work with Rick's school to help support it in working with at-risk students. A representative of the agency, Bob Boltuch, presented to his school faculty about their services. Bob asked to meet with a few teachers who might want to work with him to involve more youth at school. He talked about peer counseling, and it piqued Rick's interest. Rick wasn't familiar with this and liked what he heard. Bob talked about involving many types of students, including those who usually were not part of activities or clubs. Bob said that he needed a point person to start a program like this at the school. Rick was inspired and motivated, and he volunteered. This was the beginning of Rick's career focusing not just on teaching but on youth development and involvement. With Bob's help, Rick decided start a peer-counseling–peer-helping program at his school. As the point person who later became the program advisor, Rick initiated the process with the administration and faculty, and this program continued for many years. If Rick hadn't stepped up to take on this lead role, there might not have been a program at his school.

Element 2: Gaining School Site Buy-In

Gaining school site buy-in means securing the formal approval of designated school leaders, including the principal and other key administrators, faculty senate or site council, and possibly parent groups. Beyond this formal approval, it is vital that staff members see the value and benefit of the program and agree to support it. Buy-in involves trying to build consensus rather than just having a majority-rule vote or top-down decisions. This is best obtained through a combination of informal, one-to-one, and small-group discussions and at least one large-group presentation.

The process could start with a presentation to the staff about the value of empowering students. An effective staff presentation touches on issues important to them. It is important to help the staff understand these four main points:

- The extent of the problems at their school that empowered, involved youth could address

- How these problems affect the academic performance of their students (something teachers are held accountable for)

- Why a schoolwide initiative to empower and involve more youth is likely to be an effective strategy to address these problems

- Why students are uniquely positioned to play key roles in the strategies for solving these problems

When organizing and delivering the presentation, it is important to:

- Find common ground. Striking a common chord among most of the staff can ignite the enthusiasm needed to gain broad-based support. When people share a concern or hold a similar vision, it is easier to gain buy-in.

- Establish and agree on a goal and then discuss how to achieve it. That discussion should include exploration of what makes it hard to achieve that goal given the current school environment. For example, if the staff can agree that they want "all students feeling safe enough to learn and achieve to their full potential," then they will be more interested in exploring how the problem and costs of mistreatment get in the way of achieving that goal.

- Examine current efforts. To avoid alienating those who have already invested time addressing the issues, acknowledge the progress made while citing evidence that the problem is still not solved. In addition, provide up-to-date information about the problem and its influences and effects.

- Offer information about the importance and value of empowering students. Explain that there are resources, models, and programs that the school could be using. Discuss how students might take a more active role in addressing the current issues.

- Describe the benefits. A school with significant numbers of empowered and involved youth will see that these youth can have wide-reaching, positive effects. (See Chapter Eight for specific ways empowered youth can reduce bullying and violence and improve school climate.)

Additional information and tips on planning and delivering an effective presentation are in Appendix A. Once key staff members see the value of implementing a student empowerment program, they can help to bring others on board, which can have a snowball effect.

Element 3: Engaging Students and Adults

While it is important that a critical mass of staff are at least supportive, some of them must become inspired to step forward and take an active role in implementing the program and working with the youth in it throughout the year. These adult leaders might be teachers, counselors, parents, bus drivers, administrators, school resource officers, social workers, or other community members. Consider their passion and their skills. Are they organized? Do they follow through on their commitments and promises? Do they demonstrate that they respect and value youth? Do they relate well to students? Are they credible and approachable? (It is best to ask students this last question.)

The presentations and conversations aimed at securing buy-in are also opportunities to find those people, but it might be necessary to have some individual conversations with the people you really want to involve. In some situations, it can be more effective if the person asking is a student or peer who has some influence or long-standing relationship with that person. Selecting adults to work with the students means talking honestly about the role and commitment required. Together with the principal, the program's adult advisor should choose other adults who meet the criteria set out here and are most likely to follow through on their commitment.

Before any youth empowerment programming or activities can happen, schools need to identify, recruit, and select the students who will participate. When recruiting students, it is important to consider the social history of the different subgroups in the school. Do some traditionally clash? Are some typically left out of activities or at least underrepresented in the ranks of those who participate? Is there a hierarchy, or at least one that is perceived by many? For example, do most students think that all the perks, or "goodies," of student life go to the athletes or the student government leaders? Do some groups resent or hold grudges against others? It is likely that the answer to at least some of these questions is yes, so it becomes critically important to reach out and include non-traditional and sometimes disenfranchised students in a deliberate and inclusive way. The point person or other adults who are well connected to individual students in diverse cliques may need to have individual talks with particular student leaders to build rapport and trust and generate interest.

After students are identified, it is important that they are invited to attend an orientation meeting. This is often the first time they learn about the program, and this introduction must set the tone, establish the rationale, and invite the students to be partners in this endeavor. The attitude, tone, and words of the adults who facilitate this orientation must be in congruence with their belief in sharing power with students.

An effective orientation is engaging and dynamic, and inspires the students to get involved in the program. In the orientation, it is important that students have opportunities to express themselves with their peers and talk to adults about their concerns and opinions; it is equally important that they know adults are really listening to them.

Element 4: Training for Students and Adults

Once youth have become engaged, it is essential for them to receive appropriate training to learn new skills and support for strengthening these skills. Adults also may need to learn or sharpen skills for working with youth to engage, equip, and empower them more effectively.

Because the group of students and adults being brought together for a new program may be coming together in this way for the first time and may not know each other well or have any experience working together, team-building experiences are an important starting point. The diverse collection of students has to begin to form into a cohesive group. These exercises are designed to break down barriers and challenge stereotypes, and through them, the students come to understand the commonalities that underlie their differences, learn how to suspend their judgments about each other and get along, and unite behind their common goals. This process sets the stage for them to work together effectively on whatever task or challenge they choose to undertake.

If there is to be training for the youth, the adults could be trained alongside the students. Otherwise it is important to provide appropriate staff development for adults who lead youth empowerment programming. Without strong, committed, supportive adult leaders, the motivation that any training or experience offers the youth will have limited success and be less sustainable.

Successful and effective training and staff development workshops are:

- Skills based (communication, decision making, problem solving, facilitating meetings)
- Experiential, using role plays, dyad and small-group interactive activities, and others
- Collaborative, including and building on the knowledge and experiences of the participants
- Connective, building relationships and teamwork, creating safety, and fostering trust and full participation

Element 5: Providing Ongoing Support and Supervision

It is critical to sustain the commitment and participation of students and adults so that all successful youth empowerment programs contain features designed to make them sustainable. One of these features is meeting regularly as a group or on supervision teams. These meetings provide youth with a place to practice and sharpen their skills; meet their own developmental needs for belonging, connection, and recognition; and receive ongoing supervision and support.

Maintaining regular supervision and support meeting schedules times is often the most challenging part of sustaining a program. In most schools, it is hard to find time for adults to meet with students, and some teachers are reluctant to release students for nonacademic activities during the school day. These barriers to success can be lowered when the administration commits to giving the students and the adult group leaders release time and to providing the other staff at the school with enough information to appreciate the value of these meetings. It is at this point that the time invested earlier to build and gain staff buy-in will pay off.

When meetings are not regular or are relegated to lunchtime or before or after school, a program is less effective. Lunchtime is prime interaction and socializing time for students, and they are reluctant to give this time up. Meetings before or after school often create transportation problems and can conflict with extracurricular activities, jobs, or family commitments.

The meetings are the glue that holds a program together. Recognition, acknowledgment, practice, and sharing experiences are all critically important to the effectiveness and continuation of the program at each school site. The meetings are the place and time for these to occur.

Element 6: Collecting Data to Measure Program Effectiveness

Data drive decisions. Sustaining a program also requires having the tools to gather data to measure the program's impact. Once decision makers are given the evidence that youth empowerment programs are effective, they are more likely to re-fund it and maintain its support.

Levels of effectiveness can be assessed from a combination of methods:

• Having students record their experiences (activities, actions, and learnings) in journals or logs.

• Using surveys. Administered before the program is implemented and at regular intervals thereafter (for example, the end of each school year), these shed light on the differences in the participants' attitudes, beliefs, and behaviors. Surveys about broad issues like the friendliness of the school can be given to large groups of students, say, all entering sixth graders; more narrowly focused surveys can be given to smaller groups—perhaps the participants in the program. Surveys may also be administered to faculty and staff to gain an understanding of their views on the impact of the program. (Surveys are continually being developed and updated. A current school climate survey can be accessed on the Safe School Ambassadors Web site: www.safeschoolambassadors.org/climsurveyreg/index.php.)

• Interviewing key staff members. These are the people in the best position to see the benefits of the youth empowerment program that is being implemented. Exactly who they are depends on the nature and focus of the program. For example, in a high school program designed to help incoming freshmen adjust well, logical interviewees would be teachers of ninth-grade classes, ninth-grade counselors, administrators who have contact with freshmen, and even attendance clerks and secretaries. Anecdotal information from these key staff and administrators can reflect changes in effects or changes in occurrences related to the issues the youth have been addressing.

• Interviewing students. As with staff members, it can be illustrative to seek information from the students who are in the best position to see the impact of the program, whether they are directly involved in it or are simply beneficiaries of it. Using the previous example, it would be instructive to ask one or more representative groups of freshmen, "What has helped you feel welcome at school this year?" Each mention of the specific program would be validation that it is working.

• Collecting and analyzing related data. First, establish a baseline of data on the indicators that the program is most likely to influence. Comparisons of those indicators on a monthly, quarterly, or annual basis after the program is in place will demonstrate the effects the program is having.

Combined, this information can clearly demonstrate the effectiveness of the program to key stakeholders: staff, administration, board members, potential and actual community partners, funders, and the students themselves. It is also possible to examine the data for financial cost factors, showing the cost-effectiveness of youth empowerment programs; for example, if there is less graffiti, fewer dollars are spent to clean it up.

Element 7: Acknowledging and Celebrating the Efforts of Participants

Students who have participated in a program or initiative deserve to be recognized and acknowledged for a job well done. We believe that students who work for social change, community improvement, or justice should be appreciated and acknowledged. Traditionally most schools recognize students for their success in academics, extracurricular clubs, and sports. Having the courage to speak up for a cause or volunteering time to work on a campaign also deserves recognition at school. A commendation plaque, certificate, or even a scholarship is quite common. Athletes often receive letters to be sewn on their school jackets. Some schools give awards or certificates for community service or leadership as well.

Recognition activities can include holding a banquet or event for all participants and adult leaders and inviting parents and other interested school and community members to attend. Certificates of appreciation could be given at the all-school awards assembly. Some schools have hosted a picnic, sponsored a party, or arranged a field trip. Adults have also arranged for donated benefits, such as movie passes or restaurant coupons, to hand out with certificates.

Understanding the importance of each of the seven elements and committing the time and energy to implement them carefully will help accomplish the goal of developing a new youth empowerment program or strengthening an existing one. Putting these elements into action will improve the school's social-emotional climate and can transform the school into a more caring, connected, and compassionate community.

7

Understanding and Mobilizing Bystanders

This boy just started at our school a couple of weeks ago. I'd seen him play basketball with some other kids, but he wasn't very good. After lunch, he walked by us when we were just picking teams, and he stopped. The captains didn't pick him, so he asked, "Hey, can I play?" The captains basically told him they didn't want him on their teams, and then this one kid on the other team said something like, "Not the way you play!" and a couple of people laughed. I could see he felt really bad, and he tried not to show it. It would have been so easy to just let him play. But no one said anything. I know I probably should have, but I didn't want to get on their bad side and have them leave me out next time. So we all just started playing, and pretty soon he went away. Later on, at the end of the day, as I was walking out the door, he was right there next to me. He looked at me when I looked at him. I didn't know what to say to him; I couldn't look him in the eye. I mean, it wasn't my fault. I felt bad, so I ran to catch up with my friends.

—JULIO, EIGHTH GRADE, TEXAS

SOME ACADEMICIANS AND RESEARCHERS DEFINE *bystander* quite narrowly, making the point that the mere act of verbal encouragement transforms these bystanders into "henchmen," or accomplices of the aggressors. Others take a broader view of bystanders, saying that true accomplices have a higher degree of allegiance to the aggressor. These researchers hold instead that bystanders are any students who witness mistreatment, whether they watch it and say or do nothing, or whether they encourage it by making comments to the aggressor ("Go on, hit him!") or to the target ("You aren't going to take that from her, are you?"). In our experience, we have found it more useful to take the latter, broader definition of *bystander* because of what all bystanders have in common: they did not say or do anything to prevent or stop the mistreatment.

Researchers have found that at any given time, somewhere between 70 and 85 percent of the students at a school are neither aggressors nor targets of mistreatment. Instead, they are bystanders who witness the aggression,[1] and they outnumber aggressors and targets by roughly three to one in most schools. So the good news is that on a given day, three out of four students are not directly involved in bullying. The bad news is that this silent majority is not saying or doing anything to stop it. And since current efforts to reduce bullying by changing the behavior of the aggressors or by giving the targets defensive or coping strategies do not seem to be stemming the tide of mistreatment, it makes sense to look at the bystanders for a way to solve this problem.

The Significance of the Bystanders

It is not their numbers that make bystanders significant but rather the twofold effect they can have on the dynamic of mistreatment itself. The absence of protest from the bystanders:

- Gives immediate consent to each individual act of mistreatment
- Perpetuates a perceived norm: "It's cool to be cruel"

Immediate Impact

Students understand the significance of the bystanders and can articulate clearly the effect bystanders have on individual acts of mistreatment. In hundreds of schools, we have asked students to describe how bystanders affect what goes on between aggressors and targets. Their responses can be listed in four broad categories:

1. *Bystanders give the aggressors an audience,* meeting his or her need to be seen, and to be seen as entertaining or powerful, or both. Without an audience of bystanders watching, the mistreatment is not as satisfying to the aggressor.

2. *Bystanders make it hard for both the target and aggressor to save face,* to deescalate the situation and back away from the confrontation without violence or loss of social stature. Any target or aggressor who knows that a bystander has seen the confrontation also knows that the bystander will probably dismiss each one as a "wuss" if his or her actions are not sufficiently strong or provocative. This dynamic makes backing down a socially unacceptable choice.

3. *Bystanders' presence gives consent.* Regardless of whether they are actively encouraging or silently watching, bystanders who witness an act of mistreatment but don't say or do anything to stop it send a strong message to the aggressor and the target alike that the behavior is socially acceptable, perhaps even desirable. Many students who are silent bystanders rationalize their behavior by telling themselves that they were not really involved because they didn't say anything to encourage the aggressor; they just saw it happen. Although they are not guilty of committing the offense itself, they should understand that they are guilty of giving their consent for it to occur. "If you see it and you walk by it without saying anything, your silence says a lot. Your silence is consent," said a twelfth-grade boy from Palm Beach County, Florida.

4. *Bystanders can become accomplices.* Although they do not actually hurl the epithet or throw the punch or commit the crime, some students offer encouragement or advice to would-be aggressors, which has the effect of exacerbating the problem rather than bringing it to a rapid and peaceful conclusion. Sometimes this encouragement can be deadly. In their study of school shootings, the U.S. Secret Service and U.S. Department of Education found that 44 percent of the attackers were encouraged or dared by others to conduct their attacks:

> One attacker's original idea had been to bring a gun to school and let other students see him with it. He wanted to look tough so that the students who had been harassing him would leave him alone. When he shared this idea with two friends, however, they convinced him that exhibiting the gun would not be sufficient and that he would have to shoot at people at the school in order to get the other students to leave him alone. . . . In other cases, friends assisted the attacker in his efforts to acquire a weapon or ammunition, discussed tactics for

getting a weapon into school undetected, or helped gather information about the whereabouts of a target at a particular time during the school day.[2]

Long-Term Impact

An extensive body of literature suggests that the influence of peers has a greater impact on individual behavior than biological, personality, familial, religious, cultural, and other influences.[3] In other words, our actions are shaped most by our peers—their actions, their words, and what *we think* they think is socially acceptable. This influence is rooted in our basic human need to fit in and belong (the third level on Maslow's hierarchy discussed in Chapter Two). As it turns out, these peer influences are based more on the perceived norm (what *we think* others believe and do when we are not around) than on the actual norm (what others *actually* believe and do when we are not around).[4]

So when 70 to 85 percent of the students in a school are bystanders who say or do nothing to challenge mistreatment, their lack of opposition speaks volumes. The other students who observe them encouraging or silently condoning mistreatment conclude that those bystanders truly believe that such mistreatment is okay (which is often an incorrect conclusion). However, by acting in accord with this perceived norm that mistreatment is acceptable, bystanders reinforce it and over time make it the actual norm.

Understanding Bystanders' Behavior

To make sound decisions about how to change bystanders' behavior, it is important to understand what motivates them to act as they do. It is easy to say that bystander inaction is rooted in a lack of empathy. However, there is no reason to believe that lack of empathy is the only cause or that increasing empathy will cause bystanders to take action to stop what they see. In fact, both bystander research and reports from students suggest that several interrelated factors are at work.

Students and the schools they attend are heavily influenced by the society that surrounds them. The bystander phenomenon is not new, and it is not unique to schools. One participant in a workshop in Colorado shared the following story to illustrate his own bystander behavior:

> I recently stopped at a small local grocery store in my small town. As I turned down one of the aisles, a three- or four-year-old boy came around the corner. He was upset, and he was looking for the adult he'd come with.
>
> I will never forget how my instinctive reaction to help collided with my cautions and froze me mid-step. I wanted to bend down, hold, and comfort him, maybe pick him up if that were necessary. I wanted to offer my help in finding his adult. But in that moment, I thought about how my actions might be misinterpreted—that an equally distraught mother might see her son in my arms and presume that I was a threat, perhaps a kidnapper or pedophile. What if he started crying as I approached him? What would others in the store think?
>
> I was caught in a conflict between my natural desire to reach out to help a child and my mental reflex of self-protection. Without these fears, I would have scooped him up and helped him find his adult. Instead I stood there uncomfortably and watched. Fortunately, his mother came around the corner shortly after. I consider myself to be a practitioner of youth development and someone who wants to build a better community, but this time I was a bystander. How could that happen?

Why Students Don't Get Involved

In a culture where many believe it's cool to be cruel, some people seem to enjoy watching mistreatment, and very few speak up to stop it, it's hard not to be a bystander. Discussions with thousands of students in hundreds of training sessions have brought to light five overarching reasons, consistent with research, that students do not get involved to prevent or stop mistreatment they see:[5]

1. They fear retaliation.
2. They don't know what to do or say.

3. They are afraid of making the situation worse.

4. They are worried about losing social status, being labeled a "snitch" and becoming an object of ridicule themselves, partly because mistreatment and violence have acquired entertainment value, especially among youth.

5. They doubt that adults will believe them or that adults will handle the notification well.

Fear Factors

In addition to what our parents might have told us about minding our own business, the past few decades have produced a set of fear factors that push witnesses to be bystanders:

• *Fear of reprisal.* Urban legends or not, popular culture carries with it stories of people who have been followed, stalked, or hunted down and beaten, robbed, or worse, all because they did something to offend the attacker. What is the lesson? That every action carries with it the risk of retaliation by someone who was bothered by that action. With that mind-set, inaction becomes the least risky option.

• *Fear of litigation.* As the "Attorneys" section of the Yellow Pages has grown, so has the general fear and likelihood of being sued. Voters often encounter ballot initiatives designed to limit one type of lawsuit or another. Liability and malpractice insurance costs have skyrocketed. It is not difficult to find stories of people being sued for all sorts of reasons, many of which seem just plain spiteful. It's common knowledge that being drawn into litigation carries a huge cost of time and money, which fans the flames of fear and helps reinforce a culture where it's seen as wise not to get involved, despite the existence of Good Samaritan laws designed to protect those who intervene with good intention.

• *Fear of incompetence.* It seems that over the past generation or so, society has become much more reliant on experts and correspondingly less self-reliant. Generally people pay others to do for them many of the things their parents did for themselves—from cleaning to gardening to changing the oil in a car. When people today are confronted with a novel situation, they are more likely to think they don't know how to handle it. They don't get involved for fear of looking incompetent or making matters worse, or both.

Social Proof and Diffusion of Responsibility

In 1964, Kitty Genovese made headlines not because she was stabbed but because of the rather shocking circumstances that contributed to her death. Genovese lived in New York City's borough of Queens. At 3:15 one morning, she was returning to her home from her job as manager of a bar. As she walked from her car to her apartment, she was stabbed. In three separate attacks that night, she screamed, and lights in nearby apartments went on. Police later determined that thirty-eight people heard her cries for help, but not one person called the police or did anything substantial to help. While it is easy to jump to the conclusion that the bystanders were heartless, callous, and lacking in empathy, that particular neighborhood of Queens was actually a relatively tightly knit community of otherwise caring people. Why didn't anyone help Kitty Genovese?

This murder generated great controversy when it happened, and it led to groundbreaking research about bystanders that sheds light on two related social phenomena: social proof and diffusion of responsibility. These factors help us understand why those who witness something often fail to take action to stop it.

The essence of social proof can be understood by watching what happens in many office buildings when a fire alarm goes off. Everyone begins to look for cues as to how to behave: Do I go outside, or do I continue my work and wait for the maintenance crew to shut off the alarm? These cues might include asking these questions:

- Do others seem concerned?
- Is anyone gathering up their belongings?
- Is anyone heading for the exits?
- Has anyone seen or smelled smoke?
- Is a crowd gathering outside?

All of these bits of information, that is, the social proof, aren't obtained from objective data related to the building or a fire, but from other people's behavior and *their* assessments of the situation. In the case of Kitty Genovese, the witnesses looked for social proof that there really was an emergency—perhaps more lights going on in other apartments or more screams or the sound of a door opening, which might indicate that someone else took it seriously enough to go down and investigate. Lacking social proof, the witnesses took no action.

In school settings, it is common for students to use the elements of social proof to justify their inaction: "People do that all the time and no one says anything about it." The implied message is that because mistreatment is so common and few people speak up, it must not be a problem. This is not a logical conclusion, but it is the phenomenon of social proof at work.

Diffusion of responsibility happens when no one takes action because each person believes that others already have done so. Researchers have found that people are generally more likely to take action as the number of perceived witnesses decreases.[6] Kitty Genovese was attacked in a neighborhood, and witnesses knew that there were other witnesses (as evidenced by seeing lights go on in other apartments). This clearly influenced those witnesses. They didn't call the police because they figured someone else already had.

The Role of Empathy

Many people have proposed that bystanders don't intervene because they lack empathy, an emotional and cognitive response that emanates from the emotional state of another person.[7] For example, Lisa was just dumped by her boyfriend. She is walking out of the school building and meets up with her friend Rachel. Rachel's empathic response begins with noticing Lisa's red eyes, dejected expression, slouch, and heavy gait, and continues as she curbs her own excitement at having been named to the all-star volleyball team. Instead of sharing her good news, she asks in a kind tone, "Hey, girl, what's up?" She puts her arm around her friend's shoulders, listens attentively, feels sadness with her friend as she recalls a time she experienced a similar rejection, and shares small segments of stories or pieces of information aimed at showing her friend that she understands, cares, and will support her through this unhappy time.

Research generally supports the assumption that empathy promotes prosocial behavior and a concern for others. Although some studies do not sustain this connection, characteristics of the particular studies (for example, how empathy was assessed) are usually viewed as the reason that the link between empathy and prosocial behavior was not clearly evident.[8] However, empathy is complex, and it wouldn't be accurate to state conclusively that increasing bystanders' empathy increases the likelihood that they will actually speak up when they see mistreatment.[9]

In other words, even if empathy promotes a concern for others, is it alone enough to prompt a witness to take action? It is not hard to imagine a student feeling empathy for another who is being left out, teased, or bullied. But will that empathy trigger a desire to help? And will it result in an intervention? In one study, over half of surveyed children reported that they would intervene in a hypothetical bullying situation, but their reports did not match observed playground behavior. Researchers found that children ages five to twelve passively watched a bullying dynamic 54 percent of the time, joined in on the bullying 21 percent of the time, and intervened on behalf of the victim only 25 percent of the time.[10] Another study found that bystanders intervened in only about 11 percent of the bullying episodes they saw.[11] These percentages do not improve with age; it has been consistently reported that older children are less likely to intervene and more likely to encourage a bully than younger children are.[12]

Discussions with thousands of students have validated that this triggering happens but does not always lead to intervention. Here are the main reasons students offer for their lack of action:

- Fear of reprisal: "The bullies are bigger [or older or more popular] than I am."

- Fear factor: incompetence: "I don't know what to do, so I don't do anything."

- Social proof: "Well, it doesn't look like anyone else is too upset by this, so I figure it isn't a real problem."

- Diffusion of responsibility: "A teacher or someone else will do something. I mean, it's not *my* responsibility to stop it."

In addition, other studies have found that bystanders often identified with the intentions of the bully rather than the feelings of the victim, even after a bully prevention program that taught the opposing lesson. Over 50 percent of sixth and seventh graders felt that the victim could control the reason for being mistreated:

- "What does she expect, dressing like that?"

- "He should have known that he'd get his butt kicked for flirting with that girl."

And many bystanders believed that the victim would learn something from the encounter:[13]

- "Maybe now he'll know not to be bugging people that way!"

- "That'll teach her to be talkin' trash about other people."

The value of empathy as an impetus for action is reduced by strong social and cultural norms concerning the attribution of blame to victims in social situations. If a bystander believes the victim caused the mistreatment, then empathetic discomfort is reduced and often replaced by anger. Victims with bad reputations (those thought to be immoral or deceitful, for example) are often seen as deserving maltreatment. The most compassionate student may not feel empathy, and therefore intervene, if the victim can be blamed.[14]

In addition to this general phenomenon of blaming the victim for his or her predicament, students who seek to be accepted by a social group that supports bullying are less willing to speak up or stand up to stop it.[15] All this supports the contention that although widespread empathy training might prompt students to be nicer to each other, it is not enough to spur them to intervene when they witness bullying or other forms of mistreatment.

The Positive Power of Bystanders

While many bullying prevention efforts focus on the target or the aggressor or both, a significant body of research supports the premise that bystanders are actually in the best position to influence aggressors' behavior. For example, research has found that 57 percent of the times when a bystander objects to mistreatment, the bullying stops.[16] Promoting intervention by the student bystanders who witness mistreatment is seen as a promising way of reducing bullying in schools.[17] "Positive peer pressure is an important component of effective intervention," says Tom Tarshis, director of the Bay Area Children's Association and coauthor of the 2007 Stanford University study on the prevalence of bullying in elementary students. "When uninvolved students step up and let the perpetrator know that their behavior is not acceptable, it's a powerful message."[18]

However, accepting the proposition that bystanders are the key to reducing mistreatment and trying to use this idea in efforts to improve school climate means the challenge is tripled. Instead of trying to change the behavior of only 15 to 30 percent of a school's population (targets and aggressors), those efforts now must reach the 70 to 85 percent of the population who are the bystanders. How can that be done?

Current Bystander Mobilization Efforts

Most bystander mobilization efforts have two common themes: they are usually driven by adults and implemented by teachers, and they attempt to reach out to all bystanders equally, either en masse or in classes. Here are a few of the typical examples of such efforts:

- *Assemblies and speakers.* These are typically short-term events, lasting from an hour to a day, that have limited long-term impact. They can be expensive and take time that few schools can afford to give up.

- *Inspirational messages.* Quotes and stories of heroes and heroines are read over the PA system as part of morning announcements or placed throughout the school on posters. Unfortunately, few students remember the thought for the day once they've started thinking about what's for lunch or where that attractive girl or guy is today.

- *Behavior identification and modification campaigns.* These typically take the form of posters carrying one or more types of messages: the specific behaviors involved in bullying, the costs or consequences of bullying, don't bully others, or how to defend yourself against bullies. Although we have seen instances where student-made posters appeared to be well received (partly due to a fairly comprehensive schoolwide character development initiative), these campaigns alone generally have minimal impact on the behavior of aggressors.

- *Social-emotional curricula.* For these to be done well, three conditions must be met: the teachers must see their value, they must be trained and equipped to teach the lessons effectively, and they must do so consistently. These curricula use up instructional minutes that are already in high demand as teachers respond to pressure to teach academic subject areas.

Unfortunately, these efforts have one fundamental limitation: students, especially at the middle and high school levels, pay much more attention to the cues of their peers than the directives of adults when determining what kinds of behavior are acceptable.[19] Ken Rigby, an adjunct professor in the University of South Australia's School of Education, says, "The difficulty of promoting more proactive bystander behavior should not be underestimated. This research suggests that teachers' expectations of how students should act in bystander situations have little or no influence on student behavior. This is particularly so for secondary students. Directly instructing students about how they should behave may in fact be counter-productive, especially with boys. Teacher influence needs to be more indirect and subtle."[20]

The Missing Link: Norm Changers

Designing more effective bystander mobilization strategies requires knowing more precisely how the social norms followed by the bystanders are established and changed. Within the large set of bystanders in a given school (roughly eight hundred students in a middle school of a thousand), there exists a much smaller set of students. This smaller group comprises the socially influential opinion leaders of each of the school's diverse social cliques and groups. These are the students who shape the behavioral norms that guide other students' behavior and in some cases condone mistreatment despite all the rules adults have created to stop it. In his book, *The Tipping Point: How Little Things Can Make a Big Difference,* Malcolm Gladwell identified the processes by which social norms are established and changed. Several important insights in his book can be applied to student-on-student mistreatment.

First, as Gladwell writes, "Epidemics are sensitive to the conditions and circumstances of the times and places in which they occur."[21] He makes the case that an afternoon ride for Paul Revere would not have been as significant; the fact that Revere delivered his message late at night and had to wake people up increased the recipients' sense of its importance, and thus how they responded. The fact that seemingly subtle environmental messages have significant impact on people's behavior is confirmed by the "broken windows" theory, developed by criminologists James Q. Wilson and George Kelling that is credited with triggering the sharp decline in New York City's crime rate in the 1990s. Wilson and Kelling argued, and subsequently proved, that when the little things like broken windows and graffiti are left unattended, people sense from the environment that no one cares, no one is in charge, and the rules and laws cannot be enforced because the norms have deteriorated. Making seemingly small improvements to the environment had huge positive repercussions throughout the city. The same can be said for schools: cleaning up the more subtle and relatively benign mistreatment that happens below the waterline will have a powerful influence on visible violence. But who is best to do that cleanup?

The second insight Gladwell makes is that students have something adults don't: "We all want to believe that the key to making an impact on someone lies with the inherent quality of the ideas we present."[22] But the many examples and studies Gladwell cites show that the impact or "stickiness" of a message is vastly increased not by presenting new or more compelling information but by tinkering in some small way with the presentation of the idea. "There is a simple way to package information that, under the right circumstances, can make it irresistible. All you have to do is find it."[23] So while adults would naturally think that they have the knowledge and life experience to develop the high-quality ideas that will help prevent or stop the below-the-waterline mistreatment, their relative lack of success in this arena suggests that they might not have found the irresistible packaging yet. And looking at the way ideas race through popular youth culture further suggests that students might know something adults don't, and can't, know, especially the students who have that knack for saying the right thing in the right way at the right time.

The third insight comes from Gladwell's Law of the Few, which holds that the spread of an epidemic, whether an idea or a disease, is influenced by three kinds of people:

- *Mavens,* who have the knowledge and social skills to start word-of-mouth epidemics[24]
- *Salesmen,* who have the skills to persuade us when we are unconvinced of what we are hearing[25]
- *Connectors,* the gregarious and intensely social people who "know everybody" and always seem to be at the center of events[26]

In a school, the mavens are often the ones other students look to for social cues; they know what's what and who's who and feed into students' desire to fit in and belong. They are the ones who can best make those little changes in the social environment (for example, encouraging a friend to step down from a confrontation). In a way, whatever they do is cool not because of what they do but because of who they are in the eyes of their peers. The salesmen promote the change, properly packaging it so it's "sticky," and the connectors spread the word.

Linda Jeffrey, professor of psychology at Rowan University in New Jersey, wrote, "Communication of pro-social values in a school community requires empowerment of mavens and connectors who carry the message that bullying is not accepted behavior."[27] Both Gladwell and Jeffrey recognized that particular students are pivotal in the process of creating, maintaining, and changing social norms.

Identifying the Norm Changers

To sift through all the bystanders and find the students who shape a school's social norms requires an awareness and understanding of their characteristics, individually and collectively. While the U.S. Secret Service found that school shooters could not be profiled[28] and other studies have determined that bullies come from all varieties of life situations, the students who shape, and thus can change, the social norms at a school are much easier to identify.

These norm changers are the true leaders of the student body. They set trends, influence opinions, and shape behaviors. They aren't only the members of the student council. They aren't only the students who always make the honor roll. They aren't only the editors of the student newspaper, the sports teams, and the cheerleaders. While they may include one or more people from each of those groups, the norm changers are also the key people in groups and cliques who are often overlooked and underrepresented. These students might identify or group themselves by ethnicity or by interest in music, style of dress, politics, or something else.

Individual Characteristics   Some of these norm changers might be aggressors at times, and others might even be targets sometimes. But mostly they are bystanders whose unique role in the cycle of mistreatment creates the social norm that says it's cool to be cruel. Each student who exerts a strong influence over the social norms at a school has the following three characteristics:

• *Social position.* Norm changers are the opinion leaders of their particular social group or clique. Within their small circles, they are the ones whom their peers look to for behavioral cues as to who's in and who's out, what's cool and what's not. They are the top dogs, the alpha boys or girls of their groups. Like the lead bird in the flock, they set the direction for the flock to follow.

- *Personality.* Norm changers are generally outspoken within their social groups. They often have high verbal skills and are not shy about speaking their minds, even if their views are not popular. Many of these adolescents are the ones who frequently put their hands up in class to state their opinions or challenge a popular perspective. However, this outspokenness is not always evident in the classroom because the student might not be sufficiently engaged or interested to demonstrate his or her verbal skills in an academic setting. They might only come out in nonclassroom settings. These students typically have quick minds, and some might even have gotten in trouble for mouthing off to a teacher or not knowing when to keep a witty comment to themselves. If asked, parents of these teens will typically say that their children always have something to say about everything. Nevertheless, not all of these teens would feel comfortable making a speech at an assembly or even in class.

- *Values.* Norm changers have a strong sense of justice and concern for others, especially as it applies to their immediate circle of peers. They are very loyal to their groups and watch out for group members. They also have a certain strength of character. This can be a difficult characteristic to discern, because it is often not evident until precipitated by some emotional event or experience, like sticking up for one of their own in an intergroup conflict. This nature to do right might have gotten them in trouble before, especially for breaking rules they may have felt at the time were relatively insignificant.

Collective Characteristic: Diversity   Like the adults they'll soon become, young people tend to affiliate with peers who share common characteristics, such as ethnicity or a common interest. This tendency grows more pronounced as students progress from elementary to middle and high school. Whether determined by race, social class, or interest, these cliques form the backbone of the social structure at almost every school.

In the previous chapter, the different groups in a school were compared to the different countries in the United Nations. As one middle school student put it in the video *Let's Get Real*,[29] "Our school is like the world. Over there is Africa where a lot of the black students hang out. The front steps are Mexico where all the Mexican students hang out. The center of the quad is America where all the white students are. Then there are all these little islands in between, like for the different

Asian groups, and the Jamaicans, and all that." A high school student in one of our training sessions described her campus this way: "You've got the jocks, and the preps; then there's the nerds or the geeks. Then there's skaters, and punks, and drinkers, and skinheads. That's all the big ones." Finding the norm changers on a campus first requires identifying and naming all of its cliques. Completing the Groups and Cliques Worksheet in Chapter Four helps to organize that process.

Together the norm changers represent the major ethnic and social groups at a school. They'll have blond hair and black hair and green hair. They'll have dark skin and light skin. They'll listen to all kinds of music. Together, as a group, they'll be no more than one or two significant relationships away from almost every other person on campus.

Mobilizing the Norm Changers

The strategies used to mobilize the norm changers to take action must address the reasons they don't stand up or speak out on behalf of others:

• *Fear of retaliation.* Have norm changers first work with their friends and other people they know, where the risk of retaliation is lower because of the bonds of trust and respect that develop between friends and because of the norm changers' awareness of and sensitivity to the issues that would trigger a friend to lose control and retaliate in anger. This constraint means that if the norm changers' efforts are going to affect an entire campus, they must be drawn from all of the cliques and groups on that campus.

• *Don't know what to say or do.* Norm changers need an array of concrete strategies they can use with their peers. They need to be taught the language of nonviolent communication and the words to artfully intervene when they see something they know isn't right. These skills need to be youth friendly: easy to learn and remember, sound and feel natural, and able to be customized to apply to the wide variety of situations that young people encounter. Chapter Eight provides several examples of these concrete skills.

• *Afraid of making the situation worse.* Norm changers need to have confidence in their skills, which comes when they intervene using language in a way that is authentically theirs. They also gain confidence when they have ample opportunity to practice those skills. This practice is best accomplished in training settings through role plays where they can experiment in a low-risk environment and receive immediate helpful feedback, and it needs to be in actual situations so they gain confidence in their skills. For that practice to be maximally effective, the norm changers need opportunities to discuss and debrief their experiences with peers and experienced coaches or mentors.

- *Worried about losing social status.* Make sure that the students who end up in the program are indeed the ones with high social status or capital. These are the students who have enough of it to risk losing some of it on their interventions; if one intervention bombs or appears socially awkward, they have enough social capital remaining to retain their position within their social group.

- *Mistrust of adults.* Involve influential adults in the program so the norm changers can develop relationships with them. Then create structured (and informal) opportunities for adults and youth to build and strengthen those relationships as they work together and get to know each other.

In addition, it is essential to integrate into that mobilization strategy three general principles:

1. *Call out their courage.* In youth culture, it is often a huge risk to give voice to ideas that run counter to popular trends or beliefs, so help students explore courage: what it is, who has it, how it has helped those people overcome adversity, and how they themselves can access their own courage. Acknowledge the risks, social and even physical. Do everything reasonable to protect against them, and invite them to "feel the fear and do it anyway." As American author and professor John Augustus Shedd wrote in 1928, "A ship in a harbor is safe, but that's not what ships are made for."

2. *Challenge them to take action.* Students need to see that individual actions matter. Many teens (and even many adults) feel powerless to influence larger issues and trends. Even this viewpoint can be changed as students explore history and their own lives for examples of people whose actions have had a positive impact on the lives of others.

3. *Empower them.* Most teens have little experience with real prosocial power, so share some power with them in age-appropriate and structured ways. (See Chapter Six for several structured strategies.) This action gives them a concrete, real-life experience of making a positive difference.

With time and experience, they will come to see that taking action has intrinsic rewards.

Conclusion

Bystanders hold the key to reducing mistreatment. Their silence (or lack of action to stop mistreatment) amounts to tacit consent, which reinforces the norm that allows cruelty and mistreatment to happen. Due to a complex set of factors, bystanders often do not use their power in positive ways. Whether they are paralyzed by their fears (of retaliation, litigation, or incompetence), do not recognize mistreatment for the problem that it is, or do not feel enough individual responsibility to do something, students who witness mistreatment typically become the silent majority that colludes with the abuse and allows it to continue as the norm.

Changing the behavior of bystanders requires a strategic approach that begins with identification of the socially influential opinion leaders of a school's diverse cliques—the students who shape the norms on a campus. Because of their high social status and self-confidence, these are the students who can best stand up to the cultural pressure to continue the current norms—to be mean or to be silent—and change them. Finding these norm changers requires the input of both staff and students. Once they are identified, they must be given a chance to understand this new opportunity to use their power and influence to speak out against bullying and violence. They must be invited to take it on, and then they must choose to be "in."

As bullying prevention efforts begin to place greater emphasis on encouraging bystanders to intervene during episodes of bullying rather than simply report them to adults, equipping youth with the knowledge and skills for effective interventions, as well as providing a network of support from peers and school staff, is of critical importance.[30] The next chapter describes Safe School Ambassadors, a program that puts into practice the principles that have been described up to this point.

chapter

8

From Bystanders to Peacemakers

I was leaving the cafeteria and I saw two boys getting ready to fight. Well, it was only three days after the training. The first thing that came to my mind was distracting. Since everyone is scared of Mr. D., I yelled that Mr. D. was coming. Everyone scattered, and the boys didn't fight. Later they forgot what they were mad about, and I saw them playing basketball together.

—ELISA, SEVENTH GRADE, EL PASO, TEXAS

This boy wanted to play in this basketball game, and the other kids wouldn't let him. They told him he was too fat, and they laughed. So I said to those kids, "How would you feel if someone left you out?" Then I told the boy to come play with us and he did, and he felt better.

—JORGE, FOURTH GRADE, RIFLE, COLORADO

I was in the PE locker room, and some kids were verbally and physically abusing other kids. I distracted the aggressors, leaving time for the target to get away. I then asked the aggressors why they did that and if they thought it made them cool, and told them that it didn't. As the days passed by, the aggressors bullied him less. Within about two weeks, after a couple more encounters, the bullying totally stopped.

—XAVIER, TENTH GRADE, PERRIS, CALIFORNIA

A friend of mine was put in a situation in which a group of girls wanted to fight her. I told her not to fight, to avoid them, and to tell her mom. I also told her the situation would soon blow over and not to worry. After a couple days, the girls soon forgot about it and moved on. It made me feel good that something I learned in school helped me in the real world.

—LISA, TWELFTH GRADE, WINTER SPRINGS, FLORIDA

THESE ARE THE WORDS OF SAFE SCHOOL AMBASSADORS, students in grades 4 through 12 who are the socially influential leaders of their schools' diverse groups and cliques. These young people are bringing voice to their values and courage to their actions to make schools safer and more welcoming for everyone.

Carefully identified by both the school staff and fellow students, these ambassadors learn powerful, nonviolent communication and intervention skills they can use to prevent and stop the bullying and violence on their campus and in their community. They intervene with their peers, in the moment, as mistreatment happens. They stop harassment and reach out to students who have been excluded or isolated. They squelch malicious rumors and gossip, and report to adults information about weapons on campus and other potentially dangerous situations.

Through regularly scheduled and ongoing small-group meetings, ambassadors sharpen their skills, process their experiences, and record their interventions. These meetings help to strengthen ambassadors' relationships with one another, solidify their commitments, and promote the sustainability of the program.

After implementing the Safe School Ambassadors program, schools typically experience a reduction in violence, mistreatment, and tensions among their students. The program also engenders increased acceptance of diversity and supports an environment that encourages higher academic achievement and attendance.

The previous chapters describe the core elements of a general model for engaging, empowering, and equipping youth to address the problem of mistreatment by changing the social norms of a school culture. Those elements can be assembled and implemented in many different ways to create similar but different programs. This chapter draws on our experience with one program model: Safe School Ambassadors (SSA). Since 1999, we have developed and refined the SSA program model in conjunction with the growing team at Community Matters, a nonprofit youth development organization based in northern California.

This powerful, student-centered program has been launched in more than six hundred schools in the United States and Canada. This chapter describes how the SSA program incorporates the seven elements of effective youth empowerment programs discussed in Chapter Six. Accordingly, what we refer to as norm changers in other chapters are referred to as *ambassadors* here. Other elements of the model described in general terms elsewhere become *action logs* and *family groups* here so we can refer to the specific features of the SSA program.

Gaining Support from Staff at All Levels

The SSA program begins when a point person is introduced to the model and sees its potential for addressing the problem of mistreatment in his or her schools. As described in element 1 in Chapter Six, the point person might be a teacher or counselor; an assistant principal, dean, or principal; or even a district-level administrator. In some cases, these people might be members of a standing or ad hoc committee or work group charged with oversight of school safety and climate issues. Board members, school resource officers, parents, and others, including youth, have also been point people for bringing information about the SSA program to a school.

As described in element 2 of Chapter 6, gaining the support of the staff is the next step, and the point person is the champion of that effort. One way of obtaining that support is to conduct a staff presentation, which has four main outcomes. After hearing a presentation, staff members will:

- Understand the need for the program by having greater knowledge of the problem of mistreatment and its costs to the students and staff at their school

- Understand how the SSA program works to meet that need

- Understand the results that can be expected—reduced incidents of peer harassment, fewer disciplinary actions like suspensions—and the effect these will have on their responsibilities

- Consider taking the next steps to do the large and small things that are necessary for the program to be successful, such as deciding how they can release students from class to attend the training and small-group meetings

In the presentation, it is important to allow time for questions and, depending on the size of the group, thoughtful discussion. Appendix B offers additional information about responding to the questions and concerns often raised about the program.

Prior to or after this presentation, the point person or a committee needs to enroll the principal and other administrators in seeing the value of the SSA program. They have to get these school leaders to agree to provide institutional and professional support for implementation. Support includes providing funding, space, and supplies for trainings and meetings, release time for students and staff to attend those trainings and meetings, and any substitutes needed for staff members involved.

Recruiting and Selecting Students and Adults

Once support from administrators and staff has been secured, it is necessary to find and enroll the right students and adults to bring the program to life. Both the students and adults must meet very specific criteria for the program to be successful and effective in reducing mistreatment on campus.

Selecting Program Advisors

One or two staff members need to take on the role of program advisor to lead and manage the activities of the participating students and adults. Although they need to have some ongoing support from school administrators, the program advisors become the main spokespeople and advocates for the SSA program. They lead the efforts to recruit and select the students, coordinate training, and provide posttraining support of students and adults involved in the program. In addition, they manage the vital organizational details, including scheduling, funding, and measuring program effectiveness.

Most program advisors are part of the school staff, serving as counselors, teachers, administrators, or in other classified roles. The advisor might (or might not) be the point person who provided the impetus to launch the program. What is important is that they have the skills and relationships, the time and resources, and the authority and support to fulfill their responsibilities.

Identifying Potential Ambassadors

The program advisor begins the process of finding the students who will be directly involved in the program as ambassadors and the staff who will support them. As described in element 3 in Chapter Six, those two processes follow parallel tracks that include identification (based on specified criteria), outreach and recruitment (helping those who were identified to understand the role and decide if they want to fulfill it), and selection (choosing the right people from the pool of those interested). This process typically takes a few weeks and extends over several rounds of communication with staff members, either individually or as a whole.

Depending on the school's decision-making process, the first (or next) staff presentation would help staff members understand the characteristics of an effective ambassador and ask for their help in identifying and nominating students they know to join the program. It would also request that a small subgroup of five to seven staff members commit to work with the ambassadors by participating in the training and facilitating the small meetings (referred to as *family group meetings*) that begin after the training and provide the supervision, further skill development, and ongoing support that are necessary to sustain the program, as described in element 5.

The process of finding the right students is critical to the program's overall success. Not all students have the social status, communication skills, personality, or esteem to challenge their friends when their friends are mistreating others. Potential ambassadors must have "the right stuff" to be effective norm changers. Selecting the social leaders who are in the best position to stand up and break the code of silence that permeates the bystander culture is what makes the program work.

Tapping the Knowledge of Staff As schools begin to implement the SSA model, they need to identify the most socially influential students of the diverse social groupings on campus. This requires the knowledge and perspectives of the staff. Heather Knighton, a teacher at the Kathryn Señor Elementary School in Colorado, notes that "we look for kids who are leaders of their groups, kids who have strong personalities, who are strong enough to take a stand and who are willing to take risks." Asking staff members to assist in finding prospective ambassadors does much more than increase the likelihood of identifying the right students. The process also helps to increase the staff's understanding and support of the whole process of empowering bystanders in climate improvement efforts. There are two possible avenues for obtaining staff input: one broad and the other more narrowly focused.

Casting a Wide Net Through a Staff Presentation To begin the process of selecting the ambassadors, the program advisor or another key staff member or administrator provides a presentation that is designed to help staff members identify the students who could be effective ambassadors. The key points covered in this presentation to staff were in the "Gaining Support from Staff at All Levels" section.

In this next presentation, the program advisor makes sure staff receive a clear explanation of the characteristics of the students who will be effective ambassadors and the research that shows the power of influential social leaders to change social norms.

Getting Help from Key Staff Members   Not all staff members see students the same way. These differences are a function of different staff job roles and also of their personal views and values. For these reasons, it is important to do more than cast a wide net by sending out a memo or speaking at a staff meeting. Many schools identify the key staff members and speak with them personally to enlist their help. These key staff members typically have nonteaching roles that allow them to see students interact in relatively unstructured and unsupervised settings. This is especially important since not all of the characteristics of effective ambassadors will show up in a classroom environment. These key staff members could be counselors, librarians or media techs, campus supervisors or yard duty personnel, cafeteria staff, coaches or physical education teachers, bus drivers and custodians.

Having a good rapport with students is important. Students see them as being approachable and supportive, which indicates that these staff members often take the time to get to know students on a more personal level, beyond the subject matter being taught in a particular class.

These staff members could have a disciplinary function. At least one adult surveyed is usually the primary disciplinarian on campus, because she or he will have firsthand knowledge of who the key players are on campus.

Typically these are people who have been on campus for at least a couple of years. This time gives them a perspective on the overall campus social structure, as well as a longitudinal perspective on student dynamics (for example, that a particular student has sustained his or her influence for a year or two).

Tapping the Knowledge of Students   When identifying ambassadors, schools typically obtain information directly from students as well as staff. Student nominations invariably help to identify key students who were been listed by the staff.

The essence of this approach is asking students to name peers they look up to or respect and also those they might turn to if they needed support or help with a personal matter. Schools approach this process in different ways, depending on the size of the school and time available to analyze the information gathered.

Here are some examples of what schools have done to begin identifying their prospective ambassadors:

- Asked counselors to survey ten students each. Although this is neither random nor comprehensive, this method does acquire some student input.
- Randomly surveyed fifty students at lunch.
- Used a formal survey tool and distributed it to a cross-section of students. One large high school surveyed two English classes in each grade level, being careful to survey a cross-section of ability levels rather than just the honors classes.
- Used the SSA program's formal survey and distributed it to all students.

When students have questioned the purpose of the survey, schools have provided a general answer about wanting to identify students who might participate in training about improving school climate and helping people get along. This protects the anonymity and role of the ambassadors.

Survey questions typically touch on several topics:

Leadership

- Who is the most influential person in your group of friends?
- What other students at our school do you and other students listen to?
- What students at our school do you admire or respect?

Trust

- If you had a personal problem or concern (maybe about something that's happening in your family), what students would you talk to for advice or help?
- What students at our school listen to and seem to understand what others are saying or feeling
- What students do you trust?

Dependability

- Who could you count on to be there for you, to stand by you?
- Which students keep their word or promises?

Courage

- What students are willing to express their opinions or ideas, even if those ideas are not popular?

- Who stands up for their friends?

Students with the most "votes" are likely to be those who are seen as socially influential leaders by other students, and thus good candidates to be ambassadors. Some schools find it helpful to create a sociogram, which uses circles and arrows to depict the social relationships between and among students and helps identify the cliques and social groups more clearly.

In a school of a thousand students or more, it is likely that these two processes (staff and student nominations) will generate fifty to a hundred names. Staff start with noticing the students who have been identified on both staff and student lists. However, it is appropriate to include a couple of students who were identified only by their peers, especially if they received a high number of check marks or if they represent a group that is not otherwise represented in this identification process. Also, it may be necessary to explain several of the student nominations to any administrators, staff, and even board members who don't yet understand SSA's criteria for selection. It is also important to explain that applying the usual criteria of good grades and good behavior would significantly reduce the power and impact of the program because it would exclude some of the socially powerful students whose participation is essential for its success.

Here is a brief list of how to select students in this process:

Do	Don't
• Select students based on social position, personality, loyalty to friends, and sense of social justice.	• Select students because they need to be "fixed."
• Select a diverse group of students based on ethnicity, interest, and clique.	• Select just aggressors and targets.
• Survey both the students and adults.	• Select students based on good behavior or good grades.

Orienting and Selecting the Ambassadors

After the potential ambassadors are identified, they need to be engaged, as described in element 3. In the SSA program model, identified students are invited to attend an orientation meeting to learn about the program. At this critical juncture, they hear the reasons they were invited to attend. The program advisor or other representative tells these students that they were nominated by their peers and adults in their school because they are viewed as powerful and influential leaders.

Students participate in discussions, activities, and exercises to learn more about their school climate and the types of bullying and violence that occur. Then they watch part of a DVD and hear about the Safe School Ambassadors program to learn what part they could play in reducing mistreatment in their school.

Since being an ambassador means volunteering to take a social, and potentially physical, risk, it is important that students see the benefits, or WIIFMs ("What's in it for me") of getting involved. Some students are motivated by gaining recognition; some may want to put this down on their college applications; some may want to learn skills that could help with employment; some want to come to a school that is a better, safer place to attend. Maybe they've been noticing and worrying about the level of cruelty and fighting on the campus and wanted to be able to make a difference but didn't know how. The program advisor therefore appeals to students' self-interest, not just their altruism. The advisor lets them know that by participating, they can address some of their individual and common concerns, such as, "I don't want my girlfriend to be hassled." "I don't want my friends to be hurt." "I don't want my friends fighting," or "Too many kids are mean to each other."

Adults respond to questions students have or reasons they are not sure about becoming ambassadors. Many have to do with common topics:

- Time commitment. After the training, there will be regularly scheduled meetings with other students for twenty to forty minutes every couple of weeks.

- Perceptions about being a snitch or a goody-two-shoes. Students will learn a handful of tools they can use with their friends; only one of the skills they will learn involves an adult.

- Wearing something that identifies this role, such as a badge, sash, vest, or clipboard. Students need to know that they will be incognito and function without being formally identified to other students. This increases their influence and effectiveness because students they intervene with see the ambassador as motivated by genuine concern rather than by some official position or designation.

The orientation is an opportunity for the adult leading it to "walk the talk." By asking for their opinions and ideas, adults demonstrate respect for students' perspectives and knowledge about their experiences. This student-centered approach has enormous power and appeal. After all, adults are inviting students to take a different role in their own school by acting as leaders for change. In the spirit of Marshall McLuhan's words—"there are no passengers on spaceship earth; we are all crew"—adults invite students to help "guide the ship" and to share in shaping the climate of the school.

Through this orientation, students have the opportunity to learn about the SSA program and get inspired to join. This choice is an essential part of the process. An effective orientation is authentic and engaging, not a "sell" but an earnest and honest conversation about things that really matter: feeling safe, preventing conflicts, and getting along with others.

After the orientation, potential ambassadors bring information about the program home to their parents or guardians. Typically schools also require these candidates to fill out an application or go through an interview process, or both. The application and interview process helps the adults determine which students are likely to feel comfortable taking on the role of ambassador and will follow through with their commitment.

Once students have demonstrated interest and gained permission from their parents or guardians, the final group of students who'll be trained still needs to be selected. The adult leaders must review and assess the potential pool to make sure that the students still in it possess the necessary individual and collective characteristics. Are all of the major cliques and social groups represented? Are the students socially influential, verbal, and loyal to their peers? This thorough and comprehensive identification, orientation, and winnowing process ensures that the most appropriate students will be selected to be ambassadors.

Training Ambassadors

For these influential students to actually *do* the interventions necessary to influence the behavior of their peers and shift the social norms on their campus, they must understand the job they are going to do, be motivated to do it, and possess the skills to do it well. The Safe School Ambassadors program training process is carefully designed to accomplish those goals.

Laying the Foundation

Before introducing the observation and intervention skills the ambassadors will use with their peers, the training lays a foundation with four distinct building blocks, each introduced at the beginning of the training and then woven throughout the process:

- Creating a safe and trusting training environment and strengthening their sense of community

- Increasing their understanding of the problem and costs of mistreatment in their school and community

- Developing a motivation to intervene with their peers

- Increasing their understanding of how they will be supported and supervised after the training, which increases participant retention and program sustainability

Building Trust and a Sense of Community   Imagine bringing twenty-five to forty diverse student leaders into a two-day training session, some of whom either don't know or don't like each other. Students and adults come to SSA training with their own unique histories, knowledge, and abilities. Attempting to work with the provocative and sensitive issues that are inherent in the training without first building a sense of safety and community is a recipe for failure. Students are less likely to participate fully if they don't feel safe or if they are worried about being ridiculed for their opinions. Creating trust and connection is accomplished through a series of discussions and ice-breaker activities.

Some of these activities are less risky, with low self-disclosure. Other activities allow students to share stories, hear the stories of others, and discover what they have in common to build stronger bonds. As students (and adults) get to know one another, their assumptions about each other tend to fall away, clearing the path for honest dialogue. These experiences encourage students to see the real person rather than holding onto the preconceptions and prejudices that they had about one another before they came to the training.

Building relationships allows participants to see people for who they are. Trust is critical for establishing social comfort as well as co-creating norms for positive behavior in the training. With this foundation firmly established, the training environment is primed for optimal learning and personal growth.

Next, participants in the training are introduced to the problem of mistreatment, the consequences of bullying and violence, the motivation to act, and the skills needed to intervene.

Understanding the Problem and Costs of Mistreatment   The second building block of the training gives students an opportunity to explore the problem of mistreatment on their campus. Consistent with the principles of the youth development formula presented in Chapter Six, this part of the training is highly interactive, so it elicits the information from students' own experiences.

Students are introduced to the framework of the five types of mistreatment presented in Chapter One. They then have several opportunities through dialogue and activities to scan their own personal experiences, at school and throughout their lives, for examples of mistreatment they have experienced as targets, aggressors, or bystanders. These exercises might generate two hundred to three hundred examples, which set the stage for a discussion of the costs or impact of mistreatment on students, staff, and the school as a whole, just as Chapter Two has done.

These are sobering moments in the training, in which students and adults alike begin to see the breadth and scope of the problems. They notice, some for the first time, that these are not isolated incidents, not relegated to a few people, infrequently occurring; their previously held beliefs and the narrowness of their perspectives are shattered. With their blinders removed, the participants are awakened to the need and inspired to act, which is the springboard for the next building block of the training.

Developing a Motivation to Act   At this point, the students and adults are aware of the seriousness and nature of the problems in their school. The students are willing and becoming ready and eager. However, the vast majority of students today, especially the socially influential opinion leaders, need to see the WIIFMs if they are going to buck the prevailing trend of passivity accepted by most and instead speak up with their peers.

Igniting the intrinsic motivation of enlightened self-interest is a multi-step process, one that accelerates noticeably with an exploration of the costs or impacts of the mistreatment. Through this process, students come to see how cruelty, bullying, and violence affect not only the targets and the aggressors, but the bystanders and the people they care most about. The process also includes giving students an opportunity to explore how other change agents throughout history—Dr. Martin Luther King Jr., Cesar Chavez, Rosa Parks, Mahatma Gandhi, Susan B. Anthony, Nelson Mandela, and less well-known figures—have become dissatisfied with the status quo and committed to change it, one action at a time. Through these experiences, students learn about the "power of one" and become ready to be Safe School Ambassadors and agents of social change.

If students are to say "*yes!*" and embrace this new role, they also need to see the big picture. How will ambassadors treat each other when they next encounter each other in the halls, classrooms, or school yard? What kind of support will I get? What kind of follow-up is there? When will they next meet? In the training, they learn more about that big picture and the support they will get as ambassadors.

Providing Support After the Training   Over the course of the two-day training, students come to understand how the SSA program actually works. Students are introduced to the ongoing small-group meetings called family groups. They hear about the next large-group gatherings of ambassadors and future training opportunities. They also learn about documenting their interventions and how they will be acknowledged for their contributions.

Students learn how the adults who have been in the training with them will become their family group facilitators. The training also provides concrete experiences that show the students that the adults involved are genuinely interested in their well-being and will be there for them when needed.

The Ambassador's Job Description

Once students are enrolled in being ambassadors, they learn the four parts of the role or job they are considering taking on:

- Notice
- Think
- Act
- Follow through

Notice   Since we can't stop what we can't see, the first responsibility of an ambassador is to notice mistreatment. The training helps students become more alert to the five types of mistreatment that are defined and discussed in Chapter One. After discussing and describing examples of the five types of mistreatment that occur on their campus, the students can more clearly discern when this kind of behavior is occurring. The training gives them a common language for these incidents, and they therefore notice more and are able to intervene. What had before been seen as normal or gone unnoticed now stands out for the newly trained ambassadors. Once they have noticed and named it, they can think about what they've seen and how to respond.

Think   Ambassadors have a healthy self-preservation instinct. That's often one of the reasons they acquired the high social capital that got them identified for the training in the first place. In practical terms, this means that before saying or doing anything to intervene, they consider three questions:

- Is it safe? (Can I do this and not get hurt?)
- Is my reputation going to be harmed? (Can I do this and maintain my status among my friends?)
- Will it be effective? (Is doing this likely to work and achieve the results I want?)

By asking these questions, ambassadors learn to think critically about different aspects of a situation they have noticed. With practice, they make these assessments in an instant, which becomes habitual as the skill of discernment.

They need to assess each situation and decide what (or whether an) action might be appropriate to take. For example, they determine their relationship to and level of comfort with the people involved. They also consider the environment and who else is around. If they can answer these questions with a yes, they take action.

Act   Once ambassadors have noticed mistreatment and thought about it, they can take action to stop it or improve the situation and defuse tensions. Ambassadors use their acquired skills with their peers, in the moment and on the spot. As they do more interventions and these are successful, their confidence grows. Ambassadors learn that they can use these skills and remain safe, cool, and effective. (The particular skills ambassadors learn and use are described in a later section.)

Follow Through   There are several situations in which the interventions ambassadors do require follow-up. Ambassadors sometimes notice an act of mistreatment and do nothing in the moment but may want to follow up later. Many incidents ambassadors notice and act on have prior histories, while others are not completely resolved after the intervention. That's why it's important for them to follow through. Therefore, after supporting a target of mistreatment, they need to go back and check to see how the target is doing or if she or he needs any further help. Follow-through also means keeping an eye on a conflict that wasn't completely resolved and could flare up again and getting help if needed.

Here are a couple of examples of situations where ambassadors had to follow through. In one of them, an ambassador noticed a girl was always left out of a game and sat watching on the sidelines. She walked up to the other girls who were playing and said, "Hey, guys, how about both of us get in the game too?" She did this for a couple of days. The next week, she went back to see if the excluded girl was still being included in the game.

In the other example, two boys were wrestling around with each other in the quad. An ambassador noticed this, walked up to them, and asked, "Is everything cool, guys?" In this situation, if one of the two boys was being targeted and didn't like what was going on, it is unlikely that he would speak up and say he was having a problem. If he had little power, he would likely say that everything was fine to save face. The ambassador checked in with the weaker student later and said, "Hey, I saw what was happening with you guys. Is everything really okay?"

With Whom to Take Action?

In the training, ambassadors come to understand and learn to identify the five types of mistreatment discussed in Chapter One: exclusion, put-downs, bullying, unwanted physical contact, and acts against everyone. They learn their role: to notice, think, act, and follow through. Outside the training, as they think and analyze each act of mistreatment they notice in order to determine the most effective response, they must consider how well they know the people involved. This concept can be illustrated through four concentric circles, each representing the different degrees of connection ambassadors have with the people they will be working with: self, friends and family, classmates and acquaintances, and anyone else in the school or community (see Figure 8.1).

It is important to remember that ambassadors are chosen because they are socially influential individuals within a certain group. It is within their groups, where they have the strongest relationships, that the ambassadors have the greatest power to influence others. Thus, these circles represent the degree of influence an ambassador is likely to have with that group or person *based on connection or relationship.* The closer to the center the person is, the more likely the ambassador is to be effective. The farther from the center the person is, the less influence the ambassador will have. Obviously, as ambassadors gain *confidence* and *competence,* they increase their ability to influence people in the outer circles.

It is important to note that these circles of influence also correspond to the level of safety ambassadors experience when they intervene. Friends and family are more likely to be receptive to the ambassador's guidance and are less likely to retaliate in anger. By contrast, going up to a member of a rival group or gang and telling her or him what to do is likely to lead to trouble. For these reasons, ambassadors are directed to begin working with people in the inner circles until they have the skills to effectively and safely extend their influence to people in the outer circles.

Self   Ambassadors have to "walk their talk." They have to watch how they themselves behave and speak because their credibility is compromised if they are perceived as being hypocritical. Their peers are less likely to listen to their words about stopping mistreatment if they are known for using put-downs or

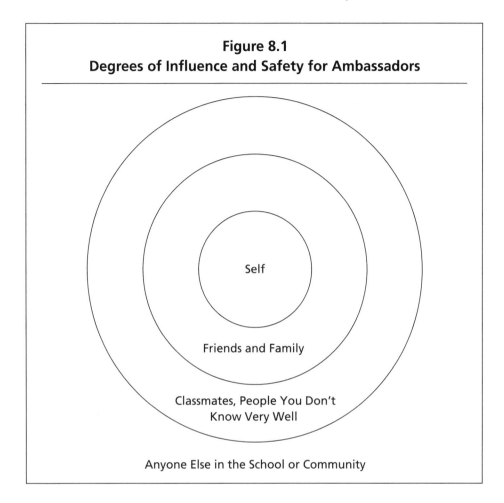

Figure 8.1
Degrees of Influence and Safety for Ambassadors

Self

Friends and Family

Classmates, People You Don't
Know Very Well

Anyone Else in the School or Community

intimidating others. Ambassadors need to be positive role models who act with integrity and are not part of the problem but part of the solution. In fact, many ambassadors report that being an ambassador has helped them become "a better person."

At the end of a Safe School Ambassadors training conducted at a high school in Florida, Eli, an eleventh grader, spoke about what this meant to him: "I didn't know I was a bully until I went through this training. It gave me a chance to see myself in a new way. My teasing, my humor . . . it was mean. I mean, people laughed and all, but it was mean. I see that now, and I'm changing that."

Friends and Family   From this foundation of integrity, ambassadors begin to say and do things to the people closest to them: their friends and family members. They already have relationships and history or "chips in the bank" with these people, and these "chips" are part of the social capital that gives ambassadors the ability to influence others. Some ambassadors will say they are *more* comfortable speaking up within that second circle, and others will say they are *less* comfortable, but either way, those existing relationships make friends and family more likely to listen to and value what the ambassadors have to say.

In addition, ambassadors are likely to be more successful intervening with friends and family because that history and prior knowledge gives them the ability to say things that are relevant to the people they are working with. For example, if an ambassador encounters a friend who is embroiled in a confrontation that is escalating, and wants to cool things down by pointing out some consequences of continuing the conflict, there are many possible consequences to choose from. Saying "You'll get suspended" might not matter to a student who has been suspended frequently, and thus wouldn't be that effective. But if the friend is a key member of the basketball team who has an important game coming up on Friday, saying "You won't be able to play in Friday's game" might carry more weight. Likewise, if the friend's parents are very strict and the friend has been on the edge of being grounded for poor choices lately, it might be more impactful to say "Look, if you keep going with this and get busted, your dad is gonna ground you for weeks!" For these reasons, it is with friends and family that ambassadors will be safer and more effective, especially at the outset.

Classmates and Acquaintances   These are people whom ambassadors know but not as well as close friends. They may be in the same classes or belong to the same large club or team. Because they are not as familiar to the ambassadors, there aren't so many "chips" to rely on. With this group, ambassadors have to be more thoughtful about whether and how to intervene. There are many situations where ambassadors can be effective working with this group, but there are also many in which they may choose to remain uninvolved. Degrees of safety, influence, connection, and emotional intensity vary widely, and ambassadors learn to assess each situation and select interventions carefully when they choose to act with this circle of people.

Anyone Else in the School or Community   Ambassadors can be effective even with people they don't know very well and are connected to only because they attend the same school or live in the same neighborhood. However, they may not be as comfortable taking action. For interventions with these people to be effective, ambassadors cannot rely on their relationships, they must rely on their skills. In these situations, the choice of words, tone of voice, and body language largely determine the success of the intervention and the safety of the ambassador. Therefore, ambassadors are taught to not intervene in any situation or with any people unless they feel sufficiently safe and believe they can be effective.

Ambassador Actions: Skills for Stopping Mistreatment

The average bullying incident lasts thirty-eight seconds. To the target, these thirty-eight seconds can seem like an eternity of feeling pain or being in fear. But if someone speaks up against the bullying, the time of the average incident drops by more than 70 percent, from thirty-eight seconds to just ten seconds.[1] In the usual bystander culture, many caring students do not speak up when they witness mistreatment. Why not? As mentioned in Chapter Six, many students will say, "I don't know what to say or do." The SSA training tackles that objection directly. It equips students with effective, practical, and field-tested actions that students can use with their peers, in the moment, to interrupt or stop the mistreatment they notice.

These actions can be used when someone is being excluded, put down, harassed, bullied, or even when there is some unwanted physical contact. Some can be used with the aggressor, others work better with the target, and still others work well with both. Some work with the heart and the emotions of the moment, and others work with the head and the thoughts of the rational mind. Some are serious and forceful, and others lighter and even humorous. One of the actions can be used when the incident is too big, complicated, or dangerous for a young person to handle alone. Together, these actions are like the tools on a carpenter's tool belt, providing the ambassadors with a range of options they can use to handle different situations.

Many of the interventions ambassadors use are designed to prevent mistreatment from escalating. For example, offering a supportive comment can take some of the pain out of a put-down or other hurtful act, which might prevent the target from wanting to retaliate. Counseling restraint might also stop an aggressor from continuing to harass the target or others.

This part of the chapter describes five intervention strategies, or actions, that ambassadors are trained to use to prevent, interrupt, or stop mistreatment:

- Distracting
- Balancing
- Supporting
- Reasoning
- Getting help

These are not all the skills ambassadors learn in the training. Other skills are included that meet the developmental needs and abilities of elementary, middle, and high school ambassadors.

Each action is introduced here through a brief story of a young person who has used the strategy.

Action 1: Distracting

> Someone in class was making mean comments about another student in my class. They were going back and forth for a while, and the situation was getting more serious. I said a joke so the whole class could hear, and everyone laughed. I know I was effective because the two students didn't say anything more to each other.
>
> —Toni, eleventh grade, California

> A girl was being cornered at her locker by a few other girls who were bullying and scaring her. I went up to one of the bullies and started a conversation. When I did this, the girl being bullied slowly left the situation.
>
> —Sandra, eighth grade, New York

Probably the simplest action an ambassador can take to interrupt an act of cruelty or mistreatment is to distract someone from the situation. Distracting is the act of changing the subject or focus of an interaction, often with humor or a simple request or comment. Distracting can often include the act of physically separating the people involved—not by force but by guile, request, suggestion, or invitation. Distracting can be used to stop exclusion, put-downs, bullying, unwanted physical contact, and sometimes even acts against the school community.

Here are some ways ambassadors have distracted others in different types of mistreatment situations:

• *Put-down situation.* In class, a small group of girls was sitting behind a fellow student named Christina. They were talking about Christina behind her back but loud enough for Christina to hear them: "Did you see what Christina is wearing today? I can't believe she would wear that." Another girl said: "Yeah, looks like she buys her clothes at the Salvation Army." Then they all laughed. An ambassador interrupted and distracted the group by asking them, "Hey, guys, did you see *American Idol* last night? (Pause) You didn't? I can't believe you missed it. It kicked ass. It's on again tonight. You've got to check it out." Then the students began to talk about something else.

• *Bullying situation.* A group of guys were cornering Jacob near his locker at school. Jacob looked nervous and afraid. An ambassador distracted in this situation by saying: "Hey, guys, did you all get what Mr. Adams told us to do for our assignment? Were we supposed to do all the questions at the end of the lessons, or just the even ones?" In other situations ambassadors have said things such as, "Hey, guys, look out, the principal's around the corner!" or "Hey, I heard they're giving away bags of chips in Ms. Garcia's room!"

Although distracting interrupts an act of cruelty, it does not resolve the underlying problem or issue between the target and the aggressor. After using a distraction, ambassadors might say or do other things that are likely to have more lasting effects; these interventions are described later in this chapter.

• *Unwanted physical contact.* Most young people don't want to get in a fight when they confront one another. If they really wanted to fight, they would immediately jump to physically hurting one another or throwing punches. This immediate move to physical contact rarely occurs, particularly with younger teens. More often, these students will "square off," exchange words, begin posturing, and then start pushing one another. When this happens, other students often see the developing situation and begin to gather around and encourage it by yelling: "Fight! Fight! Fight!" or "Go! Go! Go!" The students squaring off then find themselves in a difficult and pressure-filled situation. Backing down at that point would cause each of them to lose face and status. Word would quickly spread that they were too afraid to fight. Ambassadors have reported that they used distraction by changing the subject and moving one of the potential combatants out of the confrontation, an intervention that helps both students save face. The ambassador doing the distraction also shows the aggressor that the target is not friendless or alone and therefore is not a perfect target.

Action 2: Balancing

> A bunch of us were just hanging out on the steps in front of school like we always do. A group of Mexican kids walked by, and one of my friends made a racist comment, something about like how they're a bunch of low lifes, and I could just tell that some of the other people were going to go off on that. So before any of them jumped in, I said, "Yeah, well, I dunno about that, but you know Miguel Garcia, man, he played soccer with me, and he kicked some butt. He was one of the best guys on our team." A couple of people laughed because it was almost funny, but then the guy who'd started it came back with: "Yeah, that's Miguel, but the rest of them are scum." And I just said something kinda casual like, "Well, whatever, think what you want, but it's not what I know," and left it like that. Then I started talking with one of the guys about something else, and it just kinda ended. And since then, they haven't been saying that kind of stuff any more.
>
> —Scott, tenth grade, Colorado

Many young people have been in the presence of friends and heard someone put down another person who is not around, spread a rumor, or "talk trash about someone," as it is often called. The tendency is for those nearby either to say nothing or to add other negative comments about the target. This ambassador action involves countering a negative comment with a positive comment in order to balance such a put-down. It does not involve telling someone that he or she is wrong or directly challenging the person who made the comments. It is the simple act of offering a comment, often from personal experience or belief, that "puts-up" or balances the put-down. In effect, it says, "My experience is different from yours." This helps prevent the negative comments from spreading and becoming "the truth." In the minds of other students. ambassadors have used balancing to redirect a rumor, racist remark, negative gay comment, or other put-down about a person or a group.

In one situation a student said, "I can't believe Margie. She thinks she is so-o-o smart. She is such a stuck-up snob." An ambassador interjected: "You know what, Margie was in my summer program, and I saw her a lot. She was really easy to talk to and funny! I mean, she had some hilarious stories." Ambassadors can act quickly with a balancing comment before the negative talk can escalate or gain credibility.

The skill of balancing can serve adults as well. One evening I was in a store purchasing staplers the night before a scheduled training. When I placed all the staplers on the counter, a woman behind me asked, "So why are you buying so many staplers?" I replied: "I'm conducting a training session tomorrow of a large group of teens." She said: "Teens? Oh, boy, I sympathize. Teens can be such a pain, I have this nephew of mine, and he is such a nuisance. He thinks he knows it all, and he doesn't care about anything it seems." You can imagine she probably expected me to agree with her by saying, "Yeah, you're right," or to side with her by adding to the put-downs. Instead, I said: "Well, I've worked with thousands of teens around the country, and my experience is most young people really care a lot about what is going on. Most teens I've met want to make a difference. They just don't know how to do it, and they need our help. Most of the teens I have worked with are amazing, caring, and creative people." The woman paused and then replied, "Well, I know all teens aren't bad. I do have this niece who is really sweet."

This skill of balancing works best when the target of the put-down or rumor is not around to hear it. But sometimes the target is nearby and the aggressor is deliberately trying to hurt his or her feelings. This is a situation in which ambassadors may have to say something directly to the target, using the next action: supporting.

Action 3: Supporting

> Alex was made fun of a lot because he has glasses and talks a little funny. He was a freshman too, so the seniors made fun of him sometimes. Alex wasn't very coordinated either. For fun, he mostly did school work or stuff on the computer. I mentioned to him that there

is a golf team at our school. I told him he should go out for the team, and since I was already on it, I told him that I could show him the ropes. It turned out that he liked golf and improved a lot. I'm looking forward to playing golf with him next year. I think I was successful at supporting him because it made other people realize that he's good at sports, and most people favor athletes and recognize them more. Alex made a lot more friends from our school and from other schools because of golf.

—Marcus, ninth grade, California

Students who have been mistreated are put into an unhealthy and unstable emotional state. When left alone, the hurt they feel can become more painful and affect their self-concept and self-esteem. In most incidents of school violence, students had been mistreated before they took revenge. Their pain had escalated to rage and then into a desire to retaliate. This pain-rage-revenge cycle demonstrates the need for and potential power of stepping in to relieve some of the pain, which interrupts the cycle. In this action, a target's pain is defused by having an ambassador empathize with him or her.

Exhibiting empathy is a large part of the power of showing support, and the effect of support is much greater than it initially may appear. Many young people naturally understand how to offer support and show another person that they care. Supportive comments or gestures can make a big difference and have a significant effect on the person who needs to hear something supportive or validating.

Like balancing, supporting does not challenge the aggressor directly. Supporting also is not based on putting others down. For example, if someone is being excluded, the ambassador would not want to support by saying, "Don't worry about them. They're just a bunch of losers! You wouldn't want to waste your time with them anyway." A statement like that adds to an unhealthy climate and perpetuates the cycle of mistreatment. It may also create a problem later and cause a situation to escalate if it gets back to someone that the ambassador called the aggressors "a bunch of losers." It is important to say things that will contribute to reducing the amount of pain and mistreatment, not add to it.

A more productive alternative is to say, "You know, I've been left out of things before too, and it stinks." This shows empathy and understanding, which can reduce some of the pain. Another example is, "Hey, they've left a lot of other people out of things before. They're just like that sometimes." This helps the target not to take it personally and does so by offering objective data (they've left other people out) rather than by putting down the aggressors.

Supporting works in a number of situations:

• *After a put-down.* Supporting can often be used in combination with another action, such as distracting. After distracting an aggressor during a put-down, an ambassador turned to the target and said, "Hey, she says mean stuff like that sometimes. I hope you don't think that comment is true. I don't."

Vanessa, an eleventh grader in California, told us how she used distracting followed by supporting: "I intervened in a situation when my math teacher was putting down a male classmate and saying things like: 'You're too dumb' and 'You'll never graduate.' I used a distraction in this situation by asking the teacher for some help with understanding the homework assignment she just gave. The teacher answered my question and walked back to her desk. Then I supported the student by saying: 'Hey, don't sweat her. I know you're a smart guy, and you're going to graduate with all of us.' Now that student does his work, and the teacher doesn't pick on him anymore."

Using distraction first to interrupt an act of cruelty often provides the ambassador with the opportunity afterward to offer authentic and appropriate support to the target without risking the ridicule or wrath of the aggressor.

• *After bullying.* In bullying situations, showing support can help the target bounce back more quickly. It can also help a target to understand that he or she is not alone, which helps prevent the further loss of self-esteem. Aggressors often target those who have little social capital. However, when aggressors see a target being supported by someone else, their perception of that target can change: they are less likely to see that student as vulnerable and therefore less likely to bully this person. The following comments are some things ambassadors have said to show support to a target of bullying:

"I saw what she did, and that was really mean."

"Do you know he's done that to other people too? I've seen him. Hang in there, okay?"

"It's really annoying when people do that kind of thing. It's happened to me."

- *After unwanted physical contact.* Support can still be offered when a situation involves unwanted physical contact. When a student has tripped another student or touched someone inappropriately, ambassadors have offered support by saying:

"Wow. People can be mean sometimes. I don't like what they did either."

"That sucked, what they did. I hope you don't think that everyone is like that around here."

"That was a cheap shot. Are you okay?"

Action 4: Reasoning

> These two girls were arguing, and they were going to fight. I told them that what they were arguing about wasn't worth fighting over. They would lose their trip to Magic Mountain and would get in trouble, so they may not be able to graduate from middle school this year. The two stopped, and they never got into a fight again.
>
> —Adrian, sixth grade, California

The human body's physiological response to an upsetting incident shifts the focus of brain activity from the thinking part of the brain to the feeling and reflexive parts—the classic fight-or-flight response. When people are angry, they can be considered "out of their minds" because they are not thinking clearly. By using reasoning, ambassadors can help someone think and not just react, which could prevent this person from doing something he or she might later regret.

Most students and adults can probably recall a time when they were so upset or angry that they said or did something they later regretted. They were likely in a state where they were not thinking clearly. In hindsight, most students say they might have appreciated it if someone had said or done something that made them stop and think about what they were doing or about to do.

Even if a student is unlikely to regret an act of cruelty, ambassadors may be able to get someone to think about other options or consider the consequences of their actions. Bringing attention to an act of aggression can highlight its ugliness and may help an aggressor see that some actions are not within acceptable norms or not what they really want to be doing.

One eighth-grade girl wanted to get back at another person by spreading a rumor. The trained ambassador reasoned with her by asking, "Is that really true about her?" She continued by saying, "I've had rumors spread about me, and it upset me when I heard them. How would you feel if someone spread an untrue rumor about you?" In that moment, the girl may not have cared about how she would feel or how the person she wanted to hurt would feel; she may have even been intent on hurting the other person. But by speaking to the girl about her plans, the ambassador got her to pause, rethink her plan, and choose a different action.

Through reasoning, ambassadors help aggressors know that other options are available. Ambassadors show that the consequences could really matter to the aggressor, such as being grounded, suspended, or not able to play with the rest of the team at the upcoming game. By reasoning with aggressors, ambassadors help them see that their actions might not be worth the consequences, thereby influencing aggressors to make a different choice.

Having an Exit Strategy   There are times when even the most well-planned interventions don't have the desired result. After a few verbal exchanges, it can become apparent that reasoning is going nowhere or that the proffered support is unwanted. For any number of reasons, the aggressor (or even the target) can flash with emotion and can turn on the ambassador. When this happens, the ambassador's goal shifts from helping others to self-protection.

To help ensure their physical and emotional safety, ambassadors learn an exit strategy—a combination of words and actions that help ambassadors safely remove themselves from situations in which they feel uncomfortable, perhaps because they are being ignored, challenged, or even threatened. In the words of ambassadors, this exiting might sound like:

"Hey, Sean, just tryin' to keep things cool."

"Look, I just don't want to see you guys get kicked out of school; waste of time, man."

"I'd hate to see you do something you'd regret later, but it's your call."

Words like these signal a withdrawal of influence by the ambassador. It's all done gently, without anyone losing face. The words are accompanied by a gesture that signals "no aggression" and also protects the ambassador: hands are held up at chest level and close to the body, with palms open toward the others involved. Experience shows that this type of exit helps ambassadors practice the wisdom embedded in knowing the difference between what they can change and what they can't.

If ambassadors encounter situations that they are not willing or able to handle or that are too dangerous, they know they have to turn to other resources. In these cases, they use an exit strategy to get out of the situation and then go about getting the appropriate adult help.

It is not an ambassador's job to step in and physically break up fights. Their job is to intervene with their friends and those they know well first and foremost. The role of the ambassador is like that of a country's ambassador. Ambassadors for countries do not step into the middle of the violent battlefield and ask armies to stop shooting at each other. Similarly, Safe School Ambassadors do not step into the middle of violent conflicts and tell the combatants to stop.

Action 5: Getting Help

This is the only action ambassadors are taught in the training that requires adult involvement. Getting help involves taking action by communicating with an adult whom ambassadors trust to help them deal with situations that are beyond their own comfort zone. For example, if ambassadors find out about a weapon on campus, an impending fight, drug dealing or drug use, or another threat to the campus, or even a potential suicide attempt, getting help becomes the best action to take.

Youth often believe that speaking to an adult about incidents like these is snitching. The SSA program training helps the students involved to challenge and shift that belief. They learn that snitching or tattling occurs when students go to an adult to get someone in trouble, usually about something small. Getting help occurs when students go to an adult to prevent or get someone out of trouble, usually about something big. The SSA program training helps students to see this distinction and gives them many examples in which other ambassadors have gotten help and have been glad they did. By empowering these leaders as ambassadors and offering them the action of getting help as one of the several tools available, they have a context for, and see the value of, involving adults.

Ambassadors have identified some of the most common situations they wouldn't want to handle on their own:

- Weapons on campus

- Threats

- Date rape

- Abuse (physical, emotional or verbal, or sexual)

- Drug or alcohol use or abuse

- Gang activity

- Eating disorders such as anorexia or bulimia

- Drug use and dealing

- Self-mutilation or cutting

- Fights

- Family issues like divorce, death, or abuse

- Suicide or depression

- Vandalism

- Stealing

As volunteers, ambassadors feel a strong responsibility to stop bullying and violence, and they have learned many ways to do this. So when they realize they need to tell adults, we have seen that ambassadors become comfortable with and feel natural in taking the action of getting help as one of the many actions they could take. The examples that follow show situations when ambassadors took the action of getting help and believed they made the right decision.

> At a football game, a group of students walked by and said they were going to jump my friends after the game, and instead of going after them, I talked to a school resource officer. I don't know what the officer did, but he did something because my friend didn't get jumped.
> —Marcus, tenth grade, Florida

> I tried to get these older boys to stop messing with this freshman at the bus stop. I tried reasoning with them, but they wouldn't let up.

I talked to my coach about it, and it turns out he knew the older guys. He talked to them, and they stopped.

—Phil, tenth grade, California

My friend and I overheard a boy saying that he was going to stab someone. We even saw the knife. We got help. We quietly let a teacher know. The boy didn't get stabbed. I feel like I saved his life.

—Marissa, seventh grade, California

A friend of mine was with me at the school dance. He was talking about how he wanted to kill himself, and he really looked serious. I got help by talking to the counselor. I feel like I was effective and did the right thing because my friend is still alive today.

—Jackie, sixth grade, New York

There are many examples of students' not bringing information forward to adults, perhaps based on the mistaken view of telling as snitching, that have resulted in tragedy. In most school shootings, at least some students knew about the attacker's plans before they were carried out, but these students did not share that information with people who might have been able to help.[2] Students maintained the code of silence. Recent history provides one such example.

On March 21, 2005, Jeff Weise walked into Red Lake High School in northern Minnesota. Weise, a sixteen-year-old student at the school, first shot and killed an unarmed security guard who tried to stop him at the school's entrance. Weise then went on a shooting spree. Before taking his own life, he had killed one teacher and five students and wounded seven other students, some critically. Law enforcement officers later discovered that Weise had shot and killed his grandfather and a friend of his grandfather before coming to school that day. Ten months later, U.S. attorney Thomas Heffelfinger met with school authorities and families of the victims to share specifics about the killings that came out during the subsequent investigation. Heffelfinger reported that as many as thirty-nine people knew something about Weise's plans before the shooting rampage—some for more than a year.[3] If any one of those thirty-nine had gone to an adult for help, they could have saved many lives.

Examples of getting help include:

- Speaking to a trusted adult alone about what was seen or heard, who was or is involved, and where it was or is happening
- Leaving a note on the desk or in the mailbox of a teacher, counselor, or principal
- Making a phone call to a hot line or to the police

Students often hesitate to get help because they are worried that their peers would find out and retaliate. Therefore, when talking about the action of getting help, it is important for ambassadors to hear *the adults at the school* speak about the district and school policies on confidentiality in these situations and exactly how these reports from students are handled. Ambassadors need to know that every effort will be made to preserve their anonymity when they do seek adult help.

Once ambassadors are active in a school, the culture begins to change and the code of silence loses its grip. Because of these changes, other students become more willing to speak up and bring information forward. Getting help becomes not just an ambassador action but something many students are willing to do. Two years after launching the SSA program in one California school, a student reported to an administrator the details of two other students' plans to bomb the school. The reporting student was not an ambassador, and administrators credit the program with shifting the norms on campus so it became socially acceptable to break the code of silence.

Overcoming Disbelief

Equipping ambassadors with these five and other effective nonviolent communication and intervention skills provides them with tools they need to address bullying and violence. But knowledge and even competence by themselves are not always enough to overcome the disbelief some ambassadors have. The premise—that nonviolence is possible and that individuals speaking up with their friends to promote tolerance and peace can make those the norms of a school community—is so countercultural that some of them find it hard to integrate this new way of being into their personality. In our experience of training thousands of students using this approach, we find that they sometimes need a little help believing that it will work and that they can do it. That help comes in the form of exploring, at the teachable moments in the training, three main reasons this model resonates with youth.

First, students feel comfortable using these skills and can adapt them to their individual language and style. Although the model provides a framework for each action, ambassadors learn the *framework* and then plug their *own language* into it. Through extensive simulation of real acts of mistreatment, ambassadors practice interventions and find comfortable language that fits the framework. Detailed analysis of each role play, by fellow students and an experienced trainer, provides ambassadors with specific feedback to help them improve. For these reasons, ambassadors' interventions are seen as authentic, are therefore credible, and therefore are effective.

Second, most of these actions can be done without an adult present. Ambassadors use the actions of distracting, balancing, supporting, and reasoning most often. Interestingly, these are the actions that they can take on their own without adult involvement. Ambassadors can use these four actions to address the four types of mistreatment most common at schools: exclusion, put-downs, bullying, and some cases of unwanted physical contact. Ambassadors use the action of getting help primarily to address unwanted, violent physical contact and acts against everyone. So getting help will be used less frequently but will still have a tremendous impact on the students and on the school climate. Chala, a twelfth grader in California, said, "I've been in a lot of trainings, but what you have given me is stuff that works. Now I have what I need to make things better for people. I got something that I can really use and I feel good about using it." In essence, the process of empowering young people with these skills helps to meet their need to have a sense of purpose, a sense of power, and a sense of place (a feeling of ownership).

Another important by-product of taking action is the effect these interventions can have on bystanders nearby. When students speak out, they challenge the norm that it's cool to be cruel. When these socially influential opinion leaders, the ambassadors, speak out, they begin to shift those norms over time, replacing "it's cool to be cruel" with "it's cool to care." This alters the school's social and emotional climate. Margaret, a seventh grader in California, said, "I found that I didn't even have to tell my friends how to act. They saw how I was acting and that I wasn't putting up with people hurting each other. When they saw this, they weren't as mean. And they would start helping others too." When ambassadors come to understand how this process works, they find it easier to take on the role of *being* ambassadors.

Providing Ongoing Supervision and Support Through Family Groups

The family group is a critical element of the Safe School Ambassadors program. Ambassadors are volunteers who are doing something that goes against the popular culture and is not always understood or appreciated. With each intervention, they are voluntarily risking their reputation or status and, in the worst case, their physical safety. Being an ambassador is a big "give," and they need an equally big "get" if they are to stay actively involved in the program. While some of what they get is the intrinsic reward or internal feeling of satisfaction they might feel after a successful intervention, experience has shown that it's not enough to sustain their commitment. For these reasons, ambassadors need and deserve support, particularly in the beginning when they are just starting out on this new path of being a norm changer.

At the beginning of their service, ambassadors have just been introduced to the intervention skills they'll use with their peers. Although they have some familiarity and even comfort with the skills, they are far from having mastered them. Because of their role as social leaders, the power of the training, and the strength of their commitment to be peacemakers, ambassadors will try to use their skills. If they try once but meet with resistance, try twice and meet with resistance, and perhaps repeat this pattern several times, they will likely question their effectiveness in this role and could become discouraged. People who volunteer or often go into new roles or risky situations need time to reflect, debrief, and process their feelings and get the support of others who have had similar experiences. Rookies in many professions have regular support groups they can attend. We have found that to be most effective, ambassadors need the safety net of a family group. It would be irresponsible to provide training and send them out without appropriate ongoing supervision and support.

The family group provides another important benefit to the SSA program and to the school as a whole. When students understand the difference between telling on people and getting help, they are more willing to come forward with information. What they need is a *receiver,* a trusted adult they can talk with, a person who understands the importance of preserving the anonymity of the ambassador. The family group facilitator provides that critical link between ambassadors and adults in the school.

The family groups are small: six to nine student ambassadors and one or two adults who act as facilitators with the students. These groups meet every two weeks, and sometimes more often, particularly in the month or so after the training and at the elementary school level.

The purpose of the family group is to provide the supervision and support the ambassadors need to succeed. Supervision is provided in these ways:

- Holding the ambassadors accountable by making sure that they are using what they know and that they adhere to a code of conduct

- Gathering information about what ambassadors are actually doing in the school, including the nature, frequency, and effectiveness of their interventions, which can be accomplished through written action logs or discussion

- Documenting what the ambassadors are doing, so that the aggregate results can be shared with key stakeholders and school decision makers to build support for the program

Support from the family group includes:

- Analyzing past interventions—those that worked and those that didn't

- Coaching and guiding the ambassadors so they can practice or plan interventions and continue to develop their skills and learn new ones

- Connecting ambassadors with each other and with adults who understand them, which meets their developmental needs for belonging and helps sustain their involvement

- Helping ambassadors keep the flame of their commitment burning despite temporary setbacks and discouraging encounters

While ambassadors share in the leadership of meetings in age-appropriate ways, the family group facilitator ensures that this support and supervision is provided. The facilitator must be an effective champion, cheerleader, and coach.

It is best to have regularly scheduled meetings during the school day. When ambassadors are afforded class time for these meetings, they see evidence that adults are investing in them and step into their roles with a deeper commitment. However, having class time for these meetings can be met with resistance because administrators or teachers, or both, are often reluctant to release ambassadors from instructional time.

Some schools try to fit in the meetings outside class time. However, meeting before or after school can create scheduling conflicts for ambassadors who ride a bus or participate in extracurricular activities. Ambassadors can be conflicted about meeting at lunch or on break time because they perceive it as their own time and naturally want to hang out with their friends. Moreover, these are the times ambassadors need to be out doing their jobs. It is extremely important for the family groups to meet regularly for the program to be effective and sustainable. Despite the challenges, schools are creative and find ways to make the meetings work.

In many schools, the regularity and continuation of the family group meetings ultimately determine whether the program thrives and expands. When the school aligns with the program and the family groups meet regularly and productively, the meetings become the place ambassadors recharge their batteries for another round of peacemaking.

Assessing and Measuring Program Effectiveness

Data drive decisions. With fewer dollars and resources available, especially to fund nonacademic initiatives, schools are increasingly assessing their programs to determine if their investments are yielding results. Programs that are sustained are the ones that demonstrate their effectiveness.

The SSA program uses a variety of assessment instruments to document the impact of the program on the ambassadors themselves, their peers, and the school as a whole. Some tools measure the ambassadors' activity level, while others measure the ambassadors' impact.

The tools for assessment include these:

- *Ambassador surveys.* If given before the training and again at the end of the school year, these can help identify changes in ambassadors' beliefs, attitudes, and behaviors over time. Appendix C contains an example.

- *Action logs* that ambassadors use to document the frequency, nature, and effectiveness of their interventions. Some schools make these into quarter-sheet pads that ambassadors can carry with them and access easily.

- *Climate surveys.* If given before the training and again at the end of the school year (or one year after the first administration), these can help determine if there have been any shifts in the social-emotional climate of the school over time.

- *Formal interviews* of key adults responsible for discipline at the school site, which provide another perspective on the climate of the school and factors that might have helped to change it.

- *Discipline data* that measure specific conditions or trends that ambassadors are likely to influence, including referrals, detentions, or suspensions that result from bullying, fights, and other mistreatment.

Statistical data are important indicators of program effectiveness, but so are the individual stories and examples that they represent. Chapter Nine provides a detailed overview of the effectiveness and impact of the Safe School Ambassadors program itself, with both data and anecdotal evidence.

Recognizing and Celebrating Ambassadors and Adults

To acknowledge and appreciate their ambassadors and reinforce their commitment, schools are encouraged to recognize their accomplishments and celebrate their successes in some way. One recognition event often takes place at the end of a school year, but others can be beneficial at key points *during* the year.

The agenda at a recognition event can include testimonials from students, a keynote speaker, and recognition for the ambassadors and adults. Often the media are invited and may publicly applaud students' accomplishments. A special meal or snacks may be served, which further demonstrates the value the community places on these students' service and commitment.

When the program has been implemented at more than one school in a district or region, it is very powerful and effective to bring youth and adults from all the schools together and honor them at a combined event. Throughout the year, some schools have hosted a picnic, sponsored a party, or arranged a field trip. Adults have also arranged for donated benefits, such as movie passes or restaurant coupons, to hand out with certificates.

Program advisors and family group facilitators often involve the students in planning these fun and educational special events and activities. Doing so provides additional opportunities for students to experience empowerment and refine their skills. It also helps ensure that the recognition is genuinely meaningful to the ambassadors themselves and not just something that the adults *think* the students would appreciate.

At one recognition lunch, a mother watched as her daughter was called to the front of the room to receive her certificate. She listened to the principal speak about her daughter's courage and leadership and heard her own child speak about how this experience had made a difference for her. Afterward, in a mixture of English and her native language but with crystal-clear gratitude, the mother said that she had never before heard the word *leader* and her daughter's name spoken in the same sentence. With tears in her eyes, she spoke of how proud she was that her daughter had become empowered, learned leadership skills, and turned away from the culture of gang violence in which she lived.

Conclusion

The Safe School Ambassadors program is a proven best practice that uses all seven elements of effective youth empowerment programs. Significant amounts of research and extensive field experience shaped the unique configuration of these elements that is presented in this chapter. The SSA program effectively engages student leaders and takes them from inspiration, to action, to results. Throughout the program, activities and meetings build positive relationships between the ambassadors and adults and foster increasing acceptance and understanding among diverse youth. Ambassadors improve school climate, reduce bullying and violence, and increase school safety. The next chapter provides evidence of this through the SSA program outcome data and more stories of ambassadors in action.

chapter

9

Results and Stories of Ambassadors in Action

> In the beginning, I used to like to make fun of people, but when I saw how it can affect others, I stopped and thought about their feelings. Now since we have the Safe School Ambassadors group, we can make a difference in people's perspectives of others. Every school should have this program, because one person can make a big difference.
>
> —EMILY, EIGHTH GRADE, LONG BEACH, CALIFORNIA

> In my twenty years in education, coaching and supporting student ambassadors has been the single most rewarding experience in my career.
>
> —KAREN BRESLAWSKI, STUDENT ASSISTANCE PROGRAM COORDINATOR, BROCKPORT, NEW YORK

THE PRECEDING THREE CHAPTERS HAVE outlined an innovative strategy for addressing the problem of peer mistreatment discussed in Part One of this book:

1. Identify and recruit the socially influential opinion leaders of a school's diverse cliques.

2. Help them awaken to the problem of mistreatment, understand its costs, and unleash their motivation to do something about it.

3. Equip them with powerful, nonviolent communication and intervention skills they can use with their peers, and provide them with supervision and support so they'll continue to sharpen those skills and stay committed.

The rationale or logic model at the core of this strategy goes on to say that students who have high social capital will use their skills to intervene with their peers when they witness or have heard about mistreatment, and as a result, the school's social-emotional climate will improve as discipline incidents decrease and attendance and academic achievement rise.

This chapter explores the degree to which positive outcomes occur. Do these Safe School Ambassadors use the skills they've learned? If enough of them do, will their interventions make a difference? In other words, can the inside-out approach really work?

Intervention Frequency and Effectiveness

> At the start of PE class, two boys were arguing and started pushing each other. I'm the TA [teaching assistant] in the class, so I walked up and asked one boy, "Hey, Marcus, when's the pep rally?" They stopped pushing long enough to answer me, and started in again. So then I asked something else, like, "What's it going to be about?" The boys stopped again, and one of them answered me, so I asked another question. Finally, one of them said, "Just forget it, dude," and walked away. I kept talking with the other boy.
>
> —MICHELLE, ELEVENTH GRADE, PERRIS, CALIFORNIA

If miniature video cameras could be placed on the shoulders of Safe School Ambassadors, the adults overseeing their work could review those tapes to count and assess their interventions. Until that becomes both ethical and practical, other methods will have to be used to determine what ambassadors do with the skills they've learned. These methods include action logs completed by the ambassadors, family group meetings, and year-end surveys.

Results from Action Logs

The simple forms that ambassadors complete to record their interventions capture important information:

- *What they notice.* By recording the different types of mistreatment they notice, ambassadors help adults see the prevalence of exclusion, put-downs, and bullying and help them better understand what's really going on in the social-emotional realm among students.

- *Where it happens.* This usually confirms that most mistreatment happens in places where adults aren't present and helps identify bullying hot spots. At Lawrence Middle School in Falmouth, Massachusetts, this information was used to determine the best places to post student-designed posters that named the offensive behaviors and reminded students that it was not okay to treat people that way.

- *What skills they are using.* Effective ambassadors use a full range of intervention skills, but most have a couple of interventions they are particularly comfortable using. By reviewing this information, group leaders can determine which skills are being used and in what ways further training might be beneficial.

- *How effective they were.* By rating each intervention on a 1-to-5 scale, ambassadors can notice where they need to sharpen their intervention skills. Was this a good response to the mistreatment I noticed? Was this a skill I need to improve? And group leaders can look at the overall effectiveness of each skill as a way of corroborating the need for further training.

Here are several examples of what action logs have revealed about whether ambassadors use the skills they have learned and how they rate their own effectiveness on a scale of 1 to 5:

- Riverside Middle School, New Castle, Colorado: rural, grades 5 to 8; population approximately 400 students. Safe School Ambassadors documented 258 interventions in the 110 school days between November 14, 2003, and May 18, 2004. These interventions directly involved 850 students as targets or aggressors (some obviously involved several times). In addition, 626 students witnessed the interventions. Average effectiveness: 3.86.

- Winter Springs High School, Winter Springs, Florida: suburban, grades 9 to 12; population approximately 2,700 students. Ambassadors documented 52 interventions in the 24 school days between April 12 and May 13, 2004. More than 168 students were directly involved as targets or aggressors, and more than 289 students witnessed the interventions. Average effectiveness: 4.09.

- Santa Rosa Middle School, Santa Rosa, California: urban, ethnically diverse, grades 7 and 8; population approximately 800 students. Ambassadors documented 178 interventions in the 62 school days between September 17 and

December 17, 2004. These interventions directly involved 434 students as targets or aggressors, and 683 students witnessed the interventions. Average effectiveness rating: 3.75.

Using an average of thirty active ambassadors for each of these three schools, these ambassadors documented on action logs approximately 0.4 interventions per ambassador per day, or 2 per week. This underrepresents the number of actual interventions, however, because ambassadors do not, in practice, record every intervention they do. Many students have a distinct distaste for paperwork and don't want to bother pulling out the action log form. Also, many of the interventions are subtle, spontaneous, and quick. They become a natural part of the way these students conduct themselves, and so they become less noticeable even to the students themselves.

We have used three other strategies to help determine an average daily intervention rate for ambassadors. In the first, ambassadors complete year-end surveys, in which they are asked to reflect back on the past five days of school and count the number of interventions they did. Over a three-year period, this strategy shows an average intervention rate of just over five per week, or one per day. In another strategy, at the end of family group meetings, the adult facilitators ask ambassadors to reflect back and count the number of interventions they did in the preceding three days. After adjusting for anomalies (if, for example, the ambassador was absent for one day), these estimates indicate an average intervention rate of just over two per day. The third strategy, interviews with active ambassadors, points toward an average intervention rate of approximately three per day. Using these figures, it appears that the action logs reflect somewhere between 13 and 40 percent of the interventions these students actually do.

Results from Family Group Meetings

Ambassadors need ongoing supervision and support if they are to continue using the skills they have learned in the training and eventually master and integrate them into their lives. The family group meeting is a more intimate setting in which six to nine students meet with one or two specially trained adults. These meetings provide another way to determine what students are actually doing with the intervention skills.

Many times ambassadors come to a family group meeting thinking they've done only a handful of interventions, but after reflection and discussion guided by the adult, they discover many more instances of using their skills. The meetings often include a "success round," in which the students take turns describing situations in which they have intervened. One student's report often triggers another student's memory of another intervention he or she had done. Meeting summary notes completed by the adult leaders consistently show that ambassadors are in fact using their skills regularly.

Results from Year-End Surveys

At the end of the school year, the adults and students involved in the SSA program complete surveys that provide valuable insights into the effectiveness and impact of the program. The surveys were first given in May 2002 and have since been distributed annually to every site with a program.

Year One: June 2002 In May 2002, a seven-question survey was distributed to twelve schools that had active SSA programs. Two middle schools and three high schools in California and Massachusetts were able to participate, returning surveys representing 105 ambassadors. The students were asked to estimate the number of times they intervened in a typical day and a typical week. This provided the raw numbers for a calculation of intervention frequency: 6.6 times per week on average.

Student respondents also reported examples of interventions they had done:

> Two guys walked into my American lit class having this loud argument. The teacher took them outside, and I guess she helped them work it out. But when they came back in, one guy tried to get the last word in and said something that got the other guy really mad, and a couple of people laughed a little. But before he could say anything and start up again, I said to both of them kinda loud, "So, looks like it's time to read *Huck Finn,*" which was the book we were reading. They both looked at me funny but took the hint and sat down.

> At lunch and after school, we play soccer a lot. One team is mostly Mexican, and the other is mostly white. There are lots of arguments,

and sometimes they get into fights. When that happens, I just say things like, "Hey, we all just want to play soccer. If we fight, they won't let us play. Let's work this out," or, "Just let it go; it's not worth fighting over." Then they mostly cool down and we play again.

In an open-ended question, students were asked to describe what, if any, effect the program had had on them. This structure permitted both positive and negative effects to be reported. More than 92 percent of ambassadors reported that the program had benefited them personally. The most common effects reported were increased tolerance and respect for differences, increased ability to resolve conflicts, more friends, better communication skills, and improved relationships with peers, parents, teachers, and other adults.

Year Two: June 2003   This year seventeen middle schools and eight high schools in California, Colorado, Florida, and New York returned surveys representing 384 ambassadors. The responses confirmed the information and trends that emerged from the first year's surveys. Ambassadors estimated performing more than 50,000 interventions, at a weekly average of 7.2 per ambassador per week. Exclusion and verbal abuse combined for more than two-thirds of the mistreatment reported. According to their responses, they felt that they needed adult help in only 19 percent of situations; the balance they were able to work out on their own.

Year Three: June 2004   This year, the survey was redesigned in collaboration with Omni Research and Training in Denver, Colorado, so intervention frequency numbers are not directly comparable with previous years. Thirty-five of 144 schools (24 percent) returned surveys, representing 656 ambassadors, 122 family group facilitators, and 72 program advisors. Intervention frequency data show that:

- 2.7 percent of ambassadors did not intervene at all in the month prior to the survey
- 77.1 percent intervened one to fifteen times
- 14.0 percent intervened sixteen to thirty times
- 6.2 percent intervened more than thirty-one times

Interventions in 2005–2006   Table 9.1 shows a small but representative sample of the interventions ambassadors reported on their 2006 year-end surveys. The situation the ambassador noticed is described in the second column. This prompted the response described in the third column, which had the impact noted in the fourth.

Table 9.1. Safe School Ambassador Interventions: Snapshots, 2005–2006

The Ambassador	The Situation	Ambassador Response	Effect or Impact
Age—14, female Grade—8th Santa Rosa Middle School, Santa Rosa, California	I was at a dance and I noticed a person sitting by themselves.	I basically asked them to come and join me and my friends and dance.	They began to have a lot of fun, and it made me feel good that I could help.
Age—13, male Grade—7th Basalt Middle School, Basalt, Colorado	Someone was leaving a person out of a game.	I started playing the game, so it was uneven teams, and they said I have to get another person to play so it would be even teams, so I picked the kid who was left out.	He was having fun in the game.
Age—12, female Grade—7th Oliver Middle School, Brockport, New York	A girl was called "Fatso" because she is slightly overweight.	I did active listening to listen to the girl's feelings, and I reasoned with the bully.	The aggressor said, "Sorry," to the target, and the girl felt better.
Age—15, female Grade—10th Pine Bush High School, Pine Bush, New York	People in my class were spreading rumors about another girl.	I asked them if they realized how mean they were being and then asked them to stop.	They stopped talking bad about the girl.

(continued)

Table 9.1. (*continued*)

The Ambassador	The Situation	Ambassador Response	Effect or Impact
Age—16, male Grade—10th Los Molinos High School, Los Molinos, California	There is a boy at our school that is different than others. He doesn't have many friends and is often alone, and kids often make fun of him.	I acknowledged his presence and was friendly when I saw him. I talked to him when he was alone and defended him when he was made fun of.	Toward the end of the year, he is a completely different guy. He's social, friendly, and stands up for himself.
Age—16, male Grade—11th Franklin High School, Elk Grove, California	I was at lunch. A kid was calling another kid of a different race derogatory remarks.	I told him that that wasn't cool and that he would feel bad if that kid was baggin' on him.	He stopped bullying the kid, and since then he has thanked me.
Age—12, male Grade—7th Basalt Middle School, Basalt, Colorado	Some people I knew were talking about beating up another kid who they didn't like.	I reasoned with them, reminding them of the consequences of their actions.	I think that this action was successful because they ended up not beating the kid up and leaving him alone.
Age—14, female Grade—8th Rifle Middle School, Rifle, Colorado	A girl had a hit list, and was threatening to bring her brother's gun to school.	I told her that it would ruin her life, and she didn't really want to do it; then I told a counselor.	Well, she didn't do it.
Age—13, female Grade—7th Mountain View Middle School, Lamont, California	My friend and I overheard a boy saying that he was going to stab someone. We even saw the knife.	We got help. We told a teacher or to be more specific an administrator.	The boy didn't get stabbed. I feel like I saved his life.
Age—15, female Grade—10th Brockport High School, Brockport, New York	A friend at the dance threatening suicide.	I got help from a counselor.	He is still alive.

Impact on Ambassadors

> With this program, I started just hanging out with different people, talking with them and whatever, and you learn. You learn that they're like you. Even though you might not see them on the outside like you, if you get to know them, they are.
>
> —EDDIE, TENTH GRADE, CALIFORNIA

If recruiting is done according to the model described in Chapters Seven and Eight, the students involved in this effort are the opinion leaders, trendsetters, and norm changers in a school. Other students notice and emulate what they say, do, and believe. In other words, they are at or near the center of a ripple effect. It is not far-fetched to assume that any changes in these ambassadors will ripple out across the general student population of the school. Surveys—at year end as well as pre- and posttraining—shed light on how the program has made an impact on the students involved in it, as do the hundreds of stories told by students and the adults who work with them.

Results from Year-End Surveys

The year-end surveys contain questions designed to assess how being involved in the program has affected the ambassadors themselves. The third-year responses, consistent with the two prior years, showed the percentage of students reporting improvements in:

- Empathy: 93.6 percent
- Acceptance of diversity: 90.1 percent
- Leadership skills: 94.0 percent
- Communication skills: 91.7 percent
- Grades: 68.7 percent
- Attendance: 68.4 percent

Survey responses from the adults in the program showed that they saw virtually identical results in their ambassadors.

Another way to assess how students are affected by being part of the school climate improvement efforts such as the one described here is to administer a survey prior to their involvement and then an identical survey at some point afterward, usually six to twelve months later. Several schools have used this pre- and postsurvey approach with their ambassadors, and the early results seem to confirm what the year-end surveys show. Although these findings need to be interpreted with caution due to the small sample sizes, presurvey and postsurvey data have shown these slight changes:

- Decreases in the number of ambassadors who teased or made fun of others
- Increases in the mistreatment ambassadors noticed
- Increases in the number of ambassadors who tried to help others who looked alone, isolated, sad, or depressed or were the targets of mistreatment
- Increases in the number of ambassadors who used various skills to redirect or challenge the aggressor
- Increases in the number of ambassadors who sought adult help for situations they did not feel qualified or equipped to handle on their own

Although some students reported that they had been teased or made fun of because of their interventions, none reported being physically harmed or feeling threatened as a result. And although these changes were slight, they are changes in the right direction. Moreover, they could reasonably be expected to increase in the second year since it takes a year for ambassadors to gain sufficient confidence through experience and coaching to intervene more regularly. These results are encouraging, although it is clear that more extensive research needs to be done in this area.

Ambassadors' Experiences

Year-end surveys quantify the individual actions of thousands of ambassadors in hundreds of schools. But although they allow us to make generalizations and see trends, they also filter out the details of how these actions have made a profound difference in the lives of individual students. Hundreds of stories fill in that missing information and shed light on the program's impact on the ambassadors themselves. Told by the students and the adults they work with, these stories reveal similar trends and themes. The ambassadors:

- Work through and overcome their own prejudices and stereotypes
- Gain confidence and life skills
- See their own behaviors in new ways and change behaviors accordingly
- Renounce violence

Busting Stereotypes   Despite the best efforts of educators and community members, too often schools reflect the racial divisions in our society. At one large, comprehensive high school of twenty-eight hundred students in San Bernardino County in southern California, tensions ran high between African American and Mexican American students, fueled by the activities of the more than seventy gangs that have been active in the community for generations. Several violent racial confrontations had occurred at the school in recent years, requiring police intervention and many arrests. In this environment, thirty-some students of all races began the Safe School Ambassadors training in February 2002.

One of the smaller working groups included Deszirre, an intense and dark-skinned African American girl whom many on the campus feared. It also included Elias, a quiet and powerful Latino boy whose gold chains and muscular physique sent a strong "don't mess with me" message to all in his presence. Steeped in the prejudices they had acquired from their families and friends, both began the training sitting back in their chairs with their arms crossed over their chests. Over the course of those two days, prompted by many of the activities they engaged in side-by-side, they began to see their commonalities, and those prejudices began to soften. The seeds of a friendship based on understanding and mutual respect were sown, and those seeds were cultivated in the family group meetings they attended regularly. Several months later, the two described how their friendship had affected the school. Deszirre noted, "I'm walking with my people, and I see Elias, so I say, 'Hey,' and he says, 'Hey,' back to me, and maybe I say, 'What's up?' and we talk for a minute. My people see that, and they see it every day, and they start to think, well, maybe those Mexicans aren't so bad." Elias agreed: "And my people see that I can get along with her, and they just think about it. Then they ask what's up with that, and I say she's okay, and then they aren't so quick to fight the blacks."

Samantha, an eighth grader at Basalt Middle School in Basalt, Colorado, spoke of how her eyes and heart opened: "I see people differently now. I see past the cliques, past the labels, past the color, and past the prejudice."

Confidence and Leadership   Jody, a seventh grader at Basalt Middle School, identified another common theme: "It's definitely given me more self-confidence." Seth Groveman, a counselor and program advisor at Palm Beach Central High School in Florida, agreed: "The program has given our ambassadors a tremendous boost in self-confidence. It makes them feel special, which doesn't happen to enough students in high school. It is amazing how proud they are to be selected, as they should be."

Kristin Greenstreet, counselor and SSA program advisor at Kathryn Señor Elementary School in New Castle, Colorado, noted that teachers have seen a difference in the ambassadors: "Instead of sitting idly by, the ambassadors speak up and take leadership. Each week teachers lead discussions on topics suggested by the counselor or the students themselves. Ambassadors are not just participants; they're big facilitators in these small group discussions."

Neil Williamson, dean at Belmont High School in the Los Angeles Unified School District, gave an example of the increase in self-confidence he has noticed: "One girl lives in a shelter downtown. She was born with a lot going against her, and she's struggled. But since she's become an ambassador, she's flourished. She sees that she has an important role, and she's really stepped up to it. She's intervened a lot within her peer group, and they've come to respect her even more, which has helped her tremendously." Josh Nowak, counselor at Valencia High School in Valencia, California, described how one of his ambassadors gained enough confidence and self-respect to confront a teacher about bad behavior in the classroom, and it helped the situation greatly.

These examples highlight that once ambassadors have discovered and experienced their capacities to affect and influence the behaviors and actions of their peers, they are ready and eager to tackle other issues they care deeply about. They first embrace their ambassador leadership roles, and through this, they develop increased ability and confidence to effect broader social change in the world. For example, one high school ambassador spent the summer between his junior and senior years in India, working on a project to help disadvantaged children. When he returned home, he reported that the impetus to go to India was a direct result of his having been a Safe School Ambassador since his sophomore year.

Empowering students as Safe School Ambassadors is more than a strategy to stop bullying and violence. The program experience also develops a generation of citizen leaders who want to make the world better than the one they inherited.

Awareness of Their Own Hurtful Behavior   Seth Groveman also pointed out that going through the training helps students think about the nature and consequences of their own hurtful behavior and helps them change it. Kristen Greenstreet described what happened to a boy at her school:

> When we were selecting kids to participate, one question mark for us was Timothy. He was not always the best example. He's had difficulties at home. He struggles with anger outbursts and getting into trouble since kindergarten, but he gets it and has a big heart. At first, after the training, he was a perfect role model and very active. In November, he started having problems again with his anger and inappropriate behavior. The kids and adults discussed whether to allow him to continue and decided he should. He lost privileges, but came to the Safe School Ambassador meetings anyway. At the meetings, he would own up to his behavior and what he should have done differently. The other students would encourage him, saying that he could do it. Since Christmas, he has greatly improved and is back on track to being a good example.

Jay, an eleventh grader in California, reports a similar impact: "I used to be one of the people that would tease and make fun and go along with the crowd and do what everybody else was doing. Not anymore. It's just like this overall feeling of satisfaction knowing that if this program has changed me, I know it can change other people." A family group facilitator at Valencia High School reported that "after the training, an ambassador spoke to a member of his group who was being teased and picked on. He told his friend that he thought that the teasing was wrong and that he was no longer going to participate. He reported to me that his friend was grateful, and it gave him the courage to ask the others to stop too, and they did."

Markham Middle School in the Los Angeles Unified School District is surrounded by housing projects, and students affiliated with one gang cannot safely exit the school grounds through the gates that lead into another gang's territory. Program advisor Maria Juaregi reported that "progress is being made. One student came to me and said he saw a fight and walked away. He told his friends, 'Come on, we don't need to see this.' While that may not sound like much, it's a huge change for that boy, and it must have had a big impact on his friends."

Renouncing Violence   Students who have been through the SSA training have also reported other huge changes. Standing with a group of his fellow ambassadors before a crowd of school officials, community leaders, and philanthropists in Los Angeles, Eric, an eighth grader at a nearby middle school, spoke of what it is like to be a third-generation gang member. He described the violence and the ever-present fear, and he showed the gang tattoos on his neck and knuckles. "But," he said, "I'm in a new gang now. I'm a Safe School Ambassador."

In a similar setting in northern California a few months later, Nancy, an eighth grader, described how she had come into her last year of middle school just hoping to make it through:

> I had a pretty rough seventh-grade year. I was always in trouble and almost got expelled. But, my principal invited me to be an ambassador. She had a lot of faith in me. She saw that I had a pretty big influence on other people, and I guess she thought I might as well be a good influence instead of a bad one. Being an ambassador gave me a big wake-up call. I saw that I was doing things that weren't going to get me anywhere. I decided to change, because people wouldn't take a piece of good advice coming from a troublemaker. This year, I worked really hard to keep myself out of trouble, although it wasn't easy. A lot of problems came up that I never thought I could deal with without violence, but I did. Not once did I turn to violence. I am out of gangs. That's it for me. I am tired of fighting without a reason.

Impact on Adults

> It reminds me that there are so many great students who have so much to say. So often, kids are not heard, when in reality they can teach us so many things. From listening to our ambassadors, I have come to understand what frustrates them, what inspires them, what makes them tick. That makes me a better teacher and a better person.
>
> —SETH GROVEMAN, TEACHER, PALM BEACH CENTRAL HIGH SCHOOL, PALM BEACH, FLORIDA

"The successful, long-lasting programs have one element in common: they have an on-site program advisor who owns the program and sees it as an extension of their personal sense of mission," says Rick Lewis, district training coordinator for the Safe Schools Department in Palm Beach County, Florida, where more than a thousand Safe School Ambassadors have been trained to work in twenty-one middle and high schools. But with most schools strapped for funds, providing stipends and other forms of recognition is increasingly uncommon. It becomes clear that the adults who stick with the program must be getting something besides money back in return for their efforts: personal satisfaction, job satisfaction, improved relationships with students, and more.

Some teachers have reported that their involvement in the program recharges them. In an era of education that is so strongly focused on academics and testing, working with students on interpersonal skills and social-emotional learning feeds a part of these teachers that has been starved for a long time. One facilitator said that her small-group meetings help her maintain a healthy and balanced perspective on school and the world: "I work with great kids, and they're not all the 'good kids' either. When they talk about what they've done, I feel so proud. I feel so hopeful and so positive. It's like a warm bath that washes away a lot of the dirt that gets stuck to me over the course of the week."

Other teachers describe how tired they got when so much of their energy had to focus on discipline. With trained ambassadors as allies, many teachers report that the climate inside their classrooms has improved, and they feel more energy, lightness, and even joy in their teaching.

Les Luxmore, assistant principal at Valencia High School, describes another aspect of the payback: working with his school's ambassadors aligns with one important part of his personal mission and helps him fulfill it:

> I am very excited about Safe School Ambassadors, because I had been running a program we called The Movement, which followed Dr. King's model for addressing injustice. But SSA offered training, greater student and staff participation, and a support element my program could not offer. I am committed to these kinds of programs because since Dr. King's death, I have continued to see division and conflict between people worldwide, based on ethnicity, religion, gender, sexual preference, age, size, any difference. SSA is one very effective way I can continue that healing work that is so important to me.

Kevin Crider is a counselor and program advisor at Gardena High School in the Los Angeles Unified School District. Like Belmont High, Gardena has more than its share of conflict and violence:

> In Los Angeles, what happens in the prisons directly impacts the schools. If there are race wars in the prisons—fights over territory or rights—these grievances often spill over into the schools. Recently these tensions resulted in a student bringing a gun to school. Thankfully, one of our ambassadors found out about it. He approached the campus police officer and told him who had the gun, where it was, and what the boy's intentions were. School officials were then able to remove the gun from the student's locker, thereby protecting many potential victims. After an incident like that, I felt relieved that we were able to stop students, and even me, from being harmed. Stopping violence like that changes your life. You realize that you have to stay involved if you can stop events like that from occurring.

Impact on the School

> I've noticed a huge decrease in fights and suspensions. Overall, we have a much more friendly environment on campus this year, thanks to our ambassadors.
>
> —JOSH NOWAK, COUNSELOR, VALENCIA HIGH SCHOOL, VALENCIA, CALIFORNIA

Through their interventions, which are most frequently with their peers, ambassadors have been able to reduce incidents of mistreatment, increase the flow of information to adults, and improve student relationships and connectedness.

Reduced Incidents of Mistreatment

Kevin Crider adds that "while ambassadors feel more comfortable going to an adult about big issues like guns and gang fights, they also enjoy the idea that they can put out fires without adult help." Year-end surveys consistently indicate that exclusion, put-downs, and bullying have decreased in schools where the program has been implemented. In June 2006, those surveys again showed that more than 65 percent of ambassadors reported that bullying had decreased somewhat, and a similar percentage of adults agreed. Moreover, one-third of those ambassadors felt that bullying had decreased a lot. Erica Martenson, counselor and SSA Program Advisor at American Canyon Middle School in American Canyon, California, agreed: "I notice a difference, and the police officers who are here on campus working with the students tell me the same thing. We're not dealing with teasing and bullying as much. We've been doing other things to address these issues, but our ambassadors have tipped the scales."

As assistant principal, James Corral, brought the SSA program to Kenilworth Junior High School in Petaluma, California. He reported that for the five months after the ambassadors began their work, compared to the previous year's figures, harassment was down 50 percent, bus incidents were down 25 percent, and sexual harassment was down 55 percent. Now the assistant principal at Charlotte Wood Middle School in Danville, California, Corral had launched the ambassadors program on his new campus and says he's seeing similar results. Moreover, the program has become a model that four other schools in the district have initiated. At Wamsley Elementary School in Rifle, Colorado, students whose behavior is out of line (not safe or respectful, for example) are given "Side Tracks," which are the elementary equivalent of a detention but include a conversation with an adult to help the student understand the reason for the citation and figure out how to avoid similar problems in the future. After their SSA training, counselor Matt Engel reported that Side Tracks are down 42 percent. Kristin Greenstreet adds that discipline referrals at her school are down about 30 percent since they began their program.

Trained ambassadors also seem to be able to reduce the amount of fighting on their campuses. In year-end surveys, nearly 60 percent of students and adults felt that fighting had decreased. "Our concentration has been on reducing fights," said Sheryl Stone, assistant principal at Alta Loma Junior High School in Alta Loma, California. "We compared the number of fights we have had so far this year (ten) to the number we had at this point last year (twenty-one). We are down 53 percent." Kevin Crider reports similar decreases at Gardena in Los Angeles, saying that police officers on campus tell him that there have been far fewer fights and issues for them to deal with since the SSA training.

By reducing the number of conflicts that erupt, ambassadors have also been successful at reducing suspensions. Mark Balch, safe and drug-free schools coordinator for the Kern High School District in Bakersfield, California, reports that East Bakersfield High School experienced a 20 percent drop in suspensions after ambassadors fanned out across campus. Stone reports a 40 percent decrease in suspendable incidents at Alta Loma Junior High. "Since ambassadors got started, our out-of-school suspensions are down 49 percent, and our in-school suspensions are down 69 percent," says Lex Luxmore in Valencia, California. Jack Schipper, assistant principal at Montgomery High School in Santa Rosa, California, says that he believes the program has helped to cut suspensions by 62 percent over two years. With each three-day suspension costing roughly $115 in lost average daily attendance funds, the school has been able to retain more than $45,000 in revenue that would have been lost had suspensions continued at the prior rate. That figure does not include the cost of the time the disciplinary team would have spent investigating incidents and completing paperwork. Those hours are easily worth $30,000 or more.

Increased Reporting to Adults

"I am so stoked," writes Linda Camardella, program advisor at Conniston Middle School in West Palm Beach, Florida. "One of my ambassadors did the right thing. He saw a girl in the cafeteria Friday morning showing off a knife. He didn't feel comfortable approaching her directly, so he got help from our assistant principal. They talked to the girl, got the knife, and a potentially big incident was averted. The program works!" Dozens more ambassadors have come forward to let adults know about potentially dangerous situations or hurtful situations that have been prevented or foiled. Beyond that, at El Dorado High School in northern California, a student who was *not* an ambassador came forward to let school staff know about a plot by several students to bomb the school. Administrators at the school credit the SSA program with shifting the norms and creating a school climate where breaking the code of silence and reporting information like that is seen by all students as a good thing.

A Girl and Her Dog

My fifteen-year-old daughter Ann has cerebral palsy, but thanks to her service dog, Sierra, she attends our local high school. Two weeks ago, a girl that knew of Ann overheard four kids plotting a way to take her service dog away from her on the bus and how they could get away with it. This girl, who was one of the Safe School Ambassadors, brought this information to a teacher at her school that knew Ann very well. He went to the office and called Ann in and they discussed it. The next day, the teacher, along with Ann, went directly to those four kids and confronted them with the information that they had heard about regarding what their plan was going to be. This teacher told these kids that he was aware of what they were planning, as were Ann, her parents, and the entire school administration. He tried to explain to them that Sierra is not just a dog, but a very expensively trained service dog that Ann needed in order to help her to do things that she couldn't do any other way, and that as a result of their threat, she was afraid to take him to school. They apologized, and we haven't had any problems since. Ann brought Sierra back to school the next day.—Ann's parent

---

It has been said that anger masks pain. In the cycle of pain, rage, and then revenge, the most common expressions of rage are those that aggressors act out: verbal attacks, pushing, shoving, and fighting. What's often overlooked is the rage directed back at themselves, which can be expressed in any number of self-destructive ways: eating disorders; cutting; use of alcohol, tobacco, or other drugs; premature sexual activity; and suicide. The training includes how to listen and offer support to peers in pain and how to connect them to adults who can offer further help.

Conor Cusack, one of the prevention coordinators for the Greece School District outside Rochester, New York, tells of the most powerful moment in his two-year tenure as coordinator of the district's SSA programs:

> One of our ambassadors told of how a friend had been cutting herself for a long time. She said she'd noticed the marks on her friend's arm before, but didn't have the courage to bring it up and didn't know what to say or do. After her training, she brought it up with her friend and was able to listen, offer support, and get her to see the school counselor. Now, her friend has been through some private counseling and has stopped cutting herself. Because of what she did, this ambassador was

nominated and accepted into the New York State Attorney General's Triple C (Character, Courage, Commitment) Awards Program. To me, the fact that a life was changed as a result of our program was profound.

Improved Relationships and Connectedness

Year-end surveys also show that more than 62 percent of ambassadors and 67 percent of adults felt an increased sense of safety at school since implementing the program, and 78 percent of adults felt that school climate had improved as a result. "Ambassadors have been great for our school climate," says Seth Groveman of Palm Beach Central High School. "Fights are almost nonexistent. There have been fewer than half as many fights this year than last, and that was down 60 percent from the year before. Suspensions and crime are also way down. Although we still have subgroups and cliques, there is no animosity between the groups. Students feel safe and have expressed to me how much they like Palm Beach Central."

Other impacts are harder to measure but easy to value. Christian Kingsbury, principal of Basalt Middle School, shared how one of his students took his learning home:

> One of our ambassadors reported on one of his action logs: "I told my step-brother that he is a good kid and a great reader, and that my Mom is wrong." At first glance it is easy to miss the impact of this statement. Here is a boy who not only saw the pain of a family member but spoke up to offer support and solace. It was compassion in action. Then he went further; he recognized the injustice that had caused the pain and crossed those so-called blood lines to name it, to say that his own mother was wrong in saying what she'd said to his stepbrother. A simple statement like that can have a pretty far-reaching impact.

Ambassadors as Peer Coaches

Will Peterson was in trouble. Will always got along famously with adults, but he seemed to be missing what psychologists call social cues, and he irritated other kids. He made inappropriate comments, tried too hard to be popular, and couldn't control his angry impulses. Over the years, Will pushed more and more kids away from him. He was kicked off the soccer, baseball, and snowboarding teams. Both Will and his family had visited psychologists and medical doctors. Medication for attention deficit hyperactivity disorder and depression offered some relief, but it was short-lived. After a series of poor choices, Will had just about used up his chances at our school.

We didn't want to give up, so we tried one last intervention: Will selected three students and requested that they coach him. He picked these kids because he knew them to be cool, powerful, and also compassionate. Each kid Will selected had been through the Safe School Ambassadors program the previous semester. Our hope was that if Will heard it just right from the "powerful" kids, it might help him make better choices with his behavior. I contacted the three boys, and thankfully they agreed to give it a shot.

The first meeting took place in the school library. We were all nervous. I introduced everyone and thanked them for coming. Then the three boys just took it from there. I was amazed at their ability to be at once compassionate and direct. They were clear.

"Will, you go too far, like yesterday when you pushed that kid on the bus."

"Will, when you act like this, we feel frustrated."

There were many, many specific examples. They did not hold back. Will somehow managed to listen, tears in his eyes. And then it came: the support.

"We are here to help you," the boys said. "Let's work out a system. If you need help, we are here."

"You are a great kid inside."

Keep in mind, these were the most powerful, respected students in my school advising a kid near the bottom of the social food chain.

When kids help other kids, it's amazing. When kids with power offer genuine help to those who have no power, it seems to transform. In this case, it was big motivation for Will to clean up his act, and he did. We have no illusions: Will may not become a new person. But it really has helped him to manage his emotions better and treat others more kindly. And it made a big difference for the three boys. They used their power to do something that felt right for a kid who needed help. They saw that their actions made a real difference in lots of lives and made our school a more compassionate place.—Jim Gilchrist, Principal, Aspen Community School, Woody Creek, Colorado

Conclusion

The action logs, year-end surveys, and reports from family group facilitators all point toward several important conclusions. When Safe School Ambassadors witness mistreatment, they use the skills they've learned in the training to intervene with their peers. Those same surveys indicate, and reports of dozens of school administrators confirm, that those interventions actually reduce the number of incidents of mistreatment in a school. Disciplinary referrals, fights, suspensions related to mistreatment, and other indicators all decrease when the program is implemented according to the model described in this book.

Kevin Crider, a counselor from Gardena High School, describes an experience that in many ways sums up the power and potential of this model: "I took an ambassador with me to the Community Council meeting to speak about the program. He told them that SSA had changed his life. He said, 'I understand now that I am responsible for helping stop mistreatment and violence. It's true that kids can help and make a difference.'"

Think about what would happen if forty of these carefully selected, powerful ambassadors fanned out through the school and intervened just one time each day, speaking up once to squelch a rumor or to counsel restraint and tolerance or to offer support to a classmate in pain; together they would create forty incidents of peace on a campus in one day. In the five school days of a week, they'd create two hundred such incidents, and in the thirty-five weeks of a school year, they'd create seven thousand. Each intervention directly involves at least one aggressor or target, and usually both. Experience shows that on average, it's roughly two people per incident, which means that in those seven thousand interventions, some fourteen thousand students would be directly affected by the words and actions of the ambassadors.

Research also shows that each intervention is witnessed by an average of four students, meaning that in addition, the students on that campus would have twenty-eight thousand witness experiences in which they saw with their own eyes the social norms of cruelty and violence being redefined by socially powerful ambassadors. All students then come to see that it's not so cool to be cruel and it's cooler to stand up and speak up for others.

The final chapter explores how to launch a youth-empowerment initiative on a campus. It offers a road map and tools to be a powerful champion and effective advocate—in your school, district, and community—for engaging, empowering, and equipping youth to be agents of positive social change.

PART IV

A Call to Action

Never doubt that a small, group of thoughtful, committed citizens can change the world. Indeed, it is the only thing that ever has.

—MARGARET MEAD

THE PRECEDING CHAPTERS HAVE SHOWN THAT creating safer schools requires an institutional shift—one that reexamines current policies and practices, realigns priorities, and redirects resources. Throughout the book, we have presented evidence to support the power and ability of young people to be peacemakers and norm changers.

Chapter Ten provides a road map: a set of seven steps and actions for launching an initiative. It also includes case studies that show how three courageous educators have used these steps to navigate the journey of empowering students to create safer school climates.

A Road Map for the Future

Vision without action is merely a dream.

Action without vision is busywork.

Vision with action can change the world.

—VICTOR FRANKEL

IN THE MOST GENERAL SENSE, this final chapter describes a process for initiating and sustaining meaningful change. The steps described here apply any time you are talking about involving adults and youth in your community with whatever issues you believe need to be addressed. They apply to getting your community to recycle, help prevent forest fires, or, in this case, improve school climate. Specifically, the focus of this chapter is to offer ways to navigate the political structure of a school system effectively in order to secure the commitment of decision makers to support a new policy, project, or program in which youth are engaged and empowered as participants.

This chapter is also a guide for taking action that could be used more specifically for preparing a school to implement the Safe School Ambassadors (SSA) program described in this book. However, we use that only as an example. This chapter will help you bring any powerful message forward to the right audiences clearly and effectively. We lay out a series of steps, with strategies, tools, and tips, to prepare you to be a powerful champion and effective advocate for your chosen initiative.

Taking an idea through a system such as a school is not easy, especially if that school or district has no existing mandate to engage and empower students in this way. But if you believe in youth empowerment and want to make your school a safer place, you have to become savvy about this political process. This chapter will help you work your way through the power structure of any school system.

Launching an Initiative: Steps for Success

Our work with hundreds of organizations over the past several decades has provided the rich tapestry of experience from which these seven steps are drawn. Each step is explained in greater detail later in this section:

1. Assess personal readiness.

2. Assess organizational readiness.

3. Identify potential allies and partners.

4. Build working relationships with allies and partners.

5. Identify potential or actual detractors and obstacles.

6. Develop an action plan.

7. Implement the action plan.

These steps do not necessarily apply to all situations or circumstances. Some issues are higher priorities than others; so, assess your organization and community and take the steps you need to take to get to yes. This is a guide rather than a prescription. Use what you need, and leave the rest.

In order to make these steps understandable and usable, we introduce them in detail and then present three case studies that will help you see how people in different situations used particular steps. For example, an assistant principal at a school that is working on improving its social climate would take different steps from a concerned parent who finds that few people at her child's school are even aware of the degree of mistreatment that occurs.

Why take the time to review and understand these steps? Here are some reasons. You may have worked with or known someone who was fired up about an idea and decided to do something about it, or maybe that someone was you. That person may have wanted to bring the idea forward but neglected to create a plan for the process, thinking inspiration would be the plan. But inspiration alone as a methodology rarely produces success. Often the inspired person is representing a minority position or issue that is not the top priority of those in power. If you are not the decision maker yourself, you have to prepare to get the attention of those who do make the decisions. Don't allow your inspiration or passion to send you off before you're fully prepared to be effective. You may have only one chance to get on the agenda of an important meeting or to get that decision-making person on the phone or in person. Be prepared.

Step 1: Assess Personal Readiness

In this step, you decide if you are willing to attach yourself to this particular issue or program. Begin by asking yourself a list of questions as a self-assessment:

- *How informed am I about the issue and the background surrounding it?* You must become informed, and reading this book has given you a good foundation. Various stakeholders will ask questions about every aspect of this issue and your proposed solutions. "I don't know" or "I'll have to get back to you on that" won't serve your purposes very well.

- *Do I have the time?* Assess your time availability. Promoting a new idea or plan is not something you do only once. Make sure you have the time that's needed and that you're willing to commit that time.

- *What about my other responsibilities, relationships, and commitments?* There are other issues and people to consider: your boss, spouse, children, and colleagues, for example. Perhaps you are in a position to delegate some of your work to another member of your staff or a support person. Your time working on this program may interfere with family activities and other personal responsibilities. You need to assess these factors as part of this step.

- *What role am I willing and able to play?* Consider some of the responsibilities that might come with the territory. You may need to speak publicly at meetings or give presentations to a parent-teacher group, a service club, a staff meeting, or the school board. You may need to write letters and proposals and might be called on to be a fundraiser.

- *What is my position in this community, and do I have the respect of others?* You will need others to listen to you and support your ideas. You must evaluate your social capital and decide if you are the right person to lead this effort. Some people work better behind the scenes, and others like the public eye. Know what you do well and do not do well, and be willing to involve others when you need to. If you are not comfortable in being the spokesperson or visible voice of a cause, you will need to find someone who does that well.

- *Am I up to the challenge?* You must have the courage of your convictions and not be deterred by opposition. You must also be willing to negotiate, compromise, and listen to other viewpoints. It helps to have thick skin for a job like this. You'll need staying power, because you may hear no several times before you hear yes.

Use the results of this self-assessment to determine your next actions. If need be, become more prepared, gain more knowledge, or become more able and willing in all necessary ways.

Step 2: Assess Organizational Readiness

The word *readiness* applies to organizations and communities, as well as to individuals. Assess the site, the school system, the community, the culture, and the written (and unwritten) rules of the system you are working with. Know that there are seasons during which the ground is more fertile than others and that all organizations have rhythms. Coming at an organization during a busy time can doom your endeavor. Ask yourself the following questions in an organizational assessment:

- *What is the culture of the organization?* Understand the climate of your community, school system, and school. Determine whether the prevailing values, attitudes, and beliefs are a match for what you are proposing. Evaluate how receptive or ready the organization is for your ideas or programs.

- *What is the need? Why should this plan or program be initiated?* Having a concise explanation and answer to these questions is critical to your success. The answers will help others gain a deeper understanding of the importance of what you are proposing and will increase their support.

- *What is a good time to bring these ideas forward?* If you bring the right idea forward at the wrong time, it's not likely to be well received. Or the right person can hear it but not be prepared to act. You might want to look at previous responses to similar initiatives and determine your approach accordingly.

- *How are decisions made, and who makes them?* Learn the power structure and familiarize yourself with the important players. Find out about their personalities, roles, philosophies, and beliefs: school board members, district-level administrators and staff, principals, significant teachers, key parents, community leaders, and community organizations, for example.

- *Are the decision makers open only to insiders or also to people from outside the organization?* You will need to know how and when to submit proposals and the protocol for submission. For example, you may need to submit the proposal on a certain form, electronically, by mail, or some other way. Finally, you need to be familiar with any follow-up procedures.

- *What has worked, or not worked, in the past, and why?* Find out if anything like your proposal or idea has been put forward already and what happened. Research any previous efforts made by this decision-making body.

- *What if there is a new principal or superintendent or other leader in place?* Administrators come and go. If the administrator who approved your proposal leaves or is replaced, you may have to go through the entire approval process again. For example, a new superintendent whose focus is on test results or establishing new discipline policies may eliminate any programs that don't appear to fit that mind-set. At that point, you may have to adjust your strategy.

One school district, for example, replaced its superintendent right in the middle of Community Matters' initial exploration phase for bringing the Safe School Ambassadors program to the district. Because the new superintendent's focus was primarily on academic achievement, it was no longer a good time to start a youth empowerment program there. Until there was a new mandate or a different leader, improving school climate by empowering students would not be a primary objective for this district since he was the decision maker. Two years later, a newly hired superintendent believed that school climate is a component of academic achievement, so we decided it was a good time to approach this district again. This time when we submitted our proposal, it was all green lights for SSA. Timing and understanding the political climate are important.

Step 3: Identify Potential Allies and Partners

It is hard to be a lone ranger in this endeavor and succeed. One person can be marginalized and made to appear as if he or she is operating as a solo activist who can be more easily dismissed. That's the reason that it's critical to identify and gain allies and partners. These come in all forms—a parent, an administrator, a city official, a teacher. Sometimes an ally can gain an audience with decision makers or secure support in ways the point person can't. They may be heard and listened to differently than you are. Look to build a base of diverse allies and partners who have different roles, relationships, information, talents, strengths, and ways of presenting themselves than you have. Aligning yourself with a diverse group of stakeholders is one of the keys to success. The process is not unlike that used to identify and recruit socially influential students into the Safe School Ambassadors program. Look at all of the different groups of stakeholders and then identify the key person or persons in each group. Those are the people you want as allies and partners.

Appendix D will help when you are ready to identify and recruit your allies and partners.

Step 4: Build Working Relationships with Allies and Partners

Create a sense of team among the identified allies and partners. People work well together not just because they share a common concern or vision, but because they respect and value the relationships they've built. Taking time to get to know one other and finding common ground go a long way toward creating and maintaining the commitment of team members.

Even when working with those who share your vision, there will inevitably be disagreements. To be successful, it is important for your team to set up procedures for resolving differences. Decide if you are using consensus, majority rule,

Robert's Rules of Order, or other methods you believe would be effective and efficient. The key is to have a decision-making process in place before you reach an impasse.

Step 5: Identify Potential or Actual Detractors and Obstacles

In any endeavor, there are always people with different perspectives and even some who are resistant to any change. When you identify the people whose perspectives clash with yours, remain open and willing to address their arguments and concerns. By knowing the opposition's position from the start, you can be prepared for those surprise questions that often are asked in a meeting or during a presentation. Try to use this knowledge to get the best results from each encounter you have. You can align yourself with other like-minded people whom the detractors respect or choose another route to the conclusion you seek that avoids sensitive topics. Identify what the resisters are committed to, look for places where your commitment matches theirs, and then speak to how this effort of empowering youth helps them fulfill their commitments. Find common ground, and resistance will diminish. Ask yourself:

- What bridges have already been built between my allies or me and any detractors? How can these bridges be used effectively? What new bridges can be built?

- What are the arguments against my proposal? On what are they based? What other knowledge or background do my team and I need to address these arguments?

Step 6: Develop an Action Plan

Your action plan is the series of steps you and your team will take to achieve your goal. Once you have a team, your plan might include the following:

- Conduct a complete assessment of the school's climate and discipline data (see Appendix E).

- Use the results to develop a strong presentation (see Appendix A).

- Invite the decision makers to a meeting or presentation about your issues.

- Research your audience, and make a compelling presentation or a series of them.
- Find potential sources for funding (such as, federal, state, county, district, private foundations, local business owners, civic or service clubs).

You may find it helpful to create an action planning form to guide you through the information you need in your action plan. Here are some ideas that you might consider:

- What is the task that needs to be done?
- Who will be responsible for the task?
- What needs to be done to accomplish the task?
- What are any obstacles to accomplishing the task?
- What resources are needed to accomplish the task?
- When will the task be completed?

Step 7: Implement the Action Plan

Change is not a straight line, and you and your team have to work creatively to continue to be successful. Here are some suggestions to help you and your team move forward:

- Reconvene the team to revise the action plan as needed.
- Keep fanning the flame. Don't let delays or criticism dampen your enthusiasm.
- Maintain a level of adaptability and flexibility to meet new circumstances and challenges as they arise.
- Seek support from others, including consultants who have knowledge and experience in implementing successful youth empowerment initiatives.

Case Studies

The following three case studies will help you determine which of the seven steps would best serve you. Are you a school staff member, a parent, a district or county office staff member, a school board member, a city official, or a concerned community member? Where you are in the power chain will determine what you need to do. If you are the primary decision maker and have access to unlimited funding, you may have fewer steps to take. However, if you don't have complete authority and only some or no access to funds, you will need some strategies for reaching and convincing decision makers and funders to support your cause. From these case studies, you will be able to determine the most effective course of action for your situation.

Assistant Principal Case Study

As the assistant principal of Adams Middle School, Miguel Chavez is responsible for school discipline. Over the past couple of years, he has noticed an increase in peer conflict and other incidents between students, and more and more of these problems are ending up in his office. Many of them have to do with rumors, "he said/she said" kinds of things, put-downs, and other forms of relational aggression, and some of these have led to fights at the school. Miguel is becoming increasingly aware that the school's discipline policy is not solving the problem. The thought of getting tougher, as some have suggested, raises the specter of unintended consequences—declines in test scores because more of the students who are already struggling academically would be suspended and miss more class time—and makes him reluctant to go down that path. Still, it is clear to him that the school has to do something different. Miguel begins with step 3.

Step 3: Identify Potential Allies In his first year at the school, Miguel saw that the staff had disliked and the administration had rejected one teacher's efforts to integrate service learning into the curriculum of the upper grades. He had noticed that the process got derailed not by its merits, which were many, but by the style and approach of the single person advocating for it. This teacher had not tried to find or use any allies.

Therefore, Miguel put together a list of potential allies:

- A couple of teachers he'd gotten close to over the past two years. Both were well connected in the social and political scene at the school, and one was especially well respected by his fellow teachers. He knew he could be straightforward with them and they would reciprocate.

- The administrative team (the principal, the counselor, the department chairs, the site council chairperson, and himself). One of the school's goals this year was to build a positive climate, and that was a frequent topic of discussion at administrative team meetings.

- The assistant principal at the middle school in one of the neighboring districts. He had gotten to know her when both were working on their administrative credentials and her school had recently wrestled with a similar issue.

- Some parents whose children had been aggressors or targets. All three of these parents had spoken to him of their strong desire to reverse the current trend of increasing meanness among the students.

Step 4: Build Working Relationships with Allies and Partners   Miguel spoke with everyone on his list, beginning with his colleague at the other middle school. He had working relationships with all these people, and from the conversations he sought to acquire:

- An understanding of their perspectives on the nature and extent of the problem

- Validation of his internal assessment or the ways that their perspectives differed from his

- Information they had about what actions other schools had taken

- Their ideas about what approaches they thought might be effective at Adams

He saved the administrative team for last, wanting to go there only after having done his preparation. When he brought his proposal to the team, he requested enough time on the agenda for the group to do a quick inventory of their current school climate improvement efforts, which yielded the following:

- A social skills curriculum that was being used in seventh-grade health classes

- Several parent nights, one of which focused specifically on bullying

- A three-hour staff training the previous year that had focused on increasing awareness of bullying and offered some support and guidance to teachers on how to address it in their classrooms

What emerged from that discussion was naming a missing piece: the students. The group felt that they should more directly involve students. They realized that the school had been doing things to, for, and at the students; now it was time to do things with them.

He got the group's approval to develop a proposal for an action plan and moved forward to step 6.

Step 6: Develop an Action Plan   Miguel's plan had these components:

- Develop criteria for a successful solution.

- Research options (strategies and programs).

- Assess information obtained through the research.

- Decide on a strategy or strategies.

He went back to the administrative team for their thoughts on his plan and gained their approval.

Step 7: Implement the Action Plan   First, a subgroup met to develop the criteria a solution would have to meet: it should be more than a single event, have a skills component, enable students to solve problems on their own, and be positive and proactive rather than just react to problems. Then the group members did some research into what other schools were doing and found that the activities were quite varied and included assemblies, conflict resolution programs, and a safety summit that involved diverse student leaders from the entire school. Miguel assessed what he had learned and used that information to develop a proposal to submit to the administrative team. After his presentation, his recommendation to launch a program that would train students to resolve problems on their own was supported. With their approval he went to the staff and secured their buy-in.

Counselor Case Study

Paula Thomas is a third-year counselor who has just started her dream job at an elementary school. Being new to this school, she has a fairly limited knowledge of the staff culture and politics but is learning fast. Three months into the year, she has seen some mean behavior in the halls that some teachers and hall monitors ignore or don't seem to notice. Others simply say, "Stop it!" which Paula notices temporarily interrupts the problem or moves it out of sight and earshot of the supervising adults. There is not a lot of overt fighting and conflict;

the problem is more that some children are not feeling welcome, being left out, being teased, or put down. Older students use the power of their age to harass and bully the younger students—intentionally bumping into them in the halls, tripping them, making them sit at certain tables in the cafeteria, knocking their backpacks to the floor, and so on. Also, children who are not adept athletically are being treated in a mean way in physical education classes.

Looking deeper, Paula has found that some of the children who are frequent targets during recreational time and at lunch also have spotty attendance, and teachers report that some of them are having troubles academically and socially. In addition, she has met with several parents who shared with her that their children were coming home withdrawn, having headaches, losing interest in school, and seeming to be sick more often (or at least were pretending to be).

Paula's professional ethics and her commitment to young people's healthy development and well-being compel her to tackle this problem. However, she is keenly aware that doing so in the wrong way at the wrong time could quickly turn her dream job into a lonely nightmare.

Step 1: Assess Personal Readiness   Because she had friends at several schools in the district, it was not inconceivable to think that she could request a transfer to another school and be happy and satisfied there. In other words, she had to determine for herself if this problem was one she really wanted to take on. Here are some of the questions she considered:

- *How do I navigate this carefully?* I don't want to jeopardize my career. Am I solid enough in my relationship with my colleagues? What about my reputation?

- *What are my relationships like with other staff at this school?* I don't want to have people mad at me for stirring up stuff.

- *Do I have enough information and good data so I don't look like an alarmist?* Being prepared with data and having a strong sense of purpose made it less likely that Paula's colleagues would see her that way.

Asking herself these questions helped Paula to get clear in her own mind that the risks were worth the opportunity to address the student discipline issues. She realized her concerns were well founded and that she was ready to strongly advocate that the staff take a hard look at their policies and practices. Assessing her own readiness and being able to separate emotions from facts gave her the confidence to move forward.

Step 2: Assess Organizational Readiness   Paula looked at what the school was doing. Most teachers in the school were using the district's character development curriculum. The school has antibullying posters in the halls and other common areas and held an assembly on bullying the previous year. From the reports she heard, the assembly was okay but did not have much lasting impact on the students who most needed to hear its message.

Paula noted that parent involvement is reasonably high, but most parents seem to be concerned with their children's academic progress rather than their social skills development.

Like many other educators, the staff at Paula's school feel overwhelmed by all the academic pressure. Although they are not closed to new ideas, most seem inclined to focus on the academics, partly in response to parents and partly in response to the principal's general statements about boosting the school's scores on the state tests. The principal's leadership style is laissez-faire. She is not an initiator and looks to key staff members to propose new ideas.

Doing her homework—learning what was already in place, how leadership was expressed, and what priorities parent had—put Paula in a position to make her case in a coherent, organized, and effective way. The likelihood of gaining support for her concerns was increased by the preparation she did to understand the culture, dynamics, and personalities in the school environment better.

Step 3: Identify Potential Allies and Partners   Paula did not want to do this alone and knew that she would increase her chances for success if she could gain the support of the right people, because then her ideas would be perceived as having buy-in. She identified several parents, Parent-Teacher Association leaders, and some of the teachers. The district safe schools coordinator was also on her list.

Step 4: Building Working Relationships with Allies and Partners   Paula spoke with teachers who had been at the school longer than she had and received affirmation of her observations: the atmosphere was getting worse, or at least not getting better. Paula also spoke with key parents to find out how open they would be to some changes at the school.

Step 5: Identify Potential or Actual Detractors and Obstacles   Being new at the school, it was important for Paula to go through step 5. The hall monitor aides and a couple of the older teachers were likely to minimize her concerns, but with enough evidence and a critical mass of respected staff members in support of her efforts, it was likely that the detractors would not be able to derail the process.

Step 6: Develop an Action Plan   Paula developed an action plan with these components:

- *Build the case.* She decided to be more scientific in her observations in the halls, cafeteria, PE classes, and throughout the campus and keep a file of the types of incidents she saw.
- *Conduct preliminary research.* She wanted to bring parents into the process and discuss climate-improvement options with them.
- *Share information with the principal.* Paula will invite her to a meeting of key parents, the PTA president, and Judy and Hal, fourth- and fifth-grade teachers, respectively.
- *Gather more evidence in a climate survey.* The principal agreed to conduct the survey so data will be collected.
- *Develop strategies.* Paula wants to be ready to make recommendations to the decision makers.

Step 7: Implement the Action Plan   Paula met with the principal as she had planned. The tone of her entire approach was open and positive: "I know I've only been here twelve weeks, and my perspective is in some ways more limited. However, with these fresh eyes, here's what I've noticed. We have a committed staff, one that is generally pretty aware of school climate issues but not always taking full advantage of opportunities to build that positive climate." Based on the data Paula had collected and the support of others at the meeting, the principal sensed the importance of the issue. She asked Paula and the group to bring their information to the staff.

As a result of her presentation at the staff meeting, Paula gained support to conduct a climate survey of the school. When the survey was completed and the results presented, the staff endorsed the idea of acquiring some new programs to improve the climate, and several joined what had now become the climate committee. After researching what other schools had done, they presented their recommendations:

- A refresher training in the character development curriculum, with a focus on how to adjust it to address mistreatment
- A new program to give students the skills to stop mistreatment when they see it

Seeing the staff's support and the rationale Paula and her group had established, the principal approved their recommendations.

Assistant Superintendent Case Study

An incident at the high school had made it into the local paper: tensions between some of the groups on campus had triggered a fight that involved a handful of students and required a police response. This recent escalation led to an increase in subsequent incidents both on and off campus, first at the mall, then at the movie theater, and finally at the middle school, where the younger siblings and cousins of those involved at the high school began posturing and gesturing and generally creating a lot of conflict at their school. There is now widespread concern and a small public outcry. Parents came to the most recent school board meeting and brought it up.

The board's reaction was clear: there is no need to worry. The adults at the school are in charge, the board members essentially said, and they will take care of the situation. There will be more security on campus, at least until things cool down. Policies will be reviewed and tightened, with zero tolerance for the troublemakers, who will be expelled if they don't settle down. In sum, it was a get-tough response. In recent years, the board has been focused on increasing graduation rates and test scores. Now the district is aware that there's been a long-festering, underlying problem with intergroup tension and harassment at the school.

The superintendent assigned responsibility for handling the incident's aftermath to the assistant superintendent, Tyrone Washington, who oversees school safety efforts. He also requested that Washington determine if any further changes need to be made to prevent this kind of incident from happening in the future or from escalating. Recognizing that he'd been tossed a very hot potato, Tyrone began to plan how to handle his assignment.

Step 1: Assess Personal Readiness   Tyrone saw that his options were pretty much limited to two: take on the challenge or leave his job. Having just been promoted into the position two years earlier, he did not want to go job hunting. As he mulled it over, he saw the challenge as an opportunity to do something significant for the students in the district and perhaps break the cycle of violence that he himself had known when he was in high school. It would feel very good to him to make this happen. He began to feel excitement about taking on this assignment, speaking at the board meetings, and trying to forge consensus out of disagreement. He realized that he had learned a lot about school climate and safety, especially in this post, and relished the chance to learn more. It would be very time-consuming, and that had the potential to be a sore spot at home, but with his wife's being a former teacher in some pretty harsh settings, he figured she would become excited about the project too.

Step 2: Assess Organizational Readiness   Tyrone examined three factors:

• *Timing.* The district had not made social-emotional development issues a high priority. The board had made it clear that the focus was on academic achievement, meeting state and national standards, and boosting test scores. However, Tyrone reasoned, this might be the perfect time to balance the scales. The information he'd picked up from the grapevine seemed to indicate that a good number of the staff members was getting frustrated by the discipline issues they confronted daily.

• *Decision making.* The superintendent was generally responsive to the needs of the various sites but was cautious at first. With input from the principals, he made the big decisions but had decentralized a lot of the decision-making power in the past couple of years. (This explains the get-tough response at the most recent board meeting. The superintendent didn't want to appear to be reactive or give any sign that what he had been doing wasn't working.) The superintendent had been somewhat open to new ideas that could be shown to have merit, as well as supporting different sites. It would likely all boil down to the majority of the principals' being in support of whatever new approaches were identified, and most of them would be reluctant to buck their staff. Tyrone needed an avenue to reach the staff members—a way for them to speak their minds and a way for him to show them that whatever was coming was going to help them.

• *Needs.* Other than getting the students to "chill out" a bit, the superintendent was not very clear on exactly what needed to be done. That would be something to figure out in this process.

Step 3: Identify Potential Allies and Partners   Tyrone identified a couple of key staff at each school who had influence with their principals. The school resource officer who covered the district seemed to be a pretty level-headed person who is receptive to new ideas and had the ear of the chief of police, who was close to the superintendent. That couldn't hurt.

Step 4: Build Working Relationships with Allies and Partners   Tyrone realized that it would be helpful to renew his relationships with some of the key people he identified, so he put them on his call list for the next day, just to check in and get their views on what was going on.

Step 5: Identify Potential or Actual Detractors and Obstacles   Tyrone knew that potential detractors were likely to surface during the process and realized it would be important for them to feel heard and not shut out of the process. In addition, a large number of teachers and some administrators did not believe in involving students when exploring significant issues and considering various options. They believed that student participation at this level was "coddling" the students and not an appropriate approach.

Another potential obstacle was funding. Certainly there was no fat in this year's budget. However, Tyrone might be able to make some small reallocations and possibly write a grant proposal to obtain funds.

Step 6: Develop an Action Plan   Tyrone jotted down some general items as a skeletal outline, but realized that he would be wise to involve other people in developing the plan. With their help, he came up with this basic plan:

- Gather information and perspectives from key people at each of the schools.
- Form a climate committee at the district level, and possibly at each site as well.
- Meet with the entire staff at each school.
- Meet with parents at each school.
- Hold a town hall meeting for community input.
- Summarize results.
- Research options and evaluate programs and approaches.
- Present options and recommendation to school board.

Step 7: Implement the Action Plan   It was not hard to get a strong group of people together to serve on a climate committee. Surprisingly, members supported the idea that the committee focus on the broader variable of social-emotional climate rather than discipline exclusively. Meetings with staff, parents, and members of the community yielded some fascinating commentary, common themes, and powerful ideas. Some law enforcement leaders captured the general sentiments of most staff and parents when they said that the tensions between various groups of youth could not be controlled by a "hook 'em and book 'em" approach. More police and security would only drive the problem to another place, where there wasn't a police or security presence.

It was clear that something needed to be done to change the ways students relate to and interact with each other. Some committee members proposed creating a teen council and conducting focus groups, bringing student leaders together to identify strategies and reduce tensions. Many city council members and teachers liked this idea. Committee research turned up some previously unknown programs and initiatives. The committee sifted through what they had discovered and prepared a final report to the superintendent and school board, which recommended a multipronged approach:

- Give permanent status to the district climate committee, and include students on the committee.

- Establish similar bodies at each school (or broaden the function of an existing group to include school climate issues), and draw members from students, staff, and parents.

- Review rules and policies, and their enforcement, to determine if they give administrators sufficient latitude to consider extenuating circumstances and if they are being enforced in a fair manner. Perceived inconsistency was one of the factors that had sparked the initial incident.

- Adopt a social skills curriculum in the primary grades to help students understand basic prosocial values, give them a common vocabulary to express feelings, and provide a model for communication and conflict resolution.

- Establish a youth-led program in middle school and high school that equips diverse student leaders with skills to intervene directly with their peers to prevent and stop mistreatment.

- Conduct activities on each campus to increase tolerance, understanding, and acceptance of diversity.

- Provide training for staff so they can be more aware of the problems and have tools to solve them (not just the disciplinary hammer).

- Conduct parent education in district and site forums.

Some Final Thoughts

The very things we have outlined for ambassadors to do—notice, think, act and follow through—are the same actions required for an adult to champion the cause of youth as powerful social change agents. We hope this book has given you the information to *notice* and understand the epidemic of mistreatment and its impact on students and schools. We also want you to *think* about how many adults have not fully recognized the power, skills, and abilities of young people to speak up against injustice, and assess your own readiness to be that person. Then we hope you have been inspired and informed enough to *act* courageously and advocate passionately and effectively for youth empowerment, even if it's hard to do.

Finally, we hope you will *follow through* and support, acknowledge, and celebrate the contributions of young people.

It's up to each one of us to take a stand. This means we each have to say that enough is enough and, in spite of how busy we are, recognize that the young people we work with and care about need our help and advocacy. They need us to believe in ourselves and in them. They need us to model courage, be willing to share power, and see them for the leaders they are.

Imagine a school in which students know what mistreatment is and the cost it exacts on them, their friends, the school and the whole community; a school in which compassion and inclusion are not just words on a mission statement, but are guiding principles modeled and taught by adults: a school in which students are valued as contributors, not consumers; a school in which learning flourishes and students thrive; a school in which all young people acquire the skills, support, and opportunity to be courageous and committed to speaking up and standing up for each other.

When we have accomplished these goals, we will not only have reduced violence and improved the climates of our schools, but we will have educated a generation of young people to embody an ethic of positive citizenship. We will also have raised a generation of young adults with the beliefs, intentions, and skills required to coexist peacefully in an ever-changing, diverse, and complex world, and we will have left a legacy of hope for all of our tomorrows.

Presentation Tips

WHETHER YOUR AUDIENCE IS ONE PERSON OR ONE HUNDRED, and whether you are the school superintendent or a ninth grader, the following tips will help you convey your message effectively and achieve the outcomes you desire.

Research Your Audience

Learn about their mission or purpose, history, current priorities, and activities. Acknowledge them, and link your program to what's important to them by presenting several relevant and compelling features, that is, benefits of your program.

Name the Outcomes

First, identify what you want to achieve in your presentation—for example:

- Build relationships?
- Inform, educate, or explore?
- Motivate or inspire?
- Persuade (open or change minds)?
- Take action: raise money, involve others, ask for in-kind support, develop internships, or something else?

Second, determine how you want your listeners to feel when you are finished. What is the reaction you want from your audience?

255

Decide Who Delivers

If your program is a youth-adult partnership, your presentation will be more effective if young people speak first and deliver at least half of the message. It is especially effective to have young people address three issues:

- The need: Why are we doing this? They might begin, "We realized that . . ."
- The ask: "We really want to have your help with . . ."
- The close: "So how will you support our efforts?"

Create a Structure

Your presentation begins by getting the audience's attention, and the first ninety seconds are critical. It also has these components:

- Presenting your credentials—what qualifies you to make the presentation to this audience
- Your organizational credibility—what qualifies your group or team
- Connecting with the audience by showing evidence that you know something about them: their needs, concerns, fears, issues, hopes, or dreams
- Identifying the purpose—"why we're here" and defining the problem or need and its relevance
- Mapping out the presentation—what you are going to tell them, what to expect, and how it addresses the problem or need

The middle of the presentation, that is, the body, begins by outlining the content, naming or otherwise identifying each point you'll make. To make it effective and interesting:

- Include examples and personal stories.
- Vary the media you use, incorporating handouts, video, and other formats.
- Conduct an activity to engage your audience.
- Pay attention to making bridges between points.
- Do periodic summaries or recaps.

- Help the audience visualize what you are presenting by painting a picture with words.

- Ask for what you want.

   The conclusion should wrap everything up:

- Summarize your main points.

- Identify the significance of your presentation.

- Tell another story to open their hearts.

- Identify the next steps, and ask for the action or commitment you want.

- Take questions.

- Obtain specific commitment, if possible.

Consider Multimedia

Since people have different learning styles—some prefer to listen, others need to see it in writing, or with graphics or photos—you'll increase your impact if you use more than your voice. Consider how you might use:

PowerPoint	DVD clips
Markers	Overheads
Photos	Materials for activities
Handouts	Flip charts and easels

Assemble Content

People love good stories, and you'll find it easy to deliver your message using this medium. Try using stories to explain things such as the school's genuine needs that are being met by this program, how you got involved, and why you've continued.

Make all facts, data, statistics that you use clear and relevant. Cite studies and references only to convey credibility; don't overwhelm people with numbers.

Fine-Tune Your Delivery

These tips will help with your delivery:

• *Seating.* If the group is small, arrange to sit so there are no barriers between you (say, a desk or table) so you're not creating an us-versus-them situation.

• *Greeting.* If practical, shake hands with and introduce yourself to the people with whom you are meeting. Use your first and last names and one relevant affiliation (for example, "I'm a sophomore at East High School"). Ideally, your group can be introduced to your audience by a person who knows you both.

• *Body language.* Smile in a relaxed and natural way, and stand up straight, with your shoulders back and down (this opens up your lungs). Breathe deeply, into your belly (notice that your abdomen moves when you breathe). Then make eye contact. If you need to refer to notes, do so, and then look up at your audience. If you are speaking to a group, look around at everyone rather than focusing on one or two people.

• *Enunciation.* Speak clearly, and don't mumble. If you are speaking to a group, project your voice to fill the room without shouting. If you have a microphone, watch the preceding speaker to learn how far away your mouth should be. Make sure you speak naturally, with emphasis and inflection, rather than in a monotone.

• *Speed.* Vary the pace of your words. Everyone naturally speaks more quickly when they are excited about something and more slowly when they want to emphasize a point. Like punctuation marks, pauses help add emphasis; when you pause, look at your audience.

• *Practice.* Practice in solitude, in front of a mirror, with a family member or friend, or before a group. This helps with your timing and sequencing. Ideally you want to know your subject so thoroughly that you can speak about it in a spontaneous manner, referring only to a few bullet points to sequence the main ideas of your message.

Responding to Questions and Concerns

Seek first to understand, then to be understood.

—STEVEN COVEY

IN RESPONDING TO THE QUESTIONS people ask and even the challenges they may present, it is important to remember Covey's advice. Becoming defensive is the first step down a long road of opposition; don't take it. It is not important to be right or to win a debate; what matters more is establishing common ground and taking concrete action to create schools and communities in which young people feel safer and more welcome, both physically and emotionally.

The following are typical of the questions that arise during the process of explaining the approach and program model to others, whether in a conversation or in a meeting. The responses to each question are not to be memorized, but rather understood and integrated into your own views and knowledge base.

"We really don't have a lot of problems like fights, shootings, or even much bullying."

This response often comes from a lack of awareness. Perhaps the person does not have the information that you do: discipline statistics, results from a climate survey, or even notes from a series of interviews with campus supervisors, counselors, and disciplinarians. Perhaps the person does not have the same type or level of contact with students that you have. So acknowledge this person's perspective and then share what you know. If you don't know the extent of the mistreatment, take the time before the question is asked to gather more information:

- Interview the campus supervisors, counselors, and disciplinarians; ask them to document the number of times in a given week or month they have to deal with each of the five types of peer mistreatment discussed in Chapter One or their consequences. Consider bringing them to your meetings with key decision makers to offer their testimony in support of the point you are trying to make.

- Find out how many students get detentions for harassment or are suspended for fighting in a typical month.

- Conduct a climate survey. This strategy brings the experiences of students into the full view of adults and may surprise or even shock them.

In some situations, that lack of awareness might be more than just not knowing; it might be not wanting to know. Some school officials might be reluctant to acknowledge the existence of these behaviors due to possible repercussions, perceived or actual. We have worked with schools whose district officials did not want them to report harassment or even small fights because they were concerned that the school might be deemed a "persistently dangerous school" under the No Child Left Behind Act. This designation would trigger a series of negative consequences that could include parents' pulling their children out, loss of funding, and state takeover. We have also worked in communities at the other end of the spectrum, where the expectations are very high and school leaders feel tremendous pressure to maintain the highest of standards in academics and behavior. In these schools, acknowledging the existence of mistreatment amounts to an admission of failure and may earn a not-so-golden parachute for an administrator who would go on record as saying, "We have a problem here in our school." In this case, it can be helpful to explore with the administrator what the risk or downside is of discovering and acknowledging that there is a problem with mistreatment at the school and then gain support for at least doing a checkup on the school's social-emotional climate in much the same way that people benefit from going to a doctor for regular checkups.

Another reason for this "we have no serious mistreatment problems" response can come from a misunderstanding of terms. Many schools have an epidemic of intolerance and cruelty but few signs of trouble that are visible to adults. Adults can more easily see and more often deal with pushing, physical bullying, fights, and weapons on campus. As noted in Chapter One, these issues are just the tip of the iceberg. Virtually every campus has other behavioral issues that are precursors to these more extreme kinds of violence. The mistreatment that too often goes unnoticed by adults is what grows into more significant problems, such as fights and weapons showing up on campus. The research shows that adults miss as much as 80 to 90 percent of the bullying and cruelty that occur on a school campus. Relational aggression, rumors, put-downs, deliberate exclusion, and other issues escape the view of most adults, but they have a significant negative impact on students and on learning. Schools have to address the less visible mistreatment to prevent problems from growing and in order to establish a safer school climate.

"This is just kids being kids."
This response often comes from people who see the behavior but don't see it as a problem. Perhaps they are unaware of the costs of mistreatment—how it affects not only the targets but also the aggressors and the bystanders, the school as a whole, and the larger community. Perhaps they are aware of the costs, but only intellectually; the sharp edge of the pain that targets and others feel has been dulled by age and distance. Or perhaps they experienced similar things themselves and, because they have "survived it" and perhaps even grown stronger from it, they believe that the experience will have similar outcomes for others.

To begin, it can be helpful to ask these people to imagine working in an environment where wearing a new shirt is as likely to draw an insult as it is to draw a compliment, where a bump in the hallway is as likely to trigger a standoff and a threat as it is to evoke an apology. Describe other situations that students face regularly, based on Chapter One. Then ask how they would feel, how confident they would be, how open they would be to taking on new projects, and how motivated and productive they would be.

Draw from the evidence presented in Chapter Two to help these people see the tremendous emotional and social costs of cruelty and violence to individual students, their schools, their families, and our society. This research comes from respected and unbiased professionals in education, social science, and the medical field. Over the past twenty years, it has changed many people's perceptions that bullying is a normal and necessary part of growing up; it's not. Young people have a right to be safe at school, both physically and emotionally, and we should all support that right.

It is also helpful to point out that while some types of mistreatment may have seemed okay years ago, today's world is different. Not only do we know more about the costs of mistreatment; the risks of not addressing it are greater. Today it is far more likely that a target who has had enough of mistreatment will decide to accomplish with violence what others seem unwilling or unable to accomplish with discipline, counseling, policies, and programs. Changes in society, greater access to weapons, and precedents all increase the odds that a target will come back to school armed with guns and other weapons and get even. At least two-thirds of all school shooters had been targets of bullying and harassment and perceived that the school was not doing anything to help them.

"We've done this before. We've already got a peer mediation [or conflict resolution] program."

This response is quite understandable, since many school staff feel overwhelmed and at times suffer from program burnout. Educators today are being stretched and challenged as never before: the academic bar is being raised by state standards and parental pressure, students' intellectual and social-emotional needs are increasing as nonschool supports are disappearing, and school funding is being cut. Many educators will eagerly (and perhaps cynically) recount stories of programs that have come and gone with little or no lasting effect. Acknowledging these challenges is the first part of addressing this concern.

The second part is to point out that in such times, it is helpful to enlist support from every quarter. Too often students are overlooked and underused in the search for solutions to schools' problems. Our approach harnesses the power of students it enlists them as allies in the effort to build and maintain a positive and healthy school climate for students and staff.

Next, it can be helpful to learn more about the existing peer mediation or conflict resolution program: how students are recruited and selected, what skills they have, when and where they work, how other students access their services. Based on this information, point out the ways that this approach is complementary. Empowerment programs extend the model of peer helping to situations and social groups that the vast majority of peer mediation programs will never reach. Since this approach puts empowered and skilled students out on the campus, proactively noticing and always available, they are more likely to be able to stop the kinds of trouble that won't wait for an appointment with a peer conflict mediator. Moreover, some of the students who get involved in this new effort are not already engaged in school activities. This type of program creates opportunities for them to bond with their school, feel more like owners than renters, and make a positive difference, all of which are likely to increase their academic performance and other positive behaviors.

Based on what has been presented in Chapter One and whatever data you have gathered about the need for this effort, there is probably enough student-on-student mistreatment to warrant having more than a conflict resolution program. Beyond the simple numerical need, there are many types of mistreatment that cannot be brokered through conflict resolution. Whenever the aggressor's needs—for power, prestige, or something else—are being met by the behavior, he or she will have no desire to stop it, so conflict resolution approaches will have little lasting effect. In many other interactions between students, neither party seeks help through conflict resolution until the problem is too great. Furthermore, unless the most socially influential students are brokering the conflicts through a conflict resolution program, those who are involved are less likely to be listened to. Chapter Three presents a more thorough discussion of conflict mediation programs and why they are not by themselves enough to address mistreatment on a school campus. The bottom line is that schools are better off having both efforts.

"We've already have a curriculum that we use. I don't see why we need something else."

Chapter Three discusses the strengths and limitations of curricula in greater detail, including reasons that students are typically more effective at teaching social skills and norms to their peers than adults are. In sum, if a climate survey of students and staff, coupled with interviews with counselors and disciplinarians, reveals that peer mistreatment does not occur on campus, then the current curricular approach is probably sufficient. If these assessments show that mistreatment is still happening, then the current approach is not sufficient to significantly reduce mistreatment, and for reasons discussed in Parts Two and Three, it would likely be prudent to invest in empowering students and equipping them to become allies in building a more positive campus climate.

"Campus climate and discipline are adult responsibilities. There is no need to take this to the students; the adults are in charge."

Although the rules of behavior are set by adults, the norms of behavior are largely set by the students. The ability of adults to address these issues is limited; putting students at the center of stopping mistreatment on campus is critical. Certainly adults need to be more aware and better trained to deal with cruelty. Remember, however, that adults miss approximately 80 to 90 percent of the mistreatment that occurs on a school campus. No matter how well-trained adults are, they cannot be everywhere that students are. Aggressors know how to avoid adults. It takes both a top-down approach from adults and an inside-out approach by empowering students as allies.

"How safe are students when they do these interventions? Have there been reprisals? What about liability issues?"

Students should not be asked to physically break up fights. They are asked to go about their ordinary routines with increased awareness and skill. So when they notice something that could lead to violence—deliberate exclusion, teasing, intimidation, bullying, eyeballing—they are trained to use a full spectrum of intervention strategies which include getting help from adults for situations that require more skill or strength than they alone possess. Since students' most assertive interventions are with the people they know best—their friends and family—reprisals are unlikely, and none has been reported to date by the thousands of students currently working in schools using the program on which this book is based.

As for liability, the model in this book is based on the principles of peer helping, which has an impressive record of safety. For example, throughout the entire history of the peer-helping movement in California, there has never been a single liability issue brought forward concerning students helping other students.

⌒

"We don't have the time."

It's likely that the people saying this are weighing what they know from their experience against an intangible unknown that you are proposing to them. They know well that the students who are missing class for training and meetings are the students who are not in the class that is learning the things that will be on the next round of standardized tests, so test scores could fall. In addition, setting a precedent for students in this program could open the floodgates to a multitude of requests from staff running all sorts of programs for their students to miss class for various trips and projects; in fact, this already occurs regularly for participants in team sports. They also know, perhaps personally, that staff members are stretched thin to do what is already being asked of them; adding more time for training and meetings is not very appealing. The unknown to them is the benefit of having students as allies on campus, empowered and equipped to stop mistreatment before it escalates. What will that be like? Create vivid, believable, personalized images, using numbers (the amount of time it takes to handle one suspension, for example) and testimonials from other educators whose schools have preceded them down this path. Help them grasp the benefits.

The effort of empowering youth to address mistreatment is an investment that reduces the amount of time administrators spend dealing with discipline issues, which frees that time for other purposes. When students are properly equipped for this role, they will address mistreatment before it grows into more serious problems. For example, if a student is angry about what someone said about him and brings this problem to an adult, it not only takes the adult's time but takes the adult off task. Ambassadors address mistreatment in the hallways and on the school grounds before it erupts in a classroom. When these problems do erupt in the classroom, that takes time and creates stress. The strategies presented in this book will save adults time and create more peace of mind and ease in teaching while creating a better work and learning environment.

In addition, students are doing the work and investing the time. They are an untapped resource that can be tapped to work with adults to create a safer place, and what's more, they want to be involved. Kurt Hahn, in *Readings from the Hurricane Island Outward Bound School,* said: "There are three ways of trying to win the young. There is persuasion, there is compulsion, and there is attraction. You can preach at them: that is a hook without a worm. You can say, 'You must volunteer,' and that is of the devil. You can tell them 'you are needed.' That approach hardly ever fails."[1]

"We can't take too much class time."

A huge benefit of this effort is that it takes a minimal amount of class time. Some antibullying efforts require teaching a curriculum during class time. While some readers might be tempted to take these skills to students by teaching them during class, that has not proven to be a very effective method. These skills are actually designed to be taught to socially influential leaders outside the classroom. Ambassadors need continued support for using their skills, and this can be done at any time of day and usually accomplished in brief meetings once every two weeks.

"Isn't this ambassadors group just a narc club, a bunch of kids who are going around telling on other students? Won't other students just see these kids as snitches?"

These ambassadors are there to help their friends make good choices about how to treat people and how to stay out of trouble. They learn many intervention skills, most of which they use directly with their friends and classmates. Most adults and students on campus won't even see or know what the ambassadors are saying and doing with their friends to stop mistreatment. As mentioned in Chapter Eight, only one of the skills involves tapping the support available from adults, and national survey data show that students go to adults in fewer than 20 percent of their interventions.

"Are these ambassadors just undercover student cops?"

These students have no police power or function. They have no position of authority over other students. They are simply the most influential students who are being trained to use their influence with their friends in positive ways.

Regarding the "undercover" issue, in some cliques in some schools, students will be more effective if their friends forget that they are trained in these skills. So you can help your trained students by not reminding the student body of who they are. We recommend that you:

- Do not post a list with their names.

- Do not read their names over the school PA system.

- Do not make an announcement in the middle of class that asks all the trained students to report to Mr. Smith's room for a meeting (which requires them to stand up in front of their peers and shuffle off to the meeting).

If some students are comfortable letting their peers know that they are trained in the intervention skills, then let them do so on an individual basis.

Of course, students will often want to know what this student training stuff is about. We recommend somewhat vague answers about training "to help people get along." Being too specific about being trained to stop bullying and violence can set ambassadors up to be challenged by their friends to "stop this, why don'tcha?"

"How much does it cost?"

Schools considering implementation of a youth empowerment program would need to secure funds to cover the following types of expenses:

- The cost of the program and training provided, as well as any travel expenses for trainers who would come to the school to provide the training
- Substitutes for any teachers who participate in the training
- Logistics for the training and any follow-up activities, including food, supplies, transportation, and possibly rental of a training site if it could not be done on campus
- Stipends or other compensation or acknowledgement for the adults involved

Many of these expenses can be covered through in-kind support from a school district or other community organization. Actual dollar expenditures that cannot be covered by Safe and Drug-Free Schools, Title I, or other school funds can often be written into future grants or secured through donations by local businesses, service clubs, or foundations.

It is also important to consider the cost of the time required of adults to recruit and select the students, organize the training, and provide the supervision and support the students will need. These responsibilities are more fully described in Chapter Six. Many adults get very enthused about innovative and well-conceived programs that show promise for addressing important issues like bullying and violence and are willing to put in a great deal of personal time and energy for very little additional compensation or recognition. However, it is important that the give-and-take feels equitable so the program can be sustained over the long term.

Ambassador Survey

Your School: _____ **Are you:** (*please fill in*) ○ Male ○ Female

Today's Date: ____ / ____ / ____ **Your Birth Date:** ____ / ____ / ____

What grade are you in? (*please fill in*) ○ 6 ○ 7 ○ 8 ○ 9 ○ 10 ○ 11 ○ 12

What are the first 3 letters of your last name? ____ / ____ / ____

What do you consider yourself to be? (*please check all that apply*)

○ Latino/Hispanic/Mexican   ○ Native American/American Indian, Eskimo, or Aleut

○ Black or African American   ○ White/Not of Hispanic origin

○ Asian or Pacific Islander   ○ Other _____

1. How much do you agree or disagree with each of the following statements? Fill in the circle.

	Strongly Disagree	Disagree	Neither Agree or Disagree	Agree	Strongly Agree
a. I am happy to be at this school.	○	○	○	○	○
b. I feel close to people at this school.	○	○	○	○	○
c. I feel safe at this school.	○	○	○	○	○
d. I think I am a leader.	○	○	○	○	○
e. My friends see me as a leader and usually follow me or agree with me.	○	○	○	○	○
f. I get good grades.	○	○	○	○	○

(*continued*)

	Strongly Disagree	Disagree	Neither Agree or Disagree	Agree	Strongly Agree
g. Learning and studying are important to me.	○	○	○	○	○
h. My friends are more important than learning and studying.	○	○	○	○	○
i. Before I say or do something, I think about how it will affect other people.	○	○	○	○	○
j. It is important that people are treated fairly.	○	○	○	○	○
k. I say what I think and believe, even if it's not what other people think and believe.	○	○	○	○	○
l. I will probably do well at something even if it was hard at first.	○	○	○	○	○
m. I would feel comfortable eating lunch with students from many different groups (like skaters, "jocks").	○	○	○	○	○
n. I would feel comfortable eating lunch with students from other backgrounds and races.	○	○	○	○	○
o. The adults at this school are kind and care about me.	○	○	○	○	○
p. I would like to do something to reduce teasing, bullying, and other kinds of mistreatment at school.	○	○	○	○	○
q. People my age can make a big difference in their school.	○	○	○	○	○

2. How often in the past 4 weeks of school did you notice other students:

	Never	Rarely (less than once a week)	Sometimes (a few times a week)	Often (at least once a day)
a. Leaving another student out of a conversation, game, or activity	○	○	○	○
b. Spreading mean rumors or gossip about another student	○	○	○	○
c. Using words, looks, or hand motions to make another student feel bad	○	○	○	○
d. Scaring, threatening, or bullying another student	○	○	○	○
e. Tripping, kicking, hitting, or physically hurting another student	○	○	○	○

3. How often in the past 4 weeks of school have you done the following things?

	Never	Rarely (less than once a week)	Sometimes (a few times a week)	Often (at least once a day)
a. I left another student out of a game, talk, or activity.	○	○	○	○
b. I said or did something mean to another student (teased, put down, or told a hurtful rumor). . .	○	○	○	○
c. I threatened, scared, or bullied another student.	○	○	○	○
d. I pushed, hit, or kicked another student on purpose.	○	○	○	○
e. I felt like I should have stood up for someone who was being teased or pushed around, but I did not.	○	○	○	○

4. Think about your friends at school.

How often in the past 4 weeks of school have you, yourself, said or done the following things to help YOUR FRIENDS?	Never	Rarely (less than once a week)	Sometimes (a few times a week)	Often (at least once a day)
a. I showed care and concern for a friend whose feelings had been hurt.	○	○	○	○
b. I told a friend to think about how their words or actions make other people feel.	○	○	○	○
c. I told a friend to think about the consequences of their actions (what might happen to him or her).	○	○	○	○
d. I said something positive about a friend who was being put down (being called bad names or teased).	○	○	○	○
e. I saw or heard a friend being mean and told her/him to stop.	○	○	○	○
f. I got an adult to help handle a situation I didn't think I could handle by myself.	○	○	○	○
g. I really listened to a friend who needed to talk about something that was bothering them.	○	○	○	○

5. Think about other students at your school who aren't your close friends.

How often in the past 4 weeks of school have you, yourself, said or done the following things to help OTHER STUDENTS who ARE NOT your friends?	Never	Rarely (less than once a week)	Sometimes (a few times a week)	Often (at least once a day)
a. I showed care and concern for someone whose feelings had been hurt.	○	○	○	○
b. I told someone to think about how their words or actions make other people feel.	○	○	○	○

c. I told someone to think about the consequences of their actions (what might happen to him or her).	○	○	○	○
d. I said something positive about someone who was being put down (being called bad names or teased).	○	○	○	○
e. I saw or heard another student being mean and told that student to stop.	○	○	○	○
f. I got an adult to help handle a situation I didn't think I could handle by myself.	○	○	○	○
g. I really listened to someone who needed to talk about something that was bothering them.	○	○	○	○

6. How many of these survey questions did you answer honestly?

○ None   ○ A Few   ○ About Half   ○ Most   ○ All

Thanks!

Recruiting Allies and Partners

THE WORKSHEETS IN THIS APPENDIX are designed to guide you through a process of planning how to gain allies and secure support for any new initiative. As the case studies in Chapter Ten highlighted, each person who wanted to use the model presented in this book had to get at least one other person excited about the prospect and secure support to move forward. If you are a parent, you will need to find allies in the school or district and eventually secure the support of the building principal and leadership team. If you are a principal, you'll need to get your leadership team and staff on board, as well as a few key people at the district office.

The level of planning described here may be far more than you need in your particular situation. Take the ideas that apply to you and leave the rest; don't feel obligated to do every step.

Step 1: Be Prepared

Do your homework so that when you speak with others you can be clear about your:

- Vision—for example, "a school where every student feels welcome and safe, both physically and emotionally"

- Mission—for example, "Reduce mistreatment and improve the climate"

- What you offer—for example, "A unique and powerful strategy: engaging and empowering youth to work as allies with adults"

- Your needs—for example, "The site council's vote to allocate some of their budget to cover part of the costs of a training"

Take the time to write these down, so you can be clear and so that others who come on board can catch up quickly and align their efforts with yours.

Step 2: Identify Potential Allies

As discussed in step 3 of Chapter Ten, it is helpful to identify potential allies. Do some brainstorming to come up with a list of people or organizations, or both, that might be strong advocates of youth development, violence prevention and safety, or a related area. Also identify people who have the positional power (for example, a principal) or relational power (for example, a popular teacher or vice principal who knows everyone) to make things happen. Scan for people with connections, special knowledge, or experiences that relate to your effort—perhaps a parent who has position, resources, and clout or a school board member whose child attends the school. Think about who might have a stake or vested interest in reducing mistreatment and improving the climate at the school.

After you have identified potential detractors in step 5, come back to this list to identify people who might have influence with those detractors and might help them change their minds.

Once you have your list, you might want to group them by sector—for example, school site, school district, school board, business, media, parents, and so on. Then complete the rest of the chart shown on page 277, using one line for each organization. The first line shows an example. *Linkage* is about how the person or organization is related to you and your effort. Who has a connection there? *Interest* describes why the person or organization might want to speak with you. How does their work or mission relate to you and yours? *Ability* refers to what power they hold and what they could do for you (for example, a wealthy parent or service club could write a check; a school board member could vote for what you are proposing).

Once this information is laid out, it is easier to prioritize your outreach efforts.

Step 3: Research Your Audience

Having a better understanding of the people you might be approaching allows you to connect with them and more easily gain their support. For each individual and group named in your plan, begin researching the person in order to determine how you might cultivate a relationship. You might find it helpful to

Sectors	Organizations	Individuals	Linkage	Interest	Ability
Media	*San Francisco Chronicle*	Mike Smith	Cousin	Parent	On school board

determine the characteristics listed in the worksheet here (some of which apply more to groups than to individuals). Not everyone will be researched to the same depth and level of detail. Use one copy of the worksheet on page 278 for each group or individual.

Audience Profile

Name of potential ally:_____

Name of person's organization:_____

1. Demographics: age, residence, income, education, affiliations, values, interests, other related information

2. What are the mission and purpose of:

   This individual?   This person's organization?

3. What resources does this person have to support our efforts?

4. Possible forms of involvement: What might we ask of him or her?

5. What are the hot button issues for:

   This individual?   This person's organization?

6. How do we tie or link this person's concerns or issues to our efforts? What are the WIIFMs (what's in it for me) for:

   This individual?   This person's organization?

7. What hard questions might this person ask? What objections might he or she have?

8. What are our answers or responses to those questions or objections?

9. What other potential barriers or challenges would have to be overcome to secure their involvement?

Step 4: Cultivate a Relationship

People often make decisions based on the relationship they have with the person making the request. Begin to identify ways you might develop or strengthen your relationship with this individual. Consider letters or informational updates, calls, meetings, or invitations to activities, for example.

Step 5: Ask for Support

Eventually it will be necessary to ask the person for support. Give some consideration to these issues:

- Who might ask: a close friend of the person, a member of your group, a student?

- When the person should be asked. How soon? How much time do you need to cultivate the relationship?

- Where should the person be asked, that is, in what forum: one-to-one informal or formal? Large meeting? At one of your activities or events?

- What information or materials would support and strengthen your request?

- What do you need from this person? How might he or she be involved?

Needs Assessment

BUSY PEOPLE TEND to do the things that most need to be done. Launching an initiative to reduce or prevent bullying by empowering students at a school or district will require enlisting the support of many busy people. All of them will want to know why such a step is needed.

Chapter One detailed the problem of mistreatment and Chapter Two explored its costs on many levels. The idea behind a needs assessment is to do something similar for the school or schools you are concerned about. The goal of the needs assessment is to determine as specifically and concretely as possible the nature and extent of the problem of mistreatment and its costs for your school.

You might find it helpful to begin by talking with your principal about assessments of school climate and mistreatment that might have been done in the past year or two.

What You Are Looking For

Begin by naming the different types of mistreatment you and your colleagues observe or at least know occur at your school. Consider working with the five types of mistreatment articulated in Chapter One: exclusion, put-downs, bullying and intimidation, unwanted physical contact, and acts against everyone. You might find that in order to obtain meaningful data, you need to make your types of mistreatment correspond to the discipline data that your school gathers. This might lead to establishing subsets of the five types of mistreatment.

Once you have established categories for behavior, explore how they are commonly dealt with. Look at the ways that each affects teachers, counselors, and other administrators, and document what you hear.

Where to Find It

Consider drawing on the following sources of information for the needs assessment:

- *Personal experience.* What forms of mistreatment and violence do you observe and experience from your vantage point? How does that affect the teaching and learning that are supposed to happen at school?

- *Anecdotes.* Speak with the counselors, campus supervisors, assistant principals, and others on the front line of mistreatment at your school. What do they see? How much time do they spend dealing with the students involved and the resulting paperwork? What impact do they see mistreatment having on teaching and learning?

- *Discipline data.* Your school likely collects data on incidents (harassment, threats, fights, and so on) and their disposition (warning, detention, in-school suspension, out-of-school suspension, expulsion). These data not only provide hard evidence about the extent of mistreatment currently; they also provide a baseline against which to measure the impact new strategies are having. Speak with a counselor or assistant principal who handles discipline about what data are available.

- *Climate survey.* This is a more comprehensive tool for assessing how people feel at your school, the kinds of mistreatment that concern them, where and when it takes place, how well it is handled, and so on. Community Matters has developed a climate survey for this purpose (see the Resources section). In California, the California Healthy Kids Survey can also meet this need; outside California, contact your state or county educational resource center. If a climate survey has been done, it can help justify and focus your effort to put youth at the center of addressing mistreatment. If one has not been done, consider working with your school safety team to administer one.

How to Organize Your Information

Since you will want to share this information with a number of people, you will need to develop several different reports. The most basic is the "thirty-second elevator pitch," a way of using key findings to hook someone who has only a little bit of time to listen to you. You'll likely also want to put together a written summary (preferably a one-page piece) that could be distributed at a staff meeting or similar forum, as a way of substantiating what you are presenting verbally. Charts and graphs work well to convey a large amount of information in a short time.

At minimum, we suggest you write down why you believe this program is needed. What is true about:

- The way people are mistreated at your school?
- The number of discipline referrals and reasons they are given?
- The number of suspensions and expulsions, and reasons for them?

With a needs assessment in hand, it is far easier to make an effective presentation to enlist the support of other individuals and organizations.

INTRODUCTION

1. National Association of Secondary School Principals, quoted in B. Coloroso, *The Bully, the Bullied, and the Bystander: From Preschool to High School: How Parents and Teachers Can Help Break the Cycle of Violence* (New York: HarperCollins, 2002), 50.

2. J. H. Hoover, R. Oliver, and R. J. Hazler, "Bullying: Perceptions of Adolescent Victims in Midwestern USA," *School Psychology International,* 1991, *13,* 5–16.

3. R. H. Shaffer, "The Inspiration Behind the Gift: A Short Biography of Robert H. Shaffer," Indiana University Foundation, retrieved from http://iufoundation.iu.edu/Places_to_Give/Class_Campaigns/Robert_Shaffer.html.

CHAPTER ONE

1. J. DeVoe and others, *Indicators of School Crime and Safety: 2005* (Washington, D.C.: U.S. Department of Education, National Center for Education Statistics, 2005), Table 2.1, 72.

2. DeVoe and others, 2005, 42.

3. DeVoe and others, 2005, Table 5.1, 78.

4. DeVoe and others, 2005, Table 6.1, 79.

5. DeVoe and others, 2005, Table 6.2, 80.

6. R. Fein and others, *Threat Assessment in Schools: A Guide to Managing Threatening Situations and to Creating Safe School Climates* (Washington, D.C.: U.S. Department of Education Office of Elementary and Secondary

Education, Safe and Drug-Free Schools Program and U.S. Secret Service, National Threat Assessment Center, 2004), 11.

7. "The In Crowd and Social Cruelty," *ABC News Special*, ABC, Feb. 15, 2002.

8. "The In Crowd and Social Cruelty," 2002.

9. P. M. Greenfield and J. Juvonen, "A Developmental Look at Columbine," *APA Monitor*, 1999, *30*(7), 1.

10. T. R. Nansel and others, "Bullying Behaviors Among US Youth: Prevalence and Association with Psychosocial Adjustment," *Journal of the American Medical Association*, 2001, *285*, 2094–2100.

11. U.S. Department of Health and Human Services, Health Resources and Services Administration, *U.S. Teens in Our World* (Washington, D.C.: U.S. Department of Health and Human Services, 2003), retrieved from http://www.mchb.hrsa.gov/mchirc/_pubs/us_teens/main_pages/ch_6.htm.

12. T. P. Tarshis and L. C. Huffman, "Psychometric Properties of the Peer Interactions in Primary School (PIPS) Questionnaire," *Journal of Developmental and Behavioral Pediatrics*, 2007, *28*, 125–132.

13. D. Pepler and C. Smith, "Bullying and Victimization: Experiences of Immigrant and Minority Youth," paper presented at a colloquium sponsored by the Joint Centre of Excellence for Research on Immigration and Settlement and LaMarsh Centre for Research on Violence and Conflict Resolution, Feb. 1999, CERIS Report: Bullying and Harassment: Experiences of Minority and Immigrant Youth, retrieved from http://ceris.metropolis.net/Virtual%20Library/education/pepler1/pepler1.html.

14. National Center for Student Aspirations, *The Students Speak Survey* (Orono: College of Education and Human Development, University of Maine, 2001), quoted in National School Safety Center Review of School Safety Research, National School Safety Center, Westlake Village, California, Jan. 2006, 7–8.

15. S. Harris, "Bullying at School Among Older Adolescents," *Prevention Researcher*, 2004, *11*(3), 12–14.

16. E. Galinsky and K. Salmond, *Youth and Violence: Students Speak Out for a More Civil Society: Summary and Discussion Guide* (New York: Families and Work Institute, 2002), 2.

17. "National Survey of Teens Shows Anti-Gay Bullying Common in Schools," National Mental Health Association, Dec. 12, 2002, retrieved from http://www1.nmha.org/newsroom/system/news.vw.cfm?do=vw&rid=474.

18. American Association of University Women Educational Foundation, *Hostile Hallways: Bullying, Teasing, and Sexual Harassment in School 2001,* retrieved from http://www.aauw.org/research/hostile.cfm.

19. DeVoe and others, 2005, Table 17.1.

20. National Crime Prevention Council, "Teens and Cyberbullying," Feb. 28, 2007, retrieved from http://vocuspr.vocus.com/VocusPR30/Newsroom/ViewAttachment.aspx?SiteName=NCPCNew&Entity=PRAsset&AttachmentType=F&EntityID=99295&AttachmentID=57d58695–7e1d-404c-a0f0-d5f6d0b18996.

21. M. J. Boulton and K. Underwood, "Bully/Victim Problems Among Middle School Children," *British Journal of Educational Psychology,* 1992, *62, 73*–87; I. Whitney and P. K. Smith, "A Survey of the Nature and Extent of Bullying in Junior/Middle and Secondary Schools,"*Educational Research,* 1993, *35*(1) 3–25; G. B. Melton and others, *Violence Among Rural Youth* (Washington, D.C.: Office of Juvenile Justice and Delinquency Prevention, 1998).

22. T. R. Reid, "Newly Released Columbine Writings Reveal Killers' Mind-set," *Washington Post,* July 7, 2006, A-3.

23. House Committee on Transportation and Infrastructure, Subcommittee on Surface Transportation, Hearing on Road Rage: Causes and Dangers of Aggressive Driving, 105th Cong., 1st sess., 1997, 13 retrieved from http://commdocs.house.gov/committees/Trans/hpw105-34.000/hpw105-34_0f.htm.

24. Common Sense Media, www.commonsensemedia.org/resources.

25. C. A. Anderson and B. J. Bushman, "Effects of Violent Video Games on Aggressive Behavior, Aggressive Cognition, Aggressive Affect, Physiological Arousal, and Prosocial Behavior: A Meta-Analytic Review of the Scientific Literature," *Psychological Science,* 2001, *12, 353*–359.

CHAPTER TWO

1. *NBC Dateline Special Report: On the Edge,* NBC, Jan. 7, 2003.

2. J. R. Bullock, "Bullying Among Children,"*Childhood Education,* 2002, *78*(3), 130–133.

3. R. Forero and others, "Bullying Behaviour and Psychosocial Health Among School Students in New South Wales, Australia: Cross Sectional Survey," *British Medical Journal,* 1999, *319,* 344, 348; R. Kaltiala-Heino and others, "Bullying, Depression, and Suicidal Ideation in Finnish Adolescents: School Survey," *British Medical Journal,* 1999, *319,* 348–351.

4. J. Juvonen, A. Nishina, and M. Witkow, "Sticks and Stones May Break My Bones, But Names Will Make Me Feel Sick: The Psychosocial, Somatic, and Scholastic Consequences of Peer Harassment," *Journal of Clinical Child and Adolescent Psychology,* 2005, *34,* 37–48.

5. S. Sharp, "How Much Does Bullying Hurt? The Effects of Bullying on the Personal Well-Being and Educational Progress of Secondary Aged Students," *Educational and Child Psychology,* 1995, *12,* 81–88; P. C. Scales and N. Leffert, *Developmental Assets: A Synthesis of the Scientific Research on Adolescent Development* (Minneapolis: Search Institute, 1998), 57; P. T. Slee and K. Rigby, "Australian School Children's Self Appraisal of Interpersonal Relations: The Bullying Experience," *Child Psychiatry and Human Development,* 1993, *23,* 273–282; E. M. Anderman and D.M.S. Kimweli, "Victimization and Safety in Schools Serving Early Adolescents," *Journal of Early Adolescence,* 1997, *17,* 408–438.

6. C. A. McNeely, J. M. Nonnemaker, and R. W. Blum, "Promoting Student Connectedness to School: Evidence from the National Longitudinal Study of Adolescent Health," *Journal of School Health,* 2002, *72*(4), 138–146.

7. M. Boivin, S. Hymel, and E. Hodges, "Toward a Process View of Peer Rejection and Harassment," in J. Juvonen and S. Graham (eds.), *Peer Harassment in School: The Plight of the Vulnerable and Victimized* (New York: Guilford Press, 2001), 265–289.

8. D. Olweus, "Victimization by Peers: Antecedents and Long-Term Outcomes," in K. H. Rubin and J. B. Asendorf (eds.), *Social Withdrawal, Inhibitions, and Shyness* (Mahwah, N.J.: Erlbaum, 1993), 315–341.

9. Olweus, 1993. D. Olweus, "Bully/Victim Problems in School: Facts and Effective Intervention," *Reclaiming Children and Youth,* 1996, *5*(1), 15–22.

10. P. T. Slee, "Bullying: Health Concerns of Australian Secondary School Students," *International Journal of Adolescence and Youth,* 1995, no. 5, 215–224.

11. S. P. Limber and others, "Bullying Among School Children in the United States," in M. W. Watts (ed.), *Cross-Cultural Perspectives on Youth and Violence: Contemporary Studies in Sociology* (Stamford, Conn.: JAI Press, 1998), 159–173.

12. Olweus, 1993; K. Rigby, "Consequences of Bullying in Schools," *Canadian Journal of Psychiatry,* 2003, *48,* 583–590.

13. D. Goleman, *Emotional Intelligence: Why It Can Matter More Than IQ* (New York: Bantam Books, 1995), 27.

14. Juvonen, Nishina, and Witkow, 2005; H.-S. Wei and J. H. Williams, "Relationship Between Peer Victimization and School Adjustment in Sixth-Grade Students: Investigating Mediation Effects," *Violence and Victims,* 2004, *19,* 557–571.

15. J. H. Hoover and R. Oliver, *The Bullying Prevention Handbook* (Bloomington, Ind.: National Educational Service, 1996), 10.

16. R. Banks, "Bullying in Schools," *ERIC Review,* 2000, *7*(1), 12–14.

17. B. K. Weinhold and J. B. Weinhold, "Conflict Resolution: The Partnership Way in Schools," *Counseling and Human Development,* 1998, *30*(7), 1–2.

18. H. M. Walker, "Anti-Social Behavior in School," *Journal of Emotional and Behavioral Problems,* 1993, *2*(1), 20–24.

19. L. R. Huesmann, L. D. Eron, and P. W. Yarmel, "Intellectual Functioning and Aggression," *Journal of Personality and Social Psychology,* 1987, *52*(1), 232–240.

20. Slee, 1995.

21. L. R. Huesmann and others, "Stability of Aggression over Time and Generations," *Developmental Psychology,* 1984, *20,* 1120–1134.

22. D. C. Gottfredson, G. D. Gottfredson, and L. G. Hybl, "Managing Adolescent Behavior: A Multiyear, Multischool Study," *American Educational Research Journal,* 1993, *30,* 179–215; B. Kaiser and J. S. Rasminsky, *Challenging Behavior in Young Children: Understanding, Preventing, and Responding Effectively* (Needham Heights, Mass.: Pearson, 2003), 233–245.

23. Olweus, 1993.

24. T. R. Nansel and others, "Bullying Behaviors Among U.S. Youth: Prevalence and Association with Psychosocial Adjustment," *Journal of the American Medical Association,* 2001, *285,* 2094–2100.

25. D. Seals and J. Young, "Bullying and Victimization: Prevalence and Relationship to Gender, Grade Level, Ethnicity, Self-Esteem, and Depression," *Adolescence, 38,* 735–747.

26. Nansel and others, 2001.

27. W. M. Craig and D. J. Pepler, "Observations of Bullying and Victimization in the Schoolyard," *Canadian Journal of School Psychology,* 1997, *13,* 41–59.

28. M. S. Massey, *Early Childhood Violence Prevention* (Champaign: ERIC Clearinghouse on Elementary and Early Childhood Education, University of Illinois, 1998), 2–3.

29. B. S. McEwen and R. Sapolsky, "Stress and Cognitive Function," *Current Opinion in Neurobiology,* 1995, *5,* 205–216.

30. D. A. Sousa, "The Ramifications of Brain Research," *School Administrator* Web edition, Jan. 1998, retrieved from http://www.aasa.org/publications/sa/1998_01/sousa.htm.

31. J. Gabriel, "No Learning Without Peace," *Brain Connection,* retrieved from http://incus.brainconnection.com/topics/?main=fa/learning-peace.

32. Alliance for Excellent Education, "Teacher Attrition: A Costly Loss to the Nation and to the States," retrieved from http://www.all4ed.org/publications/TeacherAttrition.pdf.

33. R. M. Ingersoll, "High Turnover Plagues Schools," *USA Today,* Aug. 14, 2002.

34. McNeely, Nonnemaker, and Blum, 2002.

35. Centers for Disease Control and Prevention, "Youth Risk Behavior Surveillance—United States, 2005, Surveillance Summaries, June 9, 2006," *MMWR,* 2006, *55*(SS-5), 48.

36. Olweus, 1993; K. Rigby, "What Children Tell Us About Bullying in Schools," *Children Australia,* 1997, *22*(2), 28–34.

37. Banks, 2000.

38. B. Coloroso, *The Bully, the Bullied, and the Bystander: From Preschool to High School: How Parents and Teachers Can Help Break the Cycle of Violence* (New York: HarperCollins, 2002), 50.

39. Healthy Kids Resources, "California Healthy Kids Survey Fact Sheet: Health Risks, Resilience, and the Academic Performance Index: Preliminary Findings," 2001, retrieved from http://www.hkresources.org/articles/apifact.pdf.

40. N. Starkman, P. C. Scales, and C. Roberts, *Great Places to Learn: How Asset-Building Schools Help Students Succeed* (Minneapolis, Minn.: Search Institute, 1999), 42.

41. Scales and Leffert, 1998, 52.

42. S. Fried and P. Fried, *Bullies, Targets and Witnesses: Helping Children Break the Pain Chain* (New York: Evans, 2003), 295.

43. E. Timms, "Rural or Urban, Teens Look for Acceptance," *Seattle Times,* Mar. 25, 1998.

44. Fried and Fried, 2003, 5.

45. *The Dr. Phil Show,* July 16, 2003.

46. B. Vossekuil and others, *Final Report and Findings of the Safe School Initiative: Implications for the Prevention of School Attacks in the United States* (Washington, D.C.: U.S. Department of Education, Office of Elementary and Secondary Education, Safe and Drug-Free Schools Program and U.S. Secret Service, National Threat Assessment Center, 2002), 24.

47. B. Vossekuil and others, 21.

48. Alliance for Excellent Education, 2005.

49. B. Tatman, director of fiscal resources, Sonoma County Office of Education, Santa Rosa, Calif., interview with author, Feb. 9, 2006; U.S. Department of Education, National Center for Education Statistics, *Digest of Education Statistics: Tables and Figures, 2004* (Washington, D.C.: U.S. Government Printing Office, 2004), Table 168, retrieved from http://nces.ed.gov/programs/digest/d04/tables/dt04_168.asp.

50. U.S. Department of Education, National Center for Education Statistics, *Digest of Education Statistics: Tables and Figures, 2005* (Washington, D.C.:

U.S. Government Printing Office, 2005), Table 143, retrieved from http://nces.ed.gov/programs/digest/d05/tables/dt05_143.asp.

51. U.S. Department of Education, National Center for Education Statistics, *Violence and Discipline Problems in U.S. Schools, 1996–1997* (Washington, D.C.: U.S. Government Printing Office, 1997), Table 6, 54.

52. National Education Association, *Danger—School Ahead: Violence in the Public Schools* (Washington, D.C.: National Education Association: 1973); G. Stoner, M. Shinn, and H. M. Walker (eds.), *Interventions for Achievement and Behavior Problems* (Silver Spring, Md.: National Association of School Psychologists, 1991), cited in K. D. Johnson, *School Vandalism and Break-Ins* (Washington, D.C.: U.S. Government Printing Office, 2005), 4.

53. *The U.S. School Security Market* (Rockville, Md.: Packaged Facts, 2000), 2.

54. F. R. Menhard, *School Violence: Deadly Lessons* (Berkeley Heights, Calif.: Enslow, 2000), 16–17.

55. "Columbine Costs," *Rocky Mountain News*, Apr. 8, 2000, retrieved from http://rockymountainnews.com/shooting/0408chart.shtml.

56. "Bullying Case Costs Oregon School District $10,000," *Seattle Times*, Jan. 18, 2004, http://archives.seattletimes.nwsource.com/cgi-bin/texis.cgi/web/vortex/display?slug=bullying18&date=20040118.

57. C. Trowbridge, "Federal Jury Awards $250,000 to Former Tonganoxie Student," *Tonganoxie Mirror*, Aug. 11, 2005, http://www.tonganoxiemirror.com/section/breaking_news/story/8135.

58. S. Marshall, "Jury Awards Gay, Ex-Poway High Students $300K," *North Country Times*, June 8, 2005, http://www.nctimes.com/articles/2005/06/09/news/top_stories/22_51_256_8_05.txt.

59. L. U. Farrell, "Workplace Bullying's High Cost: $180M in Lost Time, Productivity," *Orlando Business Journal*, Mar. 18, 2002.

60. B. Egeland, D. Jacobovitz, and A. Sroufe, "Breaking the Cycle of Abuse," *Child Development*, 1988, *59*, 1080–1088.

61. Olweus, 1993.

62. D. Pepler and W. Craig, "What Should We Do About Bullying? Research into Practice," *Peacebuilder Magazine for Educators*, 1999, http://www.child-abuse-effects.com/bullying.html.

CHAPTER THREE

1. B. Vossekuil and others, *Final Report and Findings of the Safe School Initiative: Implications for the Prevention of School Attacks in the United States* (Washington, D.C.: U.S. Department of Education, Office of Elementary and Secondary Education, Safe and Drug-Free Schools Program and U.S. Secret Service, National Threat Assessment Center, 2002), 43.

2. "School Anti-Bullying Programs Work, Zero Tolerance, Security Programs Not Supported by Evidence," Indiana University Media Relations press release, Mar. 12, 2004, retrieved from http://newsinfo.iu.edu/news/page/normal/1333.html.

3. L. Garric, director of the Safe Schools Unit, Sonoma County Office of Education, California, telephone conversation with author, Feb. 14, 2006.

4. Fairfax County Public Schools, Office of Security and Risk Management Services, *Crisis Management Workbook,* retrieved from http://www.fcps.edu/fts/safety-security/publications/cmw.pdf.

5. M. Nieto, K. Johnston-Dodds, and C. W. Simmons, *Public and Private Applications of Video Surveillance and Biometric Technologies* (Sacramento: California Research Bureau, 2002), 29.

6. *The U.S. School Security Market* (Rockville, Md.: Packaged Facts, 2000), 2.

7. C. E. Hazel, "Making Schools Safe for All Children: Let's Not Hit the Snooze Button Again," *School Psychologist,* 2005, *59*(3), 100.

8. M. J. Mayer and P. E. Leone, "A Structural Analysis of School Violence and Disruption: Implications for Creating Safer Schools," *Education and Treatment of Children,* 1999, *22*, 333–356.

9. B. Knickerbocker, "Five Years After Columbine, the Insecurity Lingers," *Christian Science Monitor,* Apr. 20, 2004, sec. 4.

10. W. Cruz and E. Yan, "City Violence, Police Fight School Crime, Criminal Incidents Are Slightly Lower on 12 Campuses After Mayor Deployed 150 Officers in January," *Newsday,* Mar. 25, 2004, sec. A18.

11. P. A. Noguera, "Preventing and Producing Violence: A Critical Analysis of Responses to School Violence," *Harvard Educational Review,* 1995, *65*, 189–212.

12. "COPS Office Announces $4.9 Million to Increase School Safety in 27 States," U.S. Department of Justice Office of Community Oriented Policing Services, press release, 2003, 1.

13. M. A. Zehr, "Legislatures Take on Bullies with New Laws," *Education Week,* 2001, *20*(36), 18, 22, retrieved from http://www.edweek.org/ew/ewstory.cfm?slug=36bully.h20.

14. National Conference of State Legislatures, *Select School Safety Enactments 1994–2004,* retrieved from http://www.ncsl.org/programs/cyf/bullyingenac.htm.

15. U.S. Department of Education, National Center for Education Statistics, *Violence and Discipline Problems in U.S. Public Schools: 1996–97* (Washington, D.C.: U.S. Government Printing Office, 1998), Table 19, Figure 8.

16. Mayer and Leone, 1999.

17. D. Horn, *Bruised Inside: What Our Children Say About Youth Violence, What Causes It, and What We Need to Do About It* (Washington, D.C.: National Association of Attorneys General, 2000), 45.

18. C. A. McNeely, J. M. Nonnemaker, and R. W. Blum, "Promoting Student Connectedness to School: Evidence from the National Longitudinal Study of Adolescent Health," *Journal of School Health,* 2002, *72*(4), 145.

19. R. J. Skiba, *Zero Tolerance, Zero Evidence: An Analysis of School Disciplinary Practice* (Bloomington: Indiana Educational Policy Center, 2000), 16–17.

20. E. Little, "Criminalizing Kids: True Tales of Zero Tolerance Overcriminalization" (Washington, D.C.: Heritage Foundation, 2003), retrieved from http://over criminalized.com/studies/case_kids1.cfm.

21. ZTNightmares, "Zero Tolerance Nightmare at Rio Rancho High School," http://www.ztnightmares.com/html/paula_s_story.htm.

22. Skiba, 2000.

23. Vossekuil and others, 2002, 34.

24. M. Bonds and S. Stoker, *Bullyproofing Your School: A Comprehensive Approach for Middle Schools* (Longmont, Colo.: Sopris West, 2000).

25. L. Van Schoiack-Edstrom, K. S. Frey, and K. Beland, "Changing Adolescents' Attitudes About Relational and Physical Aggression," *School Psychology Review,* 2002, *31,* 201–216.

26. K. Rigby and B. Johnson, "Bystander Behavior of South Australian School Children: Observing Bullying Behavior and Sexual Coercion," retrieved from http://www.education.unisa.edu.au/bullying/FocusOnBystanders.pdf.

27. S. P. Limber, "Implementation of the Olweus Bullying Prevention Program in American Schools: Lessons Learned from the Field," in D. L. Espelage and S. M. Swearer (eds.), *Bullying in American Schools: A Social-Ecological Perspective on Prevention and Violence* (Mahwah, N.J.: Erlbaum, 2004), 351–363.

28. T. S. Jones, "Conflict Resolution Education: The Field, the Findings, and the Future," *Conflict Resolution Quarterly,* 2004, *22,* 233–266.

29. J. Batton, director of education programs, Ohio Commission on Dispute Resolution and Conflict Management, e-mail to author, Feb. 21, 2006.

30. E. Ford, "Oregon's SCRIP Model: Building School Conflict Resolution Education Capacity Through Community Partnerships," *Conflict Resolution Quarterly,* 2002, *19,* 465–477; M. Tschannen-Moran, "The Effects of a State-Wide Conflict Management Initiative in Schools," *American Secondary Education,* 2001, *29* (3), 2–32.

31. Ibid.

32. P. C. Scales and N. Leffert, *Developmental Assets: A Synthesis of the Scientific Research on Adolescent Development* (Minneapolis, Minn.: Search Institute, 1998), 186.

33. U.S. Office of the Surgeon General, U.S. Department of Health and Human Services, *Youth Violence: A Report of the Surgeon General* (Washington, D.C.: U.S. Government Printing Office, 2001).

34. R. Cohen, "Stop Mediating These Conflicts Now!" *School Mediator* (School Mediation Associates), Feb. 2002, 2, http://www.schoolmediation.com/newsletters/2002/2_02.html#article1.

CHAPTER FOUR

1. Bill Bond, resident practitioner for Safe and Orderly Schools, National Association of Secondary School Principals, telephone conversation with author, Sept. 7, 2007.

2. R. Fein and others, *Threat Assessment in Schools: A Guide to Managing Threatening Situations and to Creating Safe School Climates* (Washington, D.C.: U.S. Department of Education Office of Elementary and Secondary Education, Safe and Drug-Free Schools Program and U.S. Secret Service, National Threat Assessment Center, 2004), 5–6, 12–13.

3. G. Allport, *The Nature of Prejudice* (Reading, Mass.: Addison-Wesley, 1954); L. A. Foster, "Breaking Down Racial Isolation,"*Education Leadership* 1989, *47*(2), 76–77.

4. E. Farrell, *Self and School Success, Hanging In and Dropping Out: Voices of At-Risk High School Students* (New York: Teachers College Press, 1990).

5. R. W. Blum, C. A. McNeely, and P. M. Rinehart, *Improving the Odds: The Untapped Power of Schools to Improve the Health of Teens* (Minneapolis: Center for Adolescent Health and Development, 2002), 14.

6. WestEd, "California Healthy Kids Survey," retrieved from http://www .wested.org/pub/docs/hks_resilience.html.

7. A. D. Berkowitz, "The Social Norms Approach: Theory, Research, and Annotated Bibliography," August, 2004, retrieved from http://www.alanberkowitz .com/articles/social_norms.pdf.

CHAPTER FIVE

1. J. L. McBrien and R. S. Brandt, *The Language of Learning: A Guide to Education Terms* (Alexandria, Va.: Association for Supervision and Curriculum Development, 1997), 89.

2. R. Fein and others, *Threat Assessment in Schools: A Guide to Managing Threatening Situations and to Creating Safe School Climates* (Washington, D.C.: U.S. Department of Education, Office of Elementary and Secondary Education, Safe and Drug-Free Schools Program and U.S. Secret Service, National Threat Assessment Center, 2004) 5–6.

3. Fein and others, 11.

4. N. Noddings, "Schools Face Crisis in Caring," *Education Week,* Dec. 1998, 32.

5. D. S. Rentner, "Summary and Recommendations from the Center on Education Policy's from the Capital to the Classroom: Year 4 of the No Child Left Behind Act," Center on Education Policy, retrieved from http:// www.cepdc.org/_data/global/nidocs/NCLBYear4Summary.pdf.

6. Rentner.

7. T. L. Hanson, G. Austin, and J. Lee-Bayha, *Ensuring That No Child Is Left Behind: How Are Student Health Risks and Resilience Related to the Academic Progress of Schools?* (San Francisco: WestEd, 2004), 5.

8. M. D. Resnick and others, "Protecting Adolescents from Harm: Findings from the National Longitudinal Study on Adolescent Health," *Journal of the American Medical Association,* 2004, *278,* 823–832. Also B. Benard, *Resiliency: What We Have Learned* (San Francisco: WestEd, 2004), 65–88.

9. A. S. Bryk and B. Schneider, *Trust in Schools: A Core Resource for Improvement* (New York: Russell Sage Foundation, 2002).

10. Hanson, Austin, and Lee-Bayha, 2004.

11. C. Wallis and S. Steptoe, "How to Bring Our Schools Out of the 20th Century," *Time,* Dec. 18, 2006, 53.

12. Wallis and Steptoe, 2006.

13. B. Mesaros and K. Johnstad, "Measuring School Climate: Piloting a New Search Institute Tool," paper presented at the Annual Conference of the Search Institute, Minneapolis, 2002.

14. Ohio Department of Education, "Ohio School Climate Guidelines Foreword," retrieved from http://www.ode.state.oh.us/GD/Templates/Pages/ODE/ODEDetail.aspx?page=3&TopicRelationID=433&ContentID=1841&Content=27571.

15. Ohio Department of Education, "Ohio School Climate Guidelines," retrieved from http://www.ode.state.oh.us/GD/DocumentManagement/DocumentDownload.aspx?DocumentID=8563.

16. B. Benard, presentation on the relationship between academic success and youth development, June 23, 2006, California Department of Education, retrieved May 16, 2007, from http://www.cde.ca.gov/ls/yd/tr/bbenard.asp.

CHAPTER SIX

1. R. H. Shaffer, "The Inspiration Behind the Gift: A Short Biography of Robert H. Shaffer," Indiana University Foundation, retrieved from http://iufoundation.iu.edu/Places_to_Give/Class_Campaigns/Robert_Shaffer.html.

2. B. Benard, *Fostering Resiliency in Kids: Protective Factors in the Family, School and Community* (Portland, Ore.: Western Regional Center for Drug-Free Schools and Communities, Northwest Regional Educational Laboratory, 1991).

3. A. J. Huebner, "Examining Empowerment: A How-To Guide for the Youth Development Professional," *Journal of Extension,* 1998, *36*(6), retrieved from http://www.joe.org/joe/1998december/ent.html#a1.

4. R. Fein and others, *Threat Assessment in Schools: A Guide to Managing Threatening Situations and to Creating Safe School Climates* (Washington, DC: U.S. Department of Education, Office of Elementary and Secondary Education, Safe and Drug-Free Schools Program and U.S. Secret Service, National Threat Assessment Center, 2002).

5. P. C. Scales and N. Leffert, *Developmental Assets: A Synthesis of the Scientific Research on Adolescent Development* (Minneapolis, Minn.: Search Institute, 1998).

CHAPTER SEVEN

1. R. J. Hazler, "Bystanders: An Overlooked Factor in Peer on Peer Abuse," *Journal for the Professional Counselor,* 1996, *11*(2), 11–22; W. M. Craig and D. J. Pepler, "Peer Processes in Bullying and Victimization: An Observational Study," *Exceptionality Education Canada,* 1995, *5,* 81–95.

2. B. Vossekuil and others, *Final Report and Findings of the Safe School Initiative: Implications for the Prevention of School Attacks in the United States* (Washington, D.C.: U.S. Department of Education, Office of Elementary and Secondary Education, Safe and Drug-Free Schools Program and U.S. Secret Service, National Threat Assessment Center, 2002), 26–27.

3. A. D. Berkowitz and H. W. Perkins, "Problem Drinking Among College Students: A Review of Recent Research," *Journal of American College Health,* 1986, *35*(1), 21–28; B. Borsari and K. B. Carey, "Peer Influences on College Drinking: A Review of the Research," *Journal of Substance Abuse,* 2001, *13,* 391–424; D. B. Kandel, "On Processes of Peer Influences in Adolescent Drug Use: A Developmental Perspective," *Advances in Alcohol and Substance*

Use, 1985, *4,* 139–163; H. W. Perkins, "Social Norms and the Prevention of Alcohol Misuse in Collegiate Contexts," *Journal of Studies on Alcohol,* 2002, *14*(Suppl.), 164–172.

4. A. D. Berkowitz, "The Social Norms Approach: Theory, Research, and Annotated Bibliography," August 2004, retrieved from http://www.alan berkowitz.com/articles/social_norms.pdf.

5. Hazler, 1996, 11–12; M. Bonds and S. Stoker, *Bullyproofing Your School: A Comprehensive Approach for Middle Schools* (Longmont, Colo.: Sopris West, 2000), 151.

6. R. B. Cialdini, *Influence: The Psychology of Persuasion* (New York: Morrow, 1993), 132.

7. N. D. Feshbach, "Empathy: The Formative Years—Implications for Clinical Practice," in A. C. Bohart and L. S. Greenberg (eds.), *Empathy Reconsidered: Directions for Psychotherapy* (Washington, D.C.: American Psychological Association, 1997), 35.

8. N. Eisenberg and P. A. Miller, "The Relation of Empathy to Prosocial and Related Behaviors," *Psychological Bulletin,* 1987, *101,* 91–119.

9. D. L. Espelage, S. E. Mebane, and R. S. Adams, "Empathy, Caring and Bullying: Toward an Understanding of Complex Associations," in D. L. Espelage and S. M. Swearer (eds.), *Bullying in American Schools: A Social-Ecological Perspective on Prevention and Intervention* (Mahwah, N.J.: Erlbaum, 2004), 37–61.

10. P. O'Connell, D. Pepler, and W. Craig, "Peer Involvement in Bullying: Insights and Challenges for Intervention," *Journal of Adolescence,* 1999, *22,* 437–452.

11. W. M. Craig and D. J. Pepler, "Observations of Bullying and Victimization in the School Year," in W. Craig (ed.), *Childhood Social Development: The Essential Readings* (Oxford: Blackwell, 2000), 117–136.

12. K. Rigby and P. T. Slee, "Bullying Among Australian School Children: Reported Behavior and Attitudes Toward Victims," *Journal of School Psychology,* 1992, *131,* 615–627; C. Salmivalli, "Participant Role Approach to School Bullying: Implications for Interventions," *Journal of Adolescence,* 1999, *22,* 453–459.

13. S. C. Khosropour and J. Walsh, "That's Not Teasing—That's Bullying: A Study of Fifth Graders' Conceptualization of Bullying and Teasing," paper

presented at the annual conference of the American Educational Research Association, Seattle, 2000.

14. J. C. Brigham, *Social Psychology,* 2nd ed. (New York: HarperCollins, 1991).

15. J. Sutton and E. Keogh, "Social Competition in School: Relationships with Bullying, Machiavellianism, and Personality," *British Journal of Educational Psychology,* 2000, *7,* 443–456.

16. D. L. Hawkins, D. J. Pepler, and W. M. Craig, "Naturalistic Observations of Peer Interventions in Bullying," *Social Development,* 2001, *10,* 512–527.

17. K. Rigby and B. Johnson, "Expressed Readiness of Australian Schoolchildren to Act as Bystanders in Support of Children Who Are Being Bullied," *Educational Psychology,* 2006, *26,* 425–440.

18. Stanford University Medical Center, "School Bullying Affects Majority of Elementary Students, Stanford/Packard Researchers Find," Lucille Packard Children's Hospital, press release, Apr. 12, 2007, 2.

19. B. R. Astill, N. T. Feather, and J. P. Keeves, "A Multilevel Analysis of the Effects of Parents, Teachers and Schools on Student Values," *Social Psychology of Education,* 2002, *5,* 345–363.

20. K. Rigby and B. Johnson, "Bystander Behavior of South Australian School Children: Observing Bullying Behavior and Sexual Coercion," retrieved January 23, 2006, from http://www.education.unisa.edu.au/bullying/FocusOnBystanders.pdf, 8.

21. M. Gladwell, *The Tipping Point: How Little Things Can Make a Big Difference* (New York: Little, Brown, 2002), 139.

22. Gladwell, 2002, 131.

23. Gladwell, 2002, 132.

24. Gladwell, 2002, 67.

25. Gladwell, 2002, 70.

26. Gladwell, 2002, 56.

27. Feshbach, 1997.

28. Vossekuil and others, 2002, 33.

29. *Let's Get Real,* directed by D. Chasnoff, Women's Educational Media, 2004.

30. M. Bonds and S. Stoker, *Bully Proofing Your School: A Comprehensive Approach for Elementary Schools* (Longmont, Colo.: Sopris West, 1994).

CHAPTER EIGHT

1. W. M. Craig and D. J. Pepler, "Peer Processes in Bullying and Victimization: An Observational Study," *Exceptionality Education Canada,* 1995, *5,* 81–95.

2. B. Vossekuil and others, *Final Report and Findings of the Safe School Initiative: Implications for the Prevention of School Attacks in the United States* (Washington, D.C.: U.S. Department of Education, Office of Elementary and Secondary Education, Safe and Drug-Free Schools Program and U.S. Secret Service, National Threat Assessment Center, 2002), 32.

3. T. Collins and P. Louwagie, "Many Heard of Weise's Plans to Kill," *Star Tribune,* Jan. 31, 2006, p. 1.

APPENDIX B

1. J. Miner and J. Boldt, *Outward Bound U.S.A.* (New York: William Morrow and Company, 1981), 24.

RESOURCES

THIS RESOURCE LIST IS NOT INTENDED TO BE EXHAUSTIVE or comprehensive, but can help you get started. It also does not constitute any assessment of the value of the resources that are or are not included here; there are thousands of valuable products, services, and sources of information that can be found through an Internet search or through your library, especially with the assistance of your librarian.

Instead, we offer sources of information that you—and anyone you might enlist as a champion with you: parents, teachers, administrators, community advocates—can use to deepen your knowledge of and understanding about the issue of mistreatment and become effective advocates for empowering and equipping young people to take a greater role in preventing and stopping mistreatment. Our intention is to highlight resources that have been particularly helpful to *us* in our development of this youth-centered model and ones that offer a perspective that is sometimes overlooked or harder to find.

Organizations and Web Sites

Stop Bullying Now, www.stopbullyingnow.hrsa.gov. This site is a compilation of resources for students and adults that was assembled and maintained for the U.S. Department of Health and Human Services.

Search Institute, www.search-institute.org. One of the nation's leading youth development research organizations. Their developmental assets framework can be used by all sectors of a community—schools, parents, and faith and youth-serving organizations—to organize and coordinate their efforts to provide young people with the environments, relationships, opportunities, and tools to be capable, compassionate contributors to their schools and communities.

American Medical Association, www.ama-assn.org. Bullying is a public health issue, and the American Medical Association and its volunteer arm, the American Medical Association Alliance, have made it a priority.

National School Safety Center, www.nssc1.org. This organization, established by presidential directive in 1984, serves as an advocate for safe, secure, and peaceful schools worldwide and as a catalyst for the prevention of school crime and violence.

Common Sense Media, www.commonsensemedia.org. This organization helps to inform parents, educators, and children about the media they consume and the relationship between violence in media and violent behavior.

Center for Nonviolent Communication, www.cnvc.org. This global organization takes the work of violence prevention and peacebuilding to a practical, everyday, and personal level by helping people learn a model for communication that is based on compassion and understanding rather than power and manipulation.

Teaching Tolerance, www.teachingtolerance.org. This organization provides resources to educators to help them fight bigotry and hatred and increase students' tolerance of and respect for people of different cultures, backgrounds, and beliefs.

Videos, Articles, and Books

The articles and books listed in this book's Notes strengthen the foundation on which this book is built and are well worth reading.

Videos

Let's Get Real. In this groundbreaking and powerful documentary film, middle school students speak about mistreatment they have experienced, perpetrated, or seen at their schools. Part of their Respect for All project, this compelling resource is a great discussion starter for students and can help adults understand what the world of students is like. Women's Educational Media (now Groundspark). San Francisco, 2003. www.womedia.org.

Teen Truth. This dramatic and fast-moving film is built from footage shot by five diverse teens and includes students talking about what it's like to be a teen today, along with footage from Columbine High School security cameras and audio from 911 operators during the violence there. B1 Films and Horizon Intertainment. Los Angeles, 2006. www.teentruthlive.com. Film plus curriculum guide available through HRM Video. http://www.hrmvideo.com.

The Truth About Hate. This authentic film explores the roots of hate through the eyes of today's teenagers as they come face to face with their own racism, ethnic bigotry, religious hatred, and sexual discrimination. It documents eye-opening experiences that helped teens change their perspectives and move past their own hatred of others. Aims Multimedia. Chatsworth, California, 1999. Available through the Discovery Channel teacher store. http://teacherstore.discovery.com.

Freedom Writers. This popular film chronicles the wildly successful efforts of Erin Gruwell, a teacher in Long Beach, California, who uses basic principles of youth empowerment to connect with and inspire greatness from students her colleagues considered unreachable and unteachable. Paramount, Hollywood. 2007. www.freedomwriters foundation.org.

Books

These are books we have found to be particularly helpful in understanding the issue of youth mistreatment and empowering youth to address it. Many other insightful and valuable books on this issue can be found at libraries and over the Internet.

About Norms Change

The Tipping Point. Malcolm Gladwell. New York: Little, Brown, 2002. www.gladwell.com/tippingpoint/index.html. This book examines how changes in attitude and behavior can ripple rapidly through communities and society.

About Youth Development

Fostering Resiliency in Kids: Protective Factors in the Family, School and Community. Bonnie Benard. Portland, Ore.: Western Regional Center for Drug-Free Schools and Communities, Northwest Regional Educational Laboratory, 1991.

Healthy Communities, Healthy Youth: How Communities Contribute to Positive Youth Development. Peter Benson. Minneapolis, Minn.: Search Institute, 1993.

Emotional Intelligence. Daniel Goleman. New York: Bantam Books, 1995.

Communities That Care. J. D. Hawkins and others. San Francisco: Jossey-Bass, 1992.

Reflections on a Decade of Promoting Youth Development. Karen Pittman and Merita Irby. Washington, D.C.: American Youth Policy Forum, 1998.

About Mistreatment

The Bully, the Bullied, and the Bystander: From Preschool to High School: How Parents and Teachers Can Help Break the Cycle of Violence. Barbara Coloroso. New York: HarperCollins, 2002.

Bullies, Targets and Witnesses: Helping Children Break the Pain Chain. SuEllen Fried and Paula Fried. New York: Evans, 2003.

Empowering Bystanders in Bullying Prevention, Grades K–8. Stan Davis with Julia Davis. Champaign, Ill.: Research Press, 2007.

Bullying Prevention: Creating a Positive School Climate and Developing Social Competence. Pamela Orpinas and Arthur M. Horne. Washington, D.C.: American Psychological Association, 2006. A thorough and well-documented treatise from two applied behavioral scientists that documents the problem and discusses both universal (school-wide) and individual interventions.

Murder Is No Accident: Understanding and Preventing Youth Violence in America. Deborah Prothrow-Stith. San Francisco: Jossey-Bass, 2004. This book discusses an interdisciplinary, community-based approach to preventing youth violence that has been proven effective under challenging conditions.

Queen Bees and Wannabees: Helping Your Daughter Survive Cliques, Gossip, Boyfriends, and Other Realities of Adolescence. Rosalind Wiseman. New York: Three Rivers Press. 2002. This book explores patterns of aggressive teen girl behavior and how to deal with them.

Lost Boys: Why Our Sons Turn Violent and How We Can Save Them. James Garbarino. New York: Free Press, 1999. This inquiry into youthful male violence analyzes its roots and causes and concludes with a catalogue of strategies to address the problem.

Nineteen Minutes. Jodi Picoult. New York: Atria Books, 2007. This fictional account of a school shooting provides vivid insights into the problem of mistreatment from the perspective of teens and adults.

Materials and Tools

Climate Survey   A school climate survey can provide a snapshot of how students (and staff) feel at school and can become the springboard for developing and implementing a plan to build a safer school climate. One school climate survey is available from Community Matters. To download the latest version, visit www .community-matters.org/climsurveyreg.

Relationship Building   These resources can enhance efforts to build and strengthen relationships among the different groups of students on campus, thereby improving the school climate.

Mix It Up Day. This project of the Southern Poverty Law Center's Teaching Tolerance program is designed to help students break down the walls of division and build bridges of understanding between the groups and cliques at a school. On a given day in November, students are invited and challenged to sit at a different table in the lunch area and talk with students they usually don't hang out with. www.tolerance.org.

Challenge Day. A carefully designed series of innovative games, activities, group discussions, icebreakers, and trust-building exercises that help participants break down the walls of separation and create new levels of respect and communication with their peers, teachers, parents, and themselves. www.challengeday.org.

Days of Respect. A multiday schoolwide event that brings young people, teachers, parents, administrators, and the community together to build respect and stop violence. It cultivates a commitment to nonviolent behavior and promotes integrity, support for others, and student leadership. Guidebook for organizing one is available through Hunter House Publishing. www.hunterhouse.com/shopexd.asp?id=306.

Conflict Resolution   Because bullying and most other forms of mistreatment involve one person (the aggressor) having power over another (the target), these interactions are not appropriate for conflict resolution or mediation. However, when two students both want to "work it out" a conflict resolution program—especially one that utilizes trained students as mediators—can be very effective. For this reason, it is a valuable component of a schoolwide effort to reduce conflict and violence.

The Conflict Resolution Information Source. A project of the University of Colorado at Boulder, this Web site is a clearinghouse of information on all types of conflict, from international to relationship. The educational resources link leads to resources for elementary and secondary educators. www.crinfo.org.

National Center for Conflict Resolution Education (NCCRE). Supported in part by a grant from the Office of Juvenile Justice and Delinquency Prevention (OJJDP), Office of Justice Programs, U.S. Department of Justice in partnership with the Safe and Drug-Free School Program, U.S. Department of Education, NCCRE provides training and technical assistance nationwide to advance the development of conflict resolution education programs in schools, juvenile justice settings, and youth service organizations and community partnership programs. www.nccre.org.

Resolving Conflict Creatively Program (RCCP). A program of Educators for Social Responsibility in Cambridge, Massachusetts, is a well-evaluated, K–8 program in character education and social and emotional learning. It is the nation's largest and longest running school program with a special focus on conflict resolution and intergroup relations. www.esrnational.org/ index.php?location=pages&l=ele&link=27.

Social Skills

Second Step. Developed by the Seattle-based Committee for Children and based on over twenty years of research and classroom application, Second Step integrates academics with social and emotional learning for children preK–grade 8. Children learn and practice skills such as anger management, cooperation, respectful behavior, and problem solving. They also learn to recognize and respect people with different backgrounds, perspectives, and ethnicities. www.cfchildren.org/programs/ssp/overview.

Other tools and materials can be found through the organizations and Web sites listed above.

INDEX

309